Adorno, Foucault and tł

CW00920036

Adorno, Foucault and the Critique of the West

Deborah Cook

VERSO

London • New York

First published by Verso 2018
© Deborah Cook 2018

All rights reserved

The moral rights of the author have been asserted

1 3 5 7 9 10 8 6 4 2

Verso
UK: 6 Meard Street, London W1F 0EG
US: 20 Jay Street, Suite 1010, Brooklyn, NY 11201
versobooks.com

Verso is the imprint of New Left Books

ISBN-13: 978-1-78873-082-2
ISBN-13: 978-1-78873-080-8 (UK EBK)
ISBN-13: 978-1-78873-081-5 (US EBK)

British Library Cataloguing in Publication Data
A catalogue record for this book is available from the British Library

Library of Congress Cataloging-in-Publication Data
A catalog record for this book is available from the Library of Congress

Typeset in Minion Pro by Hewer Text UK Ltd, Edinburgh
Printed in CPI Mackays, UK

Contents

Acknowledgements

Three chapters in this book are based on pilot essays that were subsequently expanded and extensively revised. An early version of Chapter Two, ' "Is Power Always Secondary to the Economy?" Foucault and Adorno on Power and Exchange', appeared in *Foucault Studies*, no. 20 (2015), pp. 180-98. The pilot essay for Chapter Three, 'Notes on Individuation in Adorno and Foucault', was published in *Philosophy Today* 58, no. 3 (2014), pp. 325-44. Chapter Five is based loosely on 'Adorno, Foucault and Critique', an article published in *Philosophy and Social Criticism* 39, no. 10 (2013), pp. 963-79. I am grateful to the anonymous reviewers of these essays for their astute commentary. I should also like to thank the anonymous reviewer at Verso whose criticisms improved this book by enabling me to reframe it.

The Social Sciences and Humanities Research Council of Canada (SSHRC) provided me with research funding which enabled me to consult the Foucault Archives at the Institut Mémoires de l'Edition contemporaine (IMEC). My research at IMEC brought me into contact with scholars from all over the world with whom I enjoyed sharing ideas over meals at the Abbaye Ardenne. The SSHRC grant also allowed me to hire one of my graduate students to search for journal articles. Staicha Kidd doggedly pursued quarry that was often difficult to find, and she did so with a smile and an infectious sense of humour. Thank you, Staicha.

Thanks too to James Swindal at Duquesne University; his early encouragement meant a great deal to me. Another debt of gratitude is owed to Stefano Giacchetti Ludovisi who has organized the annual Critical Theory conference at the Rome campus of Loyola University of Chicago since its inception a decade ago. Equally deserving of mention are Stefano's colleagues at Loyola – David Ingram and Hugh Miller – along with other participants at the conference, especially Andrew Feenberg and Anne-Marie Feenberg-Dibon. For several years, Stefano, David, Hugh, Andrew and Anne-Marie helped me to improve my work by criticizing it. I have also been buoyed by many students at the Rome conference; their comments were always stimulating.

Parts of this book were presented at two other venues. In 2014, I presented a section of Chapter Two in a keynote address for 'The Frankfurt School and the Critique of Capitalist Culture', a conference in Vancouver that came about as the result of the collaborative efforts of Simon Fraser University, the University of British Columbia, and Douglas College. At Ryerson University in Toronto,

Meredith Schwartz invited me to speak in the Philosophy Department's Distinguished Speakers series in 2015, where I presented a portion of Chapter Four. In both Vancouver and Toronto, I learned much from the thoughtful questions of those who attended.

Finally, thanks to my friend, musician Terence Kroetsch, for raising my sometimes flagging spirits with music and laughter. And thanks also to the painter John (Jack) Brown for his support during the years of love and loss in which this book was written.

Preface

This book will argue that critical theory continues to offer important resources for critique and contestation during this turbulent period in our history. To assess these resources, I shall examine the work of two of the twentieth century's more prominent social theorists: Theodor W. Adorno and Michel Foucault. Although Adorno was situated squarely in the Marxist tradition that Foucault would occasionally challenge, I hope to demonstrate that their critiques of our current predicament are complementary in important respects. Among other things, these critiques converge in their focus on the historical forces – economic in Adorno and political in Foucault – that gave rise to racist and authoritarian tendencies in the West. They also offer remarkably similar answers to the perennial question: What is to be done?

With the wealth of primary material (including lectures, essays, interviews and translations) published over the last two decades, it was possible to approach Adorno's and Foucault's critical theories jointly and critically with a view to evaluating their work. Yet it was important to proceed with caution. As Friedrich Nietzsche once observed: 'He who seeks to mediate between two bold thinkers stamps himself as mediocre: he has not the eyes to see uniqueness; to perceive resemblances everywhere, making everything alike, is a sign of weak eyesight.'[1] I kept this passage in mind during this book's gestation in order to avoid, or at least to mitigate, the charge that *Adorno, Foucault and the Critique of the West* offers a mediocre comparison because it perceives resemblances everywhere and fails to appreciate the uniqueness of Adorno's and Foucault's thought. Much to my chagrin, Nietzsche's criticism was echoed by a student who, upon hearing a section of Chapter One that I had edited for a keynote address in Rome, effectively asked me – though not quite so bluntly – if I was planning to reduce Foucault to Adorno.

That I try to avoid conflating their ideas will, I hope, become apparent in the course of reading this book. For example, Chapter Two will contrast the respective targets of Adorno's and Foucault's critiques: where Adorno focused almost exclusively on exchange relations and the capitalist economy, Foucault studied power relations in the West. Moreover, Chapter Three will argue that Adorno and Foucault have very different ideas about the impact of Christianity on the

---

1 Adorno quotes this passage in *Minima Moralia*, p. 74; trans. mod. He is quoting Book III, Section 228 of Friedrich Nietzsche's *Joyful Wisdom*.

formation of the individual. In Chapter Four, I shall contrast Foucault's view that resistance to power is widespread with Adorno's claim that resistance is not just sporadic, but weak and largely ineffective when it does occur. Chapter Four will also explain why Adorno thought that political action should be deferred. Finally, Adorno and Foucault agree that we apprehend the world through a prism of concepts, but Chapter Five will show that Foucault does not share Adorno's aim of returning to things themselves.

Of course, it would be equally problematic to focus only on the differences between Adorno and Foucault. That their ideas are often complementary is hardly surprising. Chapter One will demonstrate that Adorno and Foucault were influenced by some of the same thinkers, and these shared influences help to account for the complementarity of their work. Although Adorno was more than twenty years older than Foucault, they were also shaped by similar economic, political and social conditions.[2] Equally important, they were affected profoundly by the same historical events. As I shall argue here, their experiences of fascism during the Second World War motivate their search for an *Ausgang* – a way out – of our current predicament. In fact, the similarities between their ideas are acknowledged by Foucault himself. By the late 1970s, Foucault recognized that he belonged to the Kantian tradition of critique that spawned the Critical Theory of the Frankfurt School. In the early 1980s, he also noted the parallels between Adorno's work and his own.

I remain convinced that Adorno's and Foucault's critiques of the West have much to teach us about ourselves. They take us on a voyage of critical self-discovery, attempting to make us more self-aware so that we no longer find ourselves in the situation of Nietzsche's seekers after knowledge who were unknown to themselves because they had never tried to find themselves. At the same time, and to cite René Char's *Partage formel* – a paean to those who resisted the Nazis that effectively serves as a leitmotif in Foucault's work – Adorno and Foucault invite us to 'develop our legitimate strangeness' by acquiring a better understanding of the forces that have shaped our identities and resisting them.[3] Indeed, given their concerns about a resurgence of fascism, this book will also argue that Adorno and Foucault have strong normative commitments to autonomy. If I succeed in conveying to readers at least some of the resistive force that animates these social theories, then the time that it has taken me to write this book will have been well spent.

---

2   Adorno was born in Frankfurt, Germany in 1903; Foucault was born in Poitiers, France in 1926.

3   In French, the aphorism reads: '*Développez votre étrangeté légitime*'. Foucault first quotes this aphorism in the preface to the original (1961) French edition of *The History of Madness*, *Folie et Déraison*; see also Foucault, *History of Madness*, p. xxxvi.

Abbreviations

BB   Foucault, *The Birth of Biopolitics*
MM   Adorno, *Minima Moralia*
ND   Adorno, *Negative Dialectics*
SP   Foucault, 'The Subject and Power', *Essential Works: Power*
STP   Foucault, *Security, Territory, Population*

Full references to these works, and to works cited in the footnotes, appear in the bibliography.

Chapter 1

The Critical Matrix

Adorno visited Paris several times during the 1950s and 1960s, giving lectures at the Collège de France and the Sorbonne.[1] Yet he never referred (in published work at least) to what would come to be known as poststructuralism or, more specifically, to Foucault.[2] Yet Foucault referred to the Frankfurt School – or Critical Theory – on a number of occasions. In an important interview conducted in 1978, he told Duccio Trombadori that, once he became acquainted with Critical Theory, he realized that its theorists had already said things that he had 'been trying to say for many years'. Had he known about their work earlier, there are many things that he 'would not have needed to say', and he 'would have avoided some mistakes'. He might even have been so 'captivated' by critical theorists that he 'wouldn't have done anything else but comment on them'.[3]

Although these remarks reveal that Foucault was familiar with Critical Theory, it is not at all clear which works he had read. In his interview with Trombadori, Foucault did mention a book written by lesser known theorists Otto Kirchheimer and Georg Rusche, *Punishment and Social Structure*, which he cited in *Discipline and Punish*.[4] Stating that this book first piqued his interest in Critical Theory, Foucault added, without naming them, that he had read 'a few of [Max] Horkheimer's texts'.[5] Yet he never referred, in this interview or in other published work, to any of Adorno's work. This is all the more surprising because Foucault once told Martin Jay in a private conversation in 1980 that he saw 'striking parallels between his own analysis of the disciplinary, carceral society and Adorno's administered world'.[6] His only mention of a text written by Adorno seems to have been made in the context of another unpublished conversation where he reportedly told Jürgen Habermas that he admired *Dialectic of Enlightenment* – a book that Adorno co-authored with Horkheimer.[7]

---

1   Stefan Müller-Doohm, *Adorno*, pp. 403, 407 and 448.
2   Adorno died of a heart attack a few months after Foucault's *The Archaeology of Knowledge* appeared in May 1969. Although he never mentioned poststructuralism, he was familiar enough with intellectual currents in France to mention the work of Claude Lévi-Strauss and Jacques Lacan in his 1968 lectures on sociology. See Adorno, *Introduction to Sociology*, p. 103.
3   Foucault, 'Interview with Michel Foucault', *Essential Works: Power*, p. 274.
4   Foucault, *Discipline and Punish*, p. 24. See also Rusche and Kirchheimer, *Punishment and Social Structure*.
5   Foucault, 'Interview with Michel Foucault', *Essential Works: Power*, p. 273.
6   Martin Jay, *Adorno*, p. 22.
7   James Miller reported on this conversation in *The Passion of Michel Foucault*, pp. 456–7 n. 52.

A few commentators have tried to explore the parallels between the work of Adorno and Foucault that Foucault mentions in his conversation with Jay. To cite two early attempts, Axel Honneth engaged in a brief (and somewhat uncharitable) comparative discussion of Adorno and Foucault, and David Hoy explored some of the affinities between them, though largely in the context of defending Foucault against Habermas.[8] Their assessments are noteworthy, not just because they are relatively rare in the secondary literature, but because they offer important insights into Adorno's and Foucault's work. Still, Adorno's and Foucault's lectures had not been published at the time that Honneth and Hoy were writing. Nor had numerous articles, essays and interviews that give a more precise shape to Adorno's and Foucault's thought, making possible a more thorough assessment of their ideas.

Benefiting from the publication of many more texts by Adorno and Foucault than were available even a decade ago, this book will begin with an overview of their work. I will show that Adorno and Foucault share similar philosophical backgrounds as I examine some of the thinkers with whom they engaged. This attempt to contextualize Adorno's and Foucault's work by situating some of its prominent themes historically within the philosophical tradition will be followed by a discussion of their critical approaches to the study of our present. Beginning with a description of the anti-systematic and provisional character of their work, along with an account of the pivotal role that history plays in it, I shall offer a comparative account of Adorno's negative dialectics and Foucault's genealogy that assesses the complementarity of their approaches to critique. I also aim to demonstrate, both here and throughout the book, that Adorno and Foucault address problems that we continue to confront in the twenty-first century while attempting to find viable solutions to them.

INFLUENCES AND THEMES

Some biographers of Adorno and Foucault begin with an ironic nod to Adorno's and Foucault's criticisms of the genre of biography. To the extent that this discussion of the thinkers who helped to shape central themes in their work relies on biographical accounts, it will share in the bad faith of these biographers. However, I shall also cite interviews and essays in which Adorno and Foucault name the thinkers who had a significant impact on their work. Among the more important of these is Immanuel Kant. Chapter Five will discuss Kant's impact on what Foucault calls his ontology of the present, and Adorno an ontology of the wrong state of things. Since this chapter will also show that Adorno and Foucault both situate themselves squarely within the enlightenment tradition

---

8   See Axel Honneth, *The Critique of Power*, and David Hoy and Thomas McCarthy, *Critical Theory*. Another early commentator, Peter Dews, will be mentioned later. A collection of essays comparing Adorno and Foucault, which included essays by Honneth and Dews, was also published in Italy in the early 1990s; see Franco Riccio and Salvo Vaccaro, eds, *Adorno e Foucault*.

that Kant described in his 1784 essay 'An Answer to the Question: What is Enlightenment?', I shall speak more broadly about Kant's influence here.

In an essay he dedicated to his early mentor, Siegfried Kracauer (with whom he studied philosophy while a teenager in Frankfurt), Adorno wrote that Kracauer taught him how to read Kant from a social and historical perspective. Kracauer made Kant 'come alive' for Adorno because he showed him that Kant's *Critique of Pure Reason* was not just an epistemology but 'a kind of coded text from which the historical situation of spirit could be read'.[9] This awakening to the possibility of reading philosophical texts as expressions of the *Zeitgeist* would have a lasting influence on Adorno.[10] In his reading of Kant, for example, Adorno deciphered Kant's ahistorical and disembodied transcendental subject as a figure for a society that is 'unaware of itself', a society that tries to vindicate its domination of human beings and the rest of the natural world by surreptitiously asserting its primacy.[11] In fact, Adorno highlighted a central theme in his own work when he interpreted the transcendental subject as a cipher for the preponderance (*Vorrang*) of society over individuals.[12]

Adorno became increasingly critical of Kant once he had completed a doctoral thesis under the supervision of the neo-Kantian philosopher Hans Cornelius. Nevertheless, when he returned to Germany from the United States after the Second World War, he gave lectures on Kant at the Johann Wolfgang Goethe Universität in Frankfurt until his death in 1969.[13] In some of these lectures he discussed Kant's *Critique of Practical Reason*, but Adorno also devoted an entire section of his *magnum opus*, *Negative Dialectics*, to a critical appraisal of Kant's ideas about freedom and autonomy. As the final chapters in this book will argue, this appraisal informs Adorno's views about freedom and autonomy under monopoly conditions. But Kant prompted Adorno to scrutinize other philosophical issues as well, including the idea of things-in-themselves and the epistemological relation between subject and object. Although Adorno rejects Kant's claim that the caesura or block that separates concepts from objects is unbridgeable, Chapter Five will argue that he follows Kant when he refuses to identify objects with concepts.

Foucault's intellectual relationship with Kant was equally long-lasting. The secondary thesis that he submitted for his doctorate at the Sorbonne in 1961 (his primary thesis was published in English under the title *History of Madness*) was a translation of Kant's *Anthropology from a Pragmatic Point of View*. Foucault wrote a long introductory essay for this translation in which he echoed Adorno's

---

9   Adorno, 'The Curious Realist', *Notes to Literature*, Vol. 2, p. 58.
10   For Adorno's discussion of the idea of the *Zeitgeist*, see *History and Freedom*, pp. 25–7.
11   Adorno, *Negative Dialectics*, p. 177. Cited hereafter in the text as ND. Ashton's translation may be modified.
12   Adorno, 'On Subject and Object', *Critical Models*, p. 248.
13   In their introduction to Adorno's book on Hegel, Shierry Weber Nicholsen and Jeremy Shapiro (former students of Adorno) report that Adorno's *Hauptseminar* in the 1960s was devoted 'almost exclusively' to Kant and Hegel. See Adorno, *Hegel: Three Studies*, p. xviii.

criticisms of Kant's transcendental subject when he emphasized the subject's corporeality and its embeddedness in history.[14] David Macey also notes that this essay invokes the death of man – an idea which, following Nietzsche, Foucault linked to the death of God. In what would become a central theme in his later work, Foucault argued, against Kant, that the death of man 'indicates the impossibility of continuing to think with an abstract notion of Man; the noble notion of an autonomous human subject has been rendered untenable by the discoveries of psychoanalysis, linguistics and Marxism'. Macey prefaces this comment with the observation that the reappearance of the proclamation of the death of man in *The Order of Things* should remind readers that the 'philosophical territory' that Foucault inhabited was 'marked out by Kant and Nietzsche'.[15]

Many commentators have examined Kant's influence on Foucault. In fact, Colin Koopman makes the contentious remark (contentious because Nietzsche appears just as often) that Kant is the only thinker 'who appears in all of Foucault's writings in each of his so-called periods of scholarship and who thus has unbroken central standing in Foucault's thought from the very beginning of his career right up to the tragic end of his life'.[16] To support their view that Kant is a key interlocutor, commentators (including Koopman) usually mention Foucault's search for the conditions of the possibility of phenomena such as madness and sexuality, while agreeing with John Rajchman (who was among the first to stress the links between Foucault and Kant) that Foucault's conception of conditions of possibility differs considerably from Kant's because Foucault not only purges Kant's conception 'of all anthropologism', he historicizes it when he stresses the utterly contingent emergence of things.[17] Yet this book will reveal that Kant's influence extends beyond Foucault's attempts to explore the historical conditions that have shaped individuals in the West. As in Adorno, Kant's ideas about autonomy inform Foucault's own critique of our present.

Kant had a pronounced influence on Foucault and Adorno, but it could be argued, somewhat more controversially in the case of Foucault, that Hegel also influenced them. In fact, Adorno's *Negative Dialectics* can be read as an extended critique of Hegel. Among other things, Adorno took from Hegel the idea that individuals are deeply affected by historical conditions, but he objected that Hegel went too far when he effectively identified individuals with these conditions. To be sure, when Hegel is read as an expression of the *Zeitgeist*, he was right in one sense – individuals are submerged under what Adorno often calls 'the universal': late capitalist society. Hegel's idea of absolute spirit – a totality that allows nothing to escape – points to an important dimension of our current

---

14   See Foucault, *Introduction to Kant's Anthropology*.

15   David Macey, *The Lives of Michel Foucault*, p. 90 *passim*. On the same page, Macey says that the theme of the death of man also appeared in a novel that Foucault would have read: André Malraux's *The Temptation of the West*.

16   Colin Koopman, *Genealogy as Critique*, p. 13.

17   John Rajchman, *Michel Foucault*, p. 103.

plight to the extent that it mirrors 'the experience of the superior coercive force inherent in everything that exists by virtue of its consolidation under domination'.[18] Yet this idea is also untrue because the social integration of human beings is by no means total. Just as things always elude concepts, human beings remain nonidentical with respect to society. Indeed, the idea of nonidentity, derived from Hegel but wielded against his system, lies at the thematic core of Adorno's work.

Adorno insists that the 'need to lend a voice to suffering is an expression of all truth' (ND 17). He also charges that Hegel (especially in his later work) tended to legitimate the suffering that our subordination to existing conditions has caused. Criticizing Hegel's 'theodicy', Adorno objects that Hegel apologetically takes the side 'of what exists', thereby rationalizing human suffering.[19] Furthermore, he rejects Hegel's view that 'failure, death and oppression are the inevitable essence of things' to which individuals must simply submit. Against Hegel, Adorno argues that experiences like these are not just 'avoidable' but 'criticizable' because the course that history took was by no means a necessary one.[20] The domination of human beings over the natural world, over other human beings and over themselves was neither inevitable nor predetermined (ND 321). History's trajectory could have been changed for the better at any time, and Adorno believes that it can still be changed in such a way that unnecessary suffering is eradicated.[21]

Like Adorno, Foucault also objects that Hegel's dialectical system ultimately championed identity over nonidentity. Failing to 'liberate differences', Hegel's dialectics suggests instead that differences 'can always be recaptured'.[22] I shall return to this point later, but I want to note here that, in spite of his criticisms of Hegel, Foucault said more than once that Hegel is a philosopher who must be reckoned with. His engagement with Hegel began in the late 1940s while he was a student at the École Normale Supérieure. There he was introduced to Hegel by his professor Jean Hyppolite (the French translator of Hegel's *Phenomenology of Spirit* and author of a seminal commentary on it). Two decades later, Foucault invited Hyppolite to give a lecture at the University of Tunis (where Foucault taught from 1966-8). In his opening remarks, Foucault introduced his former professor to students and faculty with these words: 'All philosophical reflection today is a dialogue with Hegel.'[23]

---

18   Adorno, *Hegel: Three Studies*, p. 87.
19   Ibid., p. 85.
20   Adorno, *Lectures on 'Negative Dialectics'*, p. 104.
21   Adorno, *History and Freedom*, p. 68.
22   Foucault, 'Theatrum Philosophicum', *Essential Works: Aesthetics*, p. 358. Cited by Clare O'Farrell in *Foucault: Historian or Philosopher?*, p. 31.
23   These remarks are cited by Didier Eribon in *Michel Foucault*, p. 189. For his part, Macey reports that the title of Foucault's thesis for the Diplôme d'études approfondies at the École Normale was *La Constitution d'un transcendental dans 'La Phénoménologie de l'Esprit' de Hegel* (The Constitution of a Transcendental in Hegel's *Phenomenology of Spirit*). See Macey, *The Lives of Michel Foucault*, p. 32.

Nevertheless, Foucault's dialogue with Hegel was originally motivated by a concerted attempt to wrest free from his influence. When he succeeded Hyppolite at the Collège de France in 1970, Foucault said in his inaugural lecture that our entire age represents an attempt to escape from Hegel. Yet he also made an important concession: whether it be through logic or epistemology, through Nietzsche or through Marx, we must nonetheless admit that what allows us to think against Hegel may actually owe much to Hegel himself.[24] Foucault's own attempt to escape from Hegel is a case in point. Although he seemed to realize it only towards the end of his life, Foucault linked his critique to the philosophical tradition that includes Hegel because, like Kant, Hegel engaged in 'a form of reflection' that 'takes the form of an ontology of ourselves, of present reality'.[25] In fact, Foucault's dialogue with Hegel takes an intriguing turn at the end of *The Hermeneutics of the Subject* when he states that 'the root of the challenge to Western thought' is: 'how can there be a subject of knowledge who takes the world as object through a *tekhnē*, and a subject of self-experience who takes this same world in the radically different form of the place of its test?' Foucault continues: 'if this really is the challenge of Western philosophy, you will see why *The Phenomenology of Mind* is the summit of this philosophy'.[26]

The following chapter will discuss at length the marked influence that Hegel's most famous student, Karl Marx, had on both Adorno and Foucault. Throughout his work, Adorno would retain Marx's interest in the capitalist economy, taking up and developing Marx's critique of capitalism's negative impact on human life. Of course, Marx always stressed that capitalism is a thoroughly historical phenomenon. As such, capitalism is constantly changing, if only in response to the crisis tendencies that are endemic to it. Supplementing his philosophical work with empirical social research that he conducted in the United States and Germany from the late 1930s until his death, Adorno sought to revise and update Marx's critique of capitalism in order to make sense of twentieth-century developments. He also thought it was necessary to supplement Marx with insights gleaned from psychoanalysis to acquire a better understanding of the rise of National Socialism in Germany.

Insisting, with Marx, on the primacy of the economy, Adorno's thought is thoroughly imbued with Marxist concepts and themes, including Marx's ideas about the commodity form, exploitation, surplus value, the stratification of society into classes, class consciousness and the antagonisms between forces and relations of production. Yet Adorno did not adopt Marx's ideas uncritically.

---

24   I am paraphrasing Foucault in *The Discourse on Language*. See Foucault, *The Archaeology of Knowledge & The Discourse on Language*, p. 235.

25   Foucault, *The Government of Self and Others*, p. 21.

26   Foucault, *The Hermeneutics of the Subject*, p. 487; trans. mod. As the editor notes (in a footnote on the same page), the manuscript of the final lecture ends with a sentence that Foucault did not utter: 'And if the task left by the Aufklärung (which the *Phenomenology* takes to the absolute) is to ask on what our system of objective knowledge rests, it is also to ask on what the modality of the experience of the self rests.'

Among other things, he charged that Marx's notions of domination and class conflict harbour idealist tendencies: Marx followed Hegel in thinking that domination and conflict were historically necessary so that something better – namely socialism, in Marx's case – could emerge. Agreeing with Marx that history can be characterized as the history of class struggle, Adorno nonetheless countered that it is an 'open question . . . whether or not the human race could only have been perpetuated by means of conflict, whether conflict was historically an absolute necessity'.[27] But the following chapters will reveal that Adorno also questioned whether the proletariat would overcome capitalism as he pointed to tendencies in the West that undermine collective action, tendencies that were glaringly apparent in Nazi Germany and the Soviet Union as well.

Like Adorno, Foucault rejected Marx's teleological conception of history. However, he was by no means as dismissive of Marx as some commentators believe. Although he often criticized the *Parti communiste français*, Foucault was politically active in a number of radical groups in France, and his work in the late 1960s and throughout the 1970s was markedly left-wing. In fact, Étienne Balibar – Foucault's colleague at the University of Vincennes in the 1960s – contends that 'the whole of Foucault's work can be seen in terms of a genuine struggle with Marx, and . . . this can be viewed as one of the driving forces behind his productivity'.[28] Yet, where Balibar views Marx's influence as largely negative – in the sense that Foucault engages with Marx only to refute him – I shall argue in the next chapter that Foucault has a far more positive assessment of Marx. As Foucault told an interviewer, he often cites 'concepts, texts and phrases from Marx, but without feeling obliged to add the authenticating label of a footnote with a laudatory phrase to accompany the quotation'. Claiming that it is 'impossible at the present time to write history without using a whole range of concepts directly or indirectly linked to Marx's thought and [without] situating oneself within a horizon of thought which has been defined and described by Marx', Foucault asks rhetorically 'what difference there could ultimately be between being an historian and being a Marxist'.[29]

Another important interview in which Foucault clarified his position on Marx, 'Méthodologie pour la Connaissance du Monde', has not yet been translated into English. In this interview, conducted in Japan in 1978, Foucault praised Marx for thematizing and prioritizing the notion of struggle. Although he complained that Marx's ideas about struggle were undeveloped, Foucault said that these ideas 'anchor' his interest in Marx because his own work is devoted to understanding, and lending support to, struggles in the West.[30] Foucault also admired Marx's historical analyses because these 'surpass by far'

27   Adorno, *History and Freedom*, p. 52.
28   Étienne Balibar, 'Foucault and Marx', *Michel Foucault Philosopher*, p. 39; trans. mod.
29   Foucault, 'Prison Talk', *Power/Knowledge*, p. 53.
30   Foucault, 'Méthodologie pour la Connaissance du Monde: Comment se débarrasser du marxisme', *Dits et écrits* III, p. 606. All translations of *Dits et écrits* III are my own.

8

the analyses of Marx's contemporaries 'in terms of their perspicuity, their efficacy, [and] their analytic qualities', and they 'radically surpass' those of Marx's predecessors.[31] Foucault expands on what he has learned from Marx's histories in 'The Meshes of Power' when he claims that *Capital* offers a history of the emergence of positive mechanisms of power and, in particular, of mechanisms of disciplinary power in a number of institutional sites, including the army and the workshop.[32]

Apart from the influences of Kant, Hegel and Marx, Nietzsche's influence on Adorno's and Foucault's work must not be overlooked. In fact, Adorno makes a revealing remark in one of his lectures on moral philosophy when he tells students that, 'of all the so-called great philosophers, I owe him [Nietzsche] by far the greatest debt – more even than to Hegel'.[33] Adorno made this remark in a discussion of Nietzsche's critique of morality. Commenting on it, Fabian Freyenhagen notes that Adorno adopted many of Nietzsche's ideas about modern morality, including his ideas about the connections between ascetic values and entrenched interests along with his views about the persistence of 'faded theological ideas' in secular values.[34] But apart from Nietzsche's influence on his ideas about morality, Adorno also adopted a Nietzschean view of domination when he cited Nietzsche's phrase 'No shepherd, and one herd'. In this phrase, Nietzsche denounced 'a completely functionalized and anonymous form of domination' that rules over the herd of sheep-like individuals 'with much greater brutality than if there were a visible bell-weather for them to follow'.[35]

Foucault has similar ideas about the sheep-like qualities of the dominated and the anonymity of domination. He and Adorno both expand on Nietzsche's observations about the levelling and conformist tendencies in the West, while noting that these tendencies only became more pronounced in the twentieth century. Highlighting these tendencies, 'Notes on Individuation' will show that Adorno also links conformity to the tendency of modern thought summarily to identify particulars with universal concepts. Here too, Nietzsche's influence made itself felt. Samir Gandesha explains that, for Adorno and Nietzsche, words originally referred to our experiences of particular things. Over time, however, words were used to identify particulars that bore only a 'superficial similarity' to the things for which they were first coined. As a result, differences between things

8

31   Ibid., p. 612.
32   Foucault, 'The Meshes of Power', *Space, Knowledge and Power*, p. 156. In this article, Foucault says that he is referring to Volume 2 of *Le Capital*. However, he seems be referring to Volume 1 of the English translation of *Capital*, and in particular to Part Four, Chapter 14. Anecdotally, my French translation of Volume 1 of *Capital* (which was extensively revised by Marx himself) ends with Part Three.
33   Adorno, *Problems of Moral Philosophy*, p. 172.
34   Fabian Freyenhagen, *Adorno's Practical Philosophy*, p. 125.
35   Adorno, *Problems of Moral Philosophy*, p. 174. See also Friedrich Nietzsche, *Thus Spoke Zarathustra* in *The Portable Nietzsche*, p. 130.

were effaced in favour of identity.[36] Calling the prevailing mode of thought 'identity thinking', Adorno avers that, when it subsumes diverse objects under a single concept, modern thought obliterates their particularity. Thought aims – to cite Nietzsche, who interpreted this behaviour as a manifestation of the will to power – to *make* all being thinkable, to force it to yield and bend to us.[37]

Following Nietzsche, Adorno is interested in our 'underground history', or the history of the body in the West. In particular, he is interested in the 'fate' of our instincts or drives once these were 'displaced and distorted by civilization'.[38] But 'Notes on Individuation' will also demonstrate that Foucault offers his own account of our underground history when he examines the impact of power on the body. In fact, Foucault says that it was Nietzsche who first articulated the relation between the body and history. Nietzsche tasked genealogy with exposing 'a body totally imprinted by history', along with 'the process of history's destruction of the body'.[39] Calling his own histories 'genealogies', Foucault follows Nietzsche when he studies the '"history of bodies" and the manner in which what is most material and most vital in them has been invested'.[40] Equally important for Foucault, it was Nietzsche who 'specified the power relation as the general focus . . . of philosophical discourse'. Nietzsche was a 'philosopher of power, a philosopher who managed to think about power without having to confine himself within a political theory in order to do so'.[41] Nietzsche also transformed our ideas about truth when he asked about its history, or the conditions under which particular modes of veridiction (or truth-telling) emerged, while linking this question to questions about power.[42]

If, to cite John Ransom, Nietzsche's genealogies seek 'to uncover the battles that gave birth to the world that we accept as natural, to make it questionable again, and to make it possible to fight over it once more', Foucault's genealogies share these goals.[43] By unearthing the historical conditions that made possible phenomena (including sexuality and madness) that have become so familiar that we simply take them for granted, genealogy aims to defamiliarize them and to distance us from them.[44] Yet Foucault also diverges from Nietzsche when he uses his genealogies to provide individuals who experience their subjection to power as intolerable with tools that may enable them to overcome it. Nietzsche often expressed disdain for the weak and the oppressed – with their 'slave morality' – but Foucault's genealogies aim to empower them.

---

36   Samir Gandesha, 'Leaving Home', *The Cambridge Companion to Adorno*, p. 109.
37   Friedrich Nietzsche, *Thus Spoke Zarathustra* in *The Portable Nietzsche*, p. 225.
38   Horkheimer and Adorno, *Dialectic of Enlightenment*, p. 231. See also the later translation: *Dialectic of Enlightenment: Philosophical Fragments*, p. 192.
39   Foucault, 'Nietzsche, Genealogy, History', *Essential Works: Aesthetics*, p. 376.
40   Foucault, *The History of Sexuality*, Vol. 1, p. 152.
41   Foucault, 'Prison Talk', *Power/Knowledge*, p. 53; trans. mod.
42   Foucault, *Wrong-doing, Truth-telling*, p. 20.
43   John S. Ransom, *Foucault's Discipline*, p. 5.
44   Ibid., pp. 80–1.

Nietzsche found another admirer in the person of Sigmund Freud. Although I shall offer an extended discussion of Freud's influence in 'Notes on Individuation', I shall make a few remarks about that influence here. Adorno's interest in Freud dates back to the mid-1920s when he wrote his *Habitationschrift* on Freud's theory of the unconscious – a dissertation that his supervisor, Cornelius, advised him to withdraw.[45] Yet Cornelius' rejection of his thesis (which Adorno replaced with a thesis on Søren Kierkegaard) by no means discouraged Adorno from pursuing his interest in Freud. From his inaugural lecture in Frankfurt in 1931, where he spoke briefly about Freud's interpretive techniques, to his final works (including his unfinished and post-humously published *Aesthetic Theory*), Adorno made use of psychoanalysis to study the psychology of individuals under late – or monopoly – capitalism. Adopting Freud's instinct theory, Adorno would focus throughout his work on the vicissitudes of the instinct of self-preservation, warning that, by remaining in thrall to untamed survival instincts, we could well end by destroying ourselves.

In an essay he wrote while an émigré in California during World War II, Adorno commented indirectly on the alleged incompatibility of Marxism and psychoanalysis. There he praised Freud for showing, albeit only implicitly, 'that the social principle of domination coincides with the psychological one of the repression of instincts both ontogenetically and phylogenetically'.[46] Upon his return to Germany after the war had ended, Adorno revisited this problem, interpreting the tension between the analysis of society and the analysis of the psyche as evidence that a tension exists between society and the psyche them-selves. On the one hand, to separate society and psyche is false because this separation 'perpetuates conceptually the split between the living subject and the objectivity that governs the subjects and yet derives from them'.[47] (To cite Simon Jarvis, the separation is false when it is treated as though it were natural and invariant.[48]) On the other hand, this separation is true to the extent that 'inner and outer life' really are 'torn apart' under late capitalism. Decoding psychoanalysis as an expression of the *Zeitgeist*, Adorno defended its focus on instincts and the unconscious – or on our 'archaic heritage' – because, by emphasizing the rift between inner and outer life, psychoanalysis says 'more about the hapless state of society than one which seeks, by its "holistic" approach or an inclusion of "social factors", to join the ranks of a no longer existing *universitas literarum*'.[49]

---

45   Müller-Doohm, *Adorno*, p. 103.

46   Adorno, 'Die Revidierte Psychoanalyse', *Soziologische Schriften* I, p. 27; my translation. This paper was originally presented in English to the Psychoanalytic Society in San Francisco in 1946.

47   Adorno, 'Sociology and Psychology', *New Left Review* 46, p. 69.

48   Simon Jarvis, *Adorno*, p. 82.

49   Adorno, 'Sociology and Psychology', *New Left Review* 46, p. 70. See also Adorno, *Introduction to Sociology*, pp. 113–14.

Foucault is thought by many commentators to be much less sympathetic to Freud, but it is important to stress that he had an extensive background in psychology. After completing a philosophy degree at the École Normale, Foucault took a second degree in psychology there in 1949. In addition, he received a diploma in psychopathology from the Institut de Psychologie in 1952. During the early 1950s, Foucault also worked at Sainte-Anne, a psychiatric hospital in Paris. While there, he helped with the translation of Ludwig Binswanger's *Traum und Existenz* – a translation for which he wrote the introduction.[50] In 1953–4, Foucault taught psychology, including psychoanalysis, at the University of Lille; he also published his first works: a book on mental illness and a short monograph that traced the history of psychology from 1850 to 1950. When he occupied the position of director of the Maison de France in Uppsala, Sweden in the mid-1950s, Foucault began to work on the history of madness that would become his primary thesis at the Sorbonne. And, after receiving his doctorate, he continued to teach psychology for several years at the University of Clermont-Ferrand.[51]

I am stressing Foucault's background in psychology to demonstrate that Foucault was hardly a novice in this field. Nor was his relation to Freud as fraught as some have claimed. Concerned that his criticisms of Freud had been misunderstood, Foucault denied that his attempts to situate psychoanalysis historically (by, for example, tracing its therapeutic techniques back to Christian confessional practices) amounted to an 'anti-psychoanalysis'.[52] In fact, far from simply rejecting psychoanalysis, Foucault admired Freud because, among other things, Freud had re-evaluated 'in the most fundamental way the somewhat sacred priority conferred on the subject, which has become established in Western thought since Descartes'.[53] Although Foucault contends that it was Jacques Lacan who made this re-evaluation explicit, he acknowledges, with Lacan, that Freud had demonstrated that the 'subject has a genesis, a formation, a history', or that the subject 'is not originary'.[54] In fact, I shall argue later that Foucault's account of individuation resembles Freud's in important respects.

For much of the twentieth century, phenomenology was in vogue in both Germany and France. Yet Foucault and Adorno criticized phenomenology on similar grounds. They both argued that phenomenology posits an originary subject that pre-exists social forces and is affected by them only externally. In fact, *Against Epistemology*, Adorno's extended critique of Edmund Husserl (based on a manuscript he wrote at Oxford as an advanced student under

---

50   Foucault's introduction first appeared in Ludwig Binswanger, *Rêve et existence*.
51   I am relying on Macey's account of Foucault's research and teaching during the 1940s, '50s and '60s in several chapters of *The Lives of Michel Foucault*.
52   Foucault, 'The History of Sexuality', *Power/Knowledge*, p. 192.
53   Foucault, 'Truth and Juridical Forms', *Essential Works: Power*, p. 3.
54   Foucault, 'La Scène de la Philosophie', *Dits et écrits* III, p. 590.

Gilbert Ryle before he emigrated to the United States in 1938), rehearsed some of Adorno's criticisms of Kant's transcendental subject. These criticisms reappear in *Negative Dialectics* where Adorno develops a materialist conception of the subject. Charging that Husserl treats consciousness as "'a sphere of absolute origins'", Adorno insists that consciousness is a function 'of the living subject', an 'empirical consciousness', a 'living I' (ND 185 *passim*). But Husserl's conception of objects was also problematic. Although he takes up Husserl's call to return to things themselves, Adorno argues against Husserl that things can be grasped only by 'reflecting, at every historical and cognitive stage, both upon what at that time is presented as subject and object as well as upon their mediations'.[55] The return to things requires that we reflect on our interaction with things under specific historical conditions.

Since much of Adorno's work is devoted to showing that individuals are thoroughly embedded in, and profoundly conditioned by, exchange relations under late capitalism, Adorno also criticizes Jean-Paul Sartre's radical claims about freedom. Yet he reserves his more splenetic criticisms for Martin Heidegger (many of which appear in *The Jargon of Authenticity*). According to Adorno, Heidegger insists that we neither think about Being speculatively – that is, 'have any thoughts that posit anything whatsoever' about Being – nor conceive of it as 'an entity' because this would compromise the 'precedence of Being'. As a result, Being is 'a complete vacuum, a capital X far emptier than the ancient transcendental subject' (ND 79). Criticisms like these make it difficult to countenance the view that Adorno was closer to Heidegger than he believed. As Brian O'Connor points out, there are 'profound difficulties in aligning Adorno with Heidegger' given Adorno's emphatic rejection of Heidegger's fundamental ontology. Since the subtlety of Adorno's position 'lies precisely in those aspects of it' that oppose Heidegger's 'version of antiepistemological philosophy', O'Connor contends (correctly, in my view) that any points of alignment are entirely 'coincidental'.[56]

Foucault is as critical as Adorno of phenomenological conceptions of the subject. Nevertheless, Peter Dews alleges (in a book that is contemporaneous with the work of Honneth and Hoy) that Foucault's critique of the subject is quite distinct from Adorno's because Foucault wanted to do away with the subject altogether whereas Adorno sought a new mode of subjectivity.[57] *Pace* Dews, however, this interpretation is problematic because (as the chapter on

---

55   Adorno, 'On Subject and Object', *Critical Models*, p. 253. Peter E. Gordon has argued that Adorno's reading of phenomenology helped to shape his philosophy. See Gordon, *Adorno and Existence*, p. 82: 'Adorno . . . would move toward the thought of negative dialectics via a critical reading of phenomenology; and it was precisely the failure of phenomenology to achieve its proposed "breakthrough" from the subject to the object that would help him to grasp "the impossibility of reducing the real to its concept" or "the object to the subject".'

56   Brian O'Connor, *Adorno's Negative Dialectic*, pp. 149–50. Perhaps the last word should go to Adorno: 'The lure of Being is as eloquent as the rustle of leaves in the wind of bad poems' (ND 77).

57   Peter Dews, *Logics of Disintegration*, p. 152.

resistance will argue) Foucault wanted 'to promote new forms of subjectivity through the refusal of this kind of individuality that has been imposed on us for several centuries'.[58] Rather than rejecting the subject *tout court*, Foucault followed Adorno when he repudiated ahistorical and foundational conceptions of it. For Foucault, moreover, a particularly reprehensible example of this view can be found in Sartre. Disputing Sartre's ideas about consciousness, Foucault repeatedly defended Freud's theory of the unconscious.[59] He also contested Sartre's radical conception of freedom when he insisted that it is impossible to ignore the 'forces' that intervene in our lives.[60] As I interpret this reference to forces, it is not just the unconscious, but the impact of power and knowledge on the formation of the subject that belie Sartrean freedom.

Denying that the subject is originary, Foucault also criticized the work of Maurice Merleau-Ponty. Hubert Dreyfus and Paul Rabinow explain that, despite Merleau-Ponty's insistence that the subject is embodied, Foucault thought that he 'ignored . . . the historical and cultural dimensions of being a body'.[61] Yet Dreyfus and Rabinow believe that Foucault was strongly influenced by Heidegger – a belief that Foucault seemed to confirm in a late interview when he said that Heidegger was 'the essential philosopher' for him in the 1950s. Still, Foucault also said that he was barely acquainted with *Being and Time* or Heidegger's recent work. In fact, he arguably implied that it was Heidegger's multi-volume *Nietzsche* that led him to the thinker whose influence would prove more decisive. After mentioning Heidegger's early influence, Foucault declared: 'I am simply Nietzschean, and I try to see on a number of points, and to the extent that it is possible, with the aid of Nietzsche's texts – but also with anti-Nietzschean theses (which are nevertheless Nietzschean!) – what can be done in this or that domain.'[62]

58   Foucault, 'The Subject and Power', *Essential Works: Power*, p. 336. Cited hereafter in the text as SP.

59   See Foucault, 'Interview with Michel Foucault', *Essential Works: Power*, p. 251. See also Foucault's defence of the unconscious in 'La Scène de la Philosophie', *Dits et écrits* III, p. 590, and 'Critical Theory/Intellectual History', *Politics, Philosophy, Culture*, pp. 21–2.

60   Foucault, 'M. Foucault. Conversation sans Complexes avec le Philosophe qui analyse les "Structures du Pouvoir"', *Dits et écrits* III, p. 671.

61   Hubert L. Dreyfus and Paul Rabinow, *Michel Foucault*, p. 166.

62   Foucault, 'The Return of Morality', *Politics, Philosophy, Culture*, pp. 250–1 *passim*. Foucault does refer to Heidegger's *The Question Concerning Technology* in the draft of a lecture he gave in New York. Frédéric Gros cites this draft in 'Course Context', *The Hermeneutics of the Subject*, p. 523: '"In Heidegger, it was on the basis of the Western *tekhnē* that knowledge of the object sealed the forgetting of Being. Let's turn the question around and ask ourselves on the basis of what tekhnai was the Western subject formed and were the games of truth and error, freedom and constraint, which characterized this subject, opened up."' Gros suggests (on page 524) that these remarks shed more light on Foucault's claim (on page 189 of *The Hermeneutics of the Subject*) that he has reflected on the relation between the subject and truth 'starting from Heidegger'. But see also Foucault, 'The Ethics of the Concern for Self as a Practice of Freedom', *Essential Works: Ethics*, pp. 294–5: 'Nothing is more foreign to me than the idea that, at a certain moment, philosophy went astray and forgot something, that somewhere in its history, there is a principle, a foundation that must be rediscovered.'

14

Adorno and Foucault both study the effects of historical conditions on the process of individuation. In contrast to Foucault, however, Adorno also conducted empirical research on various aspects of social conditioning, and he made use of sociology in his critique of socialization and social integration in the West. Among other sociologists, Adorno cited Émile Durkheim, Georg Simmel, Thorstein Veblen and David Riesman. However, J. M. Bernstein claims that Max Weber had a greater impact on Adorno; he argues that Weber's influence eclipses even Marx's because Adorno's reading of Marx was informed by 'the Weberian reading of *Capital* provided by Lukács' *History and Class Consciousness*'.[63] Yet Bernstein's view is problematic, not least because Adorno said that Weber misunderstood capitalism. Weber equated capitalism too much with its 'spirit' when he focussed almost exclusively on the rationality that underlies it. Although he agreed with Weber that capitalism has a distinct rationality, Adorno defended Marx against Weber. Among other things, Weber's emphasis on the spirit of capitalism led him to disregard the stratification of society into classes which 'reproduces itself by way of the exchange of equivalents' (ND 166).

Nevertheless, Bernstein is right to point out that, in his extensive critique of late capitalist society, Adorno adopts – though not uncritically – Weber's idea of rationalization, along with what Bernstein calls its two 'interlocking elements': the disenchantment of the world by modern science and 'the bureaucratisation of everyday life'.[64] As I shall argue in the following section, Adorno also takes up Weber's notion of ideal types, comparing them favourably to what he calls (following Walter Benjamin) constellations. Citing Weber, Adorno notes that ideal types are '"gradually composed" from "individual parts to be taken from historical reality"'; they consist in constellations of concepts that can be used to understand diverse phenomena, including capitalism itself (ND 165).[65]

For his part, Foucault criticizes ideal types on the grounds that Weber effectively saw them as ideal essences or rational principles. Contrasting his work with Weber's, Foucault claims that his genealogies of phenomena such as delinquency, madness and sexuality explore concrete historical programmes. These programmes may be based on principles, but they often deviate from them, use them selectively, or compete with other programmes. And while a more general rationality may underlie them, this rationality is not based – as in Weber – on the calculation of interests, but on a 'whole technology of human training, surveillance of behaviour, individualization of elements of a social body'. In fact,

63   J. M. Bernstein, *Adorno: Disenchantment and Ethics*, p. 7 n. 10. In this note, Bernstein says that the emphasis he places on Weber may be understood 'as a simplifying, heuristic device'. Yet he also claims that Adorno's position 'seems to develop more out of Weber's than Marx's'. Unfortunately, Bernstein never redeems this claim. Instead, he suggests that it was not Weber, but Georg Lukács' appropriation of Weber, that was more important for Adorno.
64   Ibid., p. 7.
65   See Max Weber, *The Protestant Ethic and the Spirit of Capitalism*, p. 47.

Foucault denies that discipline is an ideal type. Instead, discipline represents the 'generalization and interconnection of different techniques' – techniques which nonetheless respond 'to localized requirements'.[66]

By the end of the 1970s, however, Foucault saw himself as part of a critical tradition that includes Weber because (like Kant, Hegel and the Frankfurt School) Weber was also trying to comprehend and critique our present.[67] Indeed, Dreyfus and Rabinow point out that Foucault's criticisms of ideal types were given such 'disproportionate attention' in the secondary literature that they masked the complementarity between Weber's and Foucault's work. In this context, Dreyfus and Rabinow also observe that Foucault's assertion that 'the "problem of reason" must be treated historically and not metaphysically is certainly something with which [both] Weber and Adorno would agree'.[68] Since Adorno's and Foucault's ideas about the rationality that characterizes Western societies will be discussed at the end of this book, I shall simply note here that several commentators have shown that Foucault's analysis of disciplinary power is consonant in important respects with Weber's account of discipline.[69]

The philosopher and historian of science, Georges Canguilhem (another of Foucault's professors), also had a significant impact on Foucault. In his early histories especially, Foucault adopted Canguilhem's view that history is discontinuous (though he later said that discontinuity itself is impermanent and discontinuous[70]). Canguilhem's ideas about normativity in science also proved important: Foucault borrowed from Canguilhem the idea that, in science, 'the processes of elimination and selection of statements, theories, [and] objects are made at each instant in terms of a certain norm'.[71] Foucault also showed himself to be an adept pupil of Canguilhem when he traced the historical development of numerous social scientific concepts. Equally important, Foucault compared Canguilhem favourably to the Frankfurt School in his introduction to *The Normal and the Pathological* when he argued that they both question 'a rationality that makes universal claims while developing in contingency; that asserts its unity, and yet proceeds only by means of partial modifications, if not by general recastings [*refontes générales*]; that authenticates itself with reference to its sovereignty but which, in its history, cannot be dissociated from the inertias, weights, or coercions that subjugate it'.[72]

---

66   Foucault, 'Questions of Method', *The Foucault Effect*, p. 80.
67   Foucault, 'What is Enlightenment?', *Essential Works: Ethics*, p. 312.
68   Dreyfus and Rabinow, *Michel Foucault*, pp. 132–3.
69   See, for example, Barry Smart, *Foucault, Marxism and Critique*, pp. 123–32; John O'Neill, 'The Disciplinary Society', *The British Journal of Sociology*, pp. 42–60; and Colin Gordon, 'The Soul of the Citizen', *Max Weber*, pp. 293–316.
70   Foucault, 'Introduction' in Canguilhem, *The Normal and the Pathological*, p. 15.
71   Ibid., p. 16.
72   Ibid., p. 12; trans. mod. Foucault makes a similar remark in 'Critical Theory/Intellectual History', *Politics, Philosophy, Culture*, p. 27.

16

Of course, many other thinkers had an impact on Foucault's work, including Gaston Bachelard, Georges Bataille, Pierre Klossowski and Louis Althusser. This account of the thinkers who influenced Foucault does not pretend to be exhaustive. Other thinkers who influenced Adorno include Georg Lukács,[73] Ernst Bloch, Karl Krauss and Alfred Sohn-Rethel, not to mention Adorno's co-workers at the Frankfurt School. In fact, to round out the list of influences on Adorno and Foucault, one would need to include playwrights, novelists, poets and painters such as Samuel Beckett and Franz Kafka, Paul Celan, Édouard Manet, René Magritte and Paul Klee. A musician and composer himself, Adorno's work (and certainly his aesthetics) was also influenced by the music of Alban Berg, Arnold Schönberg and Gustav Mahler. For his part, Foucault said that the music of Jean Barraqué, Georges Messiaen and Pierre Boulez was as important for him as the philosophy of Nietzsche because it 'offered him his first escape from the dialectical universe in which he was still living', and it 'taught him a lesson that warned him against "categories of the universal"'.[74]

Finally, I remarked in the preface that certain experiences had a formative impact on Adorno and Foucault: in particular, their experiences of the Second World War and fascism. This book will demonstrate that the spectre of fascism haunts Adorno's and Foucault's critical theories. It is the threat that fascism might recur that prompts them to plumb Kant's famous essay on enlightenment to find resources to serve as a bulwark against it. Like Kant, Adorno and Foucault hope to promote maturity by encouraging individuals to engage in sustained – critical and self-critical – reflection on the social, political and economic conditions that have made them what they are. For Adorno and Foucault believe that, if people were able to see through their entanglement in these conditions, they could rise above them and more effectively resist them. For both, moreover, whatever freedom we can meaningfully be said to possess consists in such resistance. Foucault shares Adorno's view that morality today consists in resistance to the 'predominance of the merely existent, under which in fact we all must suffer today'.[75]

CRITICAL GAMBITS

Adorno and Foucault forged novel and distinct critical approaches to the study of our historical present, but their approaches are similar to the extent that they have an anti-systematic, anti-authoritarian and open-ended character. Always

---

73   Douglas Kellner argues that Lukács' appreciation of the Hegelian roots of Marxism and the importance of dialectics, his application of Marx's economic concepts to social phenomena, his enlargement of the concept of reification, his rejection of orthodox Marxism's economic determinism, and his insistence on the importance of subjectivity had a powerful impact on all critical theorists. See Kellner, *Critical Theory, Marxism, and Modernity*, pp. 10–11.

74   Macey, *The Lives of Michel Foucault*, pp. 53–4 *passim*.

75   I am quoting and paraphrasing Adorno, 'Discussion of Professor Adorno's Lecture "The Meaning of Working through the Past"', *Critical Models*, p. 297.

prepared to acknowledge their own fallibility and the provisional nature of their work, Adorno and Foucault by no means claimed to offer definitive accounts of our current predicament. Of course, they also stressed the importance of history for social theory and, specifically, the importance of understanding the historical conditions that have shaped, often to our detriment, our identities and modes of thought. Following a discussion of the character of their work, I shall examine the more significant ways in which Foucault's genealogies complement Adorno's negative dialectics. Specifically, I hope to show that there is at least one sense in which Adorno and Foucault can both be regarded as nonidentity thinkers.

Adorno was a resolutely anti-systematic philosopher; he charged that all attempts to subsume phenomena under a unitary principle (or principles) are authoritarian. He called his negative dialectics an 'anti-system' because it tries to apprehend what lies outside the 'sway of such unity' by using 'the strength of the subject to break through the fallacy of constitutive subjectivity', or to undermine the belief that particular things can simply be identified with the subject's universal concepts (ND xx). Criticizing idealism, Adorno argued that it has a 'primal history in the pre-mental, the animal life of the species' because it merely sublimates the rage that other animals direct against their prey. Praising Nietzsche for his 'liberating act' of putting 'such mysteries into words', Adorno adopted his view that idealism implicitly endorses the idea that the 'not-I, l'autrui, and finally all that reminds us of nature is inferior, so that the unity of self-preserving thought may devour it without misgivings'. In a potent metaphor, Adorno declared that the system is 'the belly turned mind, and rage is the mark of each and every idealism' (ND 22–3 passim).

The impulse to systematize has a societal counterpart in late capitalism, a socio-economic system that preponderates over individuals, affecting virtually all aspects of their thought and behaviour. According to Adorno, it is this 'negative objectivity that is a system, not the positive subject' (ND 20). Even as the subject (including philosophers and scientists) tries to subsume phenomena systematically under its concepts, it has itself already been socially assimilated. To return to an earlier point, Hegel said that spirit encompassed everything and, as Freyenhagen observes, 'something like this has indeed become reality, but in a different way from what Hegel envisaged'. For Adorno, however, 'it is not spirit but society that is the whole, and instead of constituting absolute truth, "The whole is the untrue"'.[76] Late capitalist society has become an oppressive totality.

Adorno's study of the totalizing features of late capitalist society centres on its economic tendencies and trends. By contrast (and to anticipate an idea discussed in Chapter Four), Foucault explores the totalizing features of the biopolitical state, totalizing because the state subsumes individuals under a

---

76   Freyenhagen, Adorno's Practical Philosophy, p. 36. 'The whole is untrue' is an aphorism in Adorno, Minima Moralia, p. 50.

relatively new form of collectivity: the population. Yet despite the differences in the targets of their critiques, Adorno and Foucault agree that Western societies exhibit two pernicious tendencies that promote totalization: they foster dependency and submission by virtue of unrelenting social integration, and they marginalize and exclude those who resist integration or who are otherwise insensible to its effects. Adorno and Foucault want to combat both tendencies for a number of reasons, not least because these tendencies helped to make possible the racism that continues to blight the Western world.

A critic of totalization on the societal level, Foucault is equally critical of the totalizing effects of concepts. Again, he rejects the idea of a constituent subject, and examines instead how the subject and its concepts have themselves been formed or constituted under specific historical conditions. He is especially suspicious of anthropological universals on the grounds that they ignore what is historically distinct in the phenomena – including madness, criminality and sexuality – that constitute the subject. Interested in what made phenomena like these possible, Foucault explores the 'conditions that enable people, according to the rules of true and false statements, to recognize a subject as mentally ill or to arrange that a subject recognize the most essential part of himself in the modality of his sexual desire'.[77]

Adorno's and Foucault's animus against totalizing philosophical systems also affects the character of their work. Like Nietzsche, Adorno sometimes wrote in aphorisms (such as 'The whole is the untrue'), and he addressed disparate, and often ostensibly disconnected, themes in short, pithy passages in *Minima Moralia* and other work. His rejection of systematic philosophy also helps to explain why he valued the essay form. As the word itself implies, an essay is tentative, not definitive; it does not begin or end with first principles, and it respects the nonidentical, the fragmentary and the partial because these can be conveyed neither in an 'airtight order of concepts' nor in closed 'deductive or inductive' constructions.[78] Adorno also criticizes Plato's and Hegel's view that what is transitory is unworthy of philosophy, adding that it is the nonconceptual, the individual and the particular that are 'matters of true philosophical interest at this point in history' (ND 8). In 'The Essay as Form', Adorno emphatically rejects Plato's 'notion that the result of abstraction, the temporally invariant concept indifferent to the individual phenomenon grasped by it, deserves ontological dignity'.[79]

As for Foucault, he denied that he was a theorist, by which he meant someone who 'constructs a general system, either deductive or analytical, and applies it to different fields in a uniform way'. Describing himself as an experimenter, Foucault only underscored the tentative character of his work and its

77   Maurice Florence [pseudonym for Michel Foucault], 'Foucault', *Essential Works: Aesthetics*, pp. 461–2 *passim*.

78   Adorno, 'The Essay as Form', *New German Critique* 32, p. 158.

79   Ibid.

fragmentary character.[80] Foucault's work is also anti-systematic in the sense that he explored the logic of specific mechanisms, technologies and strategies of power, along with the struggles that have been waged against these in particular sites. This research obviously requires that close attention be paid to historical conditions whose singularity defies subsumption under an overarching universal history. In contrast to Adorno, however, whose work is remarkably consistent, Foucault's ideas changed over the years. His antipathy towards systematic thought meant that he pursued enthusiastically new directions in his research (his later study of care of the self in ancient Greece and Hellenistic Rome is a case in point), and he readily acknowledged the disparities that exist between his earlier and later work.

History is central in Adorno's and Foucault's work. Trying to grasp transitory particulars, Adorno studies phenomena that run the gamut from jazz music and astrology columns in *The Los Angeles Times* to new technologies and institutions under late capitalism. Of course, Adorno argues that all particulars (including individuals) are shaped by objective historical trends that are linked to the vicissitudes of the capitalist economy, but he also insists that these more general trends do not fully capture the particular things over which they preponderate. Consequently, things must not be identified with them. At one and the same time, Adorno warns that if we immerse ourselves too much in historical details, we risk 'not seeing the forest for the trees', but 'if we distance ourselves too much, we shall be unable to grasp history because the categories we use themselves become excessively magnified to the point where they become problematic and fail to do justice to their material'.[81]

To understand our historical present, Adorno claims that we must examine closely the antagonistic interplay between universal tendencies and particulars. On his view, moreover, this interplay is the proper object of both history and philosophy.[82] In fact, Adorno declares in his lectures on history and freedom that 'philosophy should tend to become history, just as readily as history should become philosophy'.[83] He elaborates on this idea in another, unpublished, lecture, claiming that it means that history, 'raised to the realm of self-knowledge, is identical with what philosophy traditionally claims to be'.[84]

80   Foucault, 'Interview with Michel Foucault', *Essential Works: Power*, p. 240.
81   Adorno, *History and Freedom*, p. 11; trans. mod.
82   Ibid.
83   Ibid., p. 40. Rolf Tiedemann (the editor of *History and Freedom*) interprets the claim that philosophy should become history and history philosophy to mean that philosophy should realize itself in history (see *History and Freedom*, pp. 276–7 n. 14). But while Adorno did endorse Marx's claim that philosophy should realize itself in history, he suggests here that philosophy and history converge in terms of their subject matter, namely the antagonistic relations between objective historical trends (the universal) and individuals (the particular).
84   Ibid., pp. 276–7 n. 14. In this note, Tiedemann says that he is citing an unpublished lecture on the philosophy of history. He may be citing 'Einleitung in die Geschichtsphilosophie', lectures that Adorno delivered in the summer of 1957.

Although he also concedes that he is 'no historian',[85] Adorno nonetheless provides a philosophically informed analysis of the historical conditions that shape both thought and things, even as he gestures obliquely towards a future in which these conditions have been transformed so that the uniqueness of particular things and individuals is not just comprehended by thought but flourishes in reality.

Since Adorno believes that philosophy and history converge in their focus on the antagonisms that blight our historical present, the parallels between his work and Foucault's are all the more evident. For Foucault adopted a comparable view of history, especially in the last decade of his life. Yet in his interview with Trombadori, Foucault objected, with some justification, that critical theorists did not do history 'in the full sense'. Instead, they were 'eaters of history as others have prepared it'. They made use of work by professional historians – 'usually of a Marxist tendency' – which supplied them with a 'material foundation' for explaining sociological and psychological phenomena. To this criticism Foucault added – somewhat confusingly – that critical theorists assume that the sociological and psychological phenomena they study 'are not of the same order as history'. Here, however, he raised an important point that will be a major theme in the next chapter, namely that critical theorists simply presuppose the primacy of the economy in society.[86]

Although Adorno emphasizes the importance of history for philosophy, I have already noted that he admitted he was not an historian. Conversely, even as he stressed the importance of philosophy – in the form of a critical social theory – for understanding history, Foucault said at least once that he was not a philosopher.[87] Eschewing ready-made history, Foucault wrote original histories that explored power relations, including the struggles that have been waged, and continue to be waged, against disciplinary power and biopower by individuals and groups in many different sites. In fact, as I mentioned earlier, when Foucault adopted a view of human history that highlighted the antagonisms, conflicts and struggles that rend it, he openly acknowledged his debt to Marx.

Adorno's negative dialectics and Foucault's genealogies could be described as species of the genus critique: they not only try to demonstrate how we have become what we are, they cast a resolutely critical light on the historical forces that have made us what we are. To end this discussion, I want to explore some of the more important similarities and differences between these critical approaches to the study of our present. I use the phrase 'critical approaches' because Adorno often denied that he had a method. Aiming to apprehend particulars, Adorno contends that disparate phenomena cannot be grasped using a single method.[88] As for Foucault, he told Trombadori that he became aware of his methodological approach only after he had written his histories. In

85   Ibid., p. 39.
86   Foucault, 'An Interview with Michel Foucault', *Essential Works: Power*, pp. 276–7 *passim*.
87   Ibid., p. 240.
88   Adorno, *Lectures on 'Negative Dialectics'*, p. 5.

other words, his so-called methods were developed *post hoc*.[89] Consequently, it is important to note from the outset that Adorno and Foucault did not employ a well-defined method that they applied indiscriminately to all the phenomena they studied.

In a preliminary definition of negative dialectics, Adorno states that negative dialectics 'says nothing more, to begin with, than that objects do not go into concepts without leaving a remainder, that they come to contradict the traditional norm of adequacy'. This 'contradiction' of the *adequatio rei et intellectus* 'indicates the untruth of identity, the fact that the concept does not exhaust the thing conceived' (ND 5). Identity is 'untrue' because, when it identifies particular things with universal concepts, identity thinking merely indicates what a thing 'exemplifies or represents, and what, accordingly, it is not itself' (ND 149). In identity thinking, as Bernstein notes, a thing is known 'only when it is classified in some way', or 'when it is shown, via subsumption, to share characteristics or features' with other things. Similarly, 'an event is explained if it can be shown to fall within the ambit of a known pattern of occurrence, if it falls within the ambit of a known rule or is deducible from (subsumable by) a known law'. In turn, concepts, rules and laws have cognitive value only when they are 'subsumed under or shown to be deducible from higher-level concepts, rules, or laws'.[90]

Adorno objects to identity thinking, not simply on the epistemological grounds that it fails to apprehend things, but because it damages things when it effaces their particularity in favour of the characteristics that they have in common with other things. Fetishizing concepts, identity thinking imposes a conceptual identity on nonconceptual particulars that does them an injustice because it distorts them by abstracting from everything that makes them unique. By extension, once diverse things are subsumed under a particular concept, the features that they share with things that are ranged under other concepts are largely effaced or occulted. These problems are especially pernicious in the case of concepts such as women and men, for example, or blacks and whites, Muslims and Christians, but they skew our understanding of all other people and things as well.

Against identity thinking, Adorno objects that when 'B is defined as an A, it is always also *different from* and *more than* the A'.[91] In one of its principal iterations, then, negative dialectics simply emphasizes the fact that things are not concepts and concepts are not things. Contrasting his dialectics with Hegel's, Adorno says that negative dialectics is 'a dialectics not of identity, but of *non-identity*'.[92] But negative dialectics differs from Hegel's dialectics for a related reason: where Hegel tried to subsume everything under a totalizing system, negative dialectics cancels 'the subject's claim to be first' (ND 139). Negative

---

89   Foucault, 'An Interview with Michel Foucault', *Essential Works: Power*, p. 240.
90   Bernstein, *Adorno*, p. 87.
91   Adorno, *Lectures on 'Negative Dialectics'*, p. 7; italics in the text.
92   Ibid., p. 6; italics in the text.

dialectics gives 'the Copernican revolution an axial turn', or an orientation towards things themselves (ND xx).

In short, negative dialectics involves 'the consistent sense of nonidentity', or what Adorno calls nonidentity thinking (ND 5). To be sure, both identity thinking and nonidentity thinking attempt to apprehend things, but nonidentity thinking tries to grasp things by immersing 'itself in things . . . without placing those things in prefabricated categories'. Its aim, initially, is 'total self-relinquishment' (ND 13). Yet Adorno also concedes that particular things can be apprehended only by means of universal concepts. In principle, concepts can do justice to things because they are themselves 'entwined with a nonconceptual whole', or with the material world in which they originated (ND 12). Furthermore, the subjects who employ concepts are themselves embedded in the material world that they seek to understand; they belong 'a priori to the same sphere as the given thing' (ND 196). Even as it entrusts itself to experience, then, nonidentity thinking tries to approximate conceptually the things with which it is already 'akin by virtue of its own objective being'.[93]

Earlier I said that Adorno adopts a version of Weber's ideal types when he proposes (in a dense and elliptical section of Negative Dialectics) to use constellations of concepts to apprehend things (ND 162–3).[94] On David Kaufmann's interpretation of this proposal, since each concept is singular (in the sense that it is only one of many historically generated concepts), it necessarily 'misses its mark in the object', and 'other concepts need to be mobilized to correct its insufficiencies'. Of course, these concepts will miss their mark as well, but they will do so in a 'slightly different way'. By arranging concepts together in a constellation, however, Adorno thinks that it may be possible to 'form an asymptotic approximation of the truth of the object'.[95] As Adorno explains in Negative Dialectics, constellations of diverse concepts may illuminate 'the specific side of the object, the side which to a classifying procedure is either a matter of indifference or a burden' (ND 162).

Alison Stone accentuates the historical dimension of constellations when she comments on the following remark: 'Becoming aware of the constellation in which a thing stands is tantamount to deciphering the constellation which, having come to be, the thing bears within itself' (ND 163). According to Stone, this means that 'the specificity of any thing consists in the sedimentation of history in it'. In the course of history, 'any thing enters into multiple relations with other things; each such relation shapes and marks this thing; each thing, therefore, exists as a precipitate of its complex history'. Optimally, a constellation of concepts will provide 'a chart or map' of these 'sedimented past relations'. Although Stone neglects the speculative, or proleptic, dimension of negative dialectics when she says that a constellation of concepts should simply 'mirror

93   Adorno, 'On Subject and Object', Critical Models, p. 254.
94   This discussion of constellations reprises ideas in Cook, Adorno on Nature, pp. 84–5.
95   David Kaufmann, 'Correlations, Constellations and the Truth', Theodor W. Adorno, p. 170.

the relations between the many aspects of the thing,[96] she is trying to do justice to Adorno's 'cognitive utopia' which uses 'concepts to unseal the nonconceptual . . . without making it their equal' (ND 10).

Chapter Five will argue that nonidentity thinking does not simply mirror things; it also points to unrealized potentials that inhere in damaged life. According to Adorno, nonidentity thinking apprehends objects by referring to 'the possibility of which their reality has cheated the objects and which is nonetheless visible in each one' (ND 52). Again, concepts are always also more than the things that are subsumed under them. By virtue of 'overshooting' things, some concepts may reveal that 'nothing particular is true', that 'no particular is itself, as its particularity requires' (ND 152). For Adorno, then, nonidentity thinking involves, not just an immersion in things, but 'the freedom to step out of the object, a freedom which the identity claim cuts short' (ND 28). By stepping out of the object and confronting it with its better potential, nonidentity thinking reveals the inadequacy of things with respect to concepts while pointing obliquely to what the object might become.

In his lectures on *Negative Dialectics*, Adorno calls the nonidentity of concept and object the 'subjective aspect' of negative dialectics, subjective because it concerns the relation between thought and things. However, negative dialectics has an objective aspect as well. In its objective aspect, negative dialectics reveals the preponderance of another 'universal' – in this case, late capitalist society – over individuals.[97] In fact, it is the preponderance of late capitalism over individuals that accounts for the emergence of identity thinking. Noting that Adorno took this idea from philosopher and economist Sohn-Rethel, Stefan Müller-Doohm writes that, for both, the exchange of commodities under capitalism is the 'precondition of an objective process of abstraction that became . . . the precondition of the abstract nature of conceptual thought'.[98]

In other words, negative dialectics reveals both that there is 'contradiction in the realm of ideas and concepts' and that 'the world itself is antagonistic in its objective form'. In each case, moreover, we are dealing with problems that are linked to 'the principle of mastery, the mastery of nature'.[99] In their relentless attempts to dominate nature, both identity thinking and our exchange-based society end by expunging alterity, difference. Since late capitalist society reduces individuals to their economic functions when it turns them into agents and bearers of exchange value, negative dialectics is a dialectics of nonidentity under its objective aspect as well: it is a dialectics of the nonidentity of the individual and society. Indeed, just as objects do not go into concepts without leaving a remainder, individuals do not 'go into' society without remainder.

---

96   Alison Stone, 'Adorno and the Disenchantment of Nature', *Philosophy and Social Criticism*, p. 241.
97   Adorno, *Lectures on 'Negative Dialectics'*, p. 8.
98   Müller-Doohm, *Adorno*, p. 222. See also ND 177.
99   Adorno, *Lectures on 'Negative Dialectics'*, p. 9.

Expressing this idea in another way, Adorno says that there is a 'pre-established disharmony' between late capitalist society and individuals.[100] This disharmony exists, in part, because late capitalism is acting against the interests of individuals in its rapacious pursuit of profit. Simply to survive, we must perpetuate an economic system that makes our survival precarious. In fact, this system, which we perpetuate as producers and consumers, has no interest in keeping us alive *qua* individuals. 'For capital', Jarvis remarks, 'the individual's self-preservation is not itself a matter of any importance'.[101] But Adorno is also concerned that, by restricting the lives of individuals to finding food, clothing and shelter, society ties individuals to interests that blind them to the threats that capitalism also poses to the survival of our species as a whole (not to mention the survival of other species). According to Adorno, the 'very constraints that are imposed on people by the course of the world, and that compel them to attend to their own interests and nothing beyond them, is the very same force that turns against people, and asserts itself over their heads as a blind and almost unavoidable fate'.[102]

Foucault does not express himself in this way, but he would agree that there is a pre-established disharmony between Western society and the individual. To be sure, he views individuals as products of disciplinary power and biopower. These forms of power have shaped individuals by imposing on them behaviours and identities that are often coercive and constraining, especially for those who are labelled deviant and subsequently subjected to ever more intensive forms of constraint. Yet Foucault also insists that the struggles against disciplinary power and biopower that he studies throughout his work would not have been possible if society were completely totalizing. Examining the agonistic relations between society and individuals, Foucault constantly draws our attention to the 'distant roar of battle'.[103]

A critic of modern power relations, Foucault was equally interested in the formation of knowledge, or in the emergence of what he would later call regimes of truth.[104] In his early work, he called his approach to the study of these regimes 'archaeology'. Yet some commentators, including Dreyfus and Rabinow, maintain that Foucault ultimately abandoned archaeology owing to problems that he identified in it.[105] Other commentators believe that he subordinated archaeology to genealogy in later work, and still others think that archaeology remained one of Foucault's two major approaches to the study of our present. Without wishing to wade too far into these choppy waters, I shall cite some of Foucault's own remarks on this issue.

100   Ibid.
101   Jarvis, *Adorno*, p. 83.
102   Adorno, *History and Freedom*, p. 27.
103   Foucault, *Discipline and Punish*, p. 308.
104   Foucault, *On the Government of the Living*, p. 93.
105   Dreyfus and Rabinow, *Michel Foucault*, pp. 79–100.

In an interview with Gérard Raulet in the early 1980s, Foucault remarked that, although he continued to study how it was possible for phenomena to become objects of knowledge, he no longer used the word 'archaeology' to refer to this study.[106] According to James Faubion, Foucault eventually adopted a genealogical approach because his attention had turned to writing a history of the present and of the struggles that have been waged against power in the modern age. Furthermore, Foucault wanted to explore the extra-discursive conditions in which knowledge had developed. Quoting 'Nietzsche, Genealogy, History' to support his interpretation, Faubion also refers to a 1973 interview in which Foucault said that he was no longer interested exclusively in types of discourse. Instead, he was trying to understand how discourses 'were able to form in history and on what historical realities they were articulated'.[107] In Foucault's own words, he was trying to explore 'the dynastics of knowledge, the relation that exists between the major types of discourse observable in a culture and the historical conditions, economic conditions, and political conditions of their appearance and formation'.[108]

However, Stuart Elden contends that Foucault continued to make use of archaeology in later work. To support this contention, Elden quotes the introduction to the second volume of *The History of Sexuality*, *The Use of Pleasure*, where Foucault contrasts archaeology with a 'genealogy of practices of the self'. Elden also cites an unpublished discussion that took place at Berkeley in 1983 in which Foucault reportedly said that he had never stopped doing archaeology.[109] Yet, when these remarks are compared with the remarks cited above (and others like them), it becomes clear that Foucault was not entirely consistent on this point.[110] For the purposes of this discussion, moreover, deciding which position Foucault adopted is not crucial, and I shall simply stipulate here that I am using the term 'genealogy' as a cipher for Foucault's critical approach to both power and knowledge.

With respect to knowledge, Foucault's genealogies examine the historical problems to which the invention of new concepts and the recasting of old ones were meant to respond. So, for example, in his genealogy of the modern concept of sex, Foucault remarks that this concept took shape when the biopolitical state began to regulate and manage populations at the turn of the nineteenth century. At this time, sex became a central concern in many disciplines (including biology and medicine); these disciplines constructed around sex 'an immense apparatus for producing truth', turning 'the truth of sex' into

---

106   Foucault, 'Critical Theory/Intellectual History', *Politics, Philosophy, Culture*, p. 31.

107   James Faubion, 'Introduction', *Essential Works: Aesthetics*, pp. xxxiv–xxxv.

108   Foucault, 'De l'Archéologie à la Dynastique', *Dits et écrits* II, p. 406; my translation.

109   Stuart Elden, *Foucault's Last Decade*, pp. 173–4. Elden is quoting Foucault, *The History of Sexuality*, Vol. 2, p. 13.

110   To the charge of inconsistency, Foucault famously responded: 'Do not ask who I am and do not tell me to remain the same: leave it to our bureaucrats and our police to see that our papers are in order'. Foucault, *The Archaeology of Knowledge & The Discourse on Language*, p. 17.

'something fundamental' on the grounds that sex defines our core identity.[111] Correspondingly, and in direct response to these attempts to regulate and control our sexual lives, struggles were waged (and they continue to be waged). Among these are struggles that invoke the '"right" to life, to one's body, to health, to happiness, to the satisfaction of needs'.[112]

Since concepts such as sex are generated in response to specific problems at particular times, Foucault questions their universality. Again, much like Adorno, Foucault underscores the singularity of concepts, along with the relatively simple fact that the same concept may have different meanings in different historical contexts. But if Foucault suggests, with Adorno, that concepts do not do justice to things because they accentuate certain aspects of things to the exclusion of others, he also problematizes concepts on the related grounds that some of them have become coercive tools for disciplinary power and biopower. Where Adorno objects, in a Nietzschean vein, that concepts squeeze the life out of things, Foucault shows that some concepts may constrain people in ways that they experience as intolerable.

With respect to the constraints imposed by the modern concept of sex, Foucault points out that physicians, biologists, sexologists and others in the nineteenth century used concepts to diagnose individuals that categorized their behaviours as normal (monogamous heterosexuality) or perverse (homosexuality, for example). Individuals began to think of themselves in terms of these normative categories; their self-understanding was largely a function of the concepts that were applied to them. However, Foucault goes much further than this: he maintains that, once the concept of perversion was applied to diverse behaviours, experts actually created perversions by pathologizing certain behaviours and normalizing others. As 'perverse' sexualities were isolated and analyzed, turned into objects of intense scientific scrutiny and subjected to disciplinary mechanisms and biopolitical regulation, sexual practices that were formerly 'scattered [disséminées]' were 'rigidified, . . . stuck to an age, a place, a taste, a type of practice'.[113]

This is one sense in which Foucault could be said to have his own version of the nonidentical. Although Dews' reading of Foucault is sometimes problematic, he aptly points out that Foucault adopts Nietzsche's view that scientific knowledge 'imposes an order on disorder, reduces non-identity to identity'. Like Adorno, moreover, Foucault follows Nietzsche when he 'suggests that this imposition of order is motivated, at the most fundamental level, by a fear of the chaotic and unclassifiable'.[114] To be sure, Foucault rarely thematized the nonidentity of objects and concepts, but his genealogies are devoted to exploring the conditions under which 'something can become an object for a possible

111   Foucault, *The History of Sexuality*, Vol. 1, p. 56.
112   Ibid., p. 145.
113   Ibid., p. 48; trans. mod.
114   Dews, *Logics of Disintegration*, p. 186.

knowledge [*connaissance*], how it may have been problematized as an object to be known, to what selective procedure [*procédure de découpage*] it may have been subjected, and what part of it was regarded as pertinent'.[115] In other words, his genealogies reveal that concepts only grasp specific features in objects, while ignoring or concealing others.

Foucault's genealogies have a counterpart in the subjective side of negative dialectics, but they are just as consonant with its objective side. To cite David Weberman's gloss on Foucault's claims about our subjection to power, when power ties us to particular identities and modes of conduct, it gives 'us a sense of who we are and who we ought to be, and this normative sense of self and of ownership for our actions becomes an instrument by which power relations, in various institutions and spheres of life, are able to gain a hold on us'.[116] However, Foucault also contends that power entails 'at least in potentia, a strategy of struggle'. Just as power constitutes 'a kind of permanent limit, a point of possible reversal' for struggles, struggles represent both a limit and point of possible reversal for existing forms of power (SP 346; trans. mod.). If history involves myriad clashes between opposing forces, struggles against power represent a form of power in their own right. On the one side is institutional and state power; it 'incites, . . . induces, . . . seduces, . . . makes easier or more difficult; it releases or contrives, makes more probable or less; in the extreme, it constrains or forbids absolutely, but it is always a way of acting upon one or more acting subjects' (SP 341). On the other side are multifarious struggles against these incitements, inducements, seductions, constraints and prohibitions.

Adorno and Foucault also agree that history, which traditionally gave pride of place to victors, should give a voice to those who suffer. For Adorno, nonidentity manifests itself in 'the opposition between whatever is held down and the universal domination that is condemned to identity'. To this he adds that, 'if history is looked at materialistically, not as the history of victories but of defeats, we will become incomparably more conscious of this non-identity than was true of idealism'.[117] Foucault makes similar remarks in *Society Must be Defended* where he inverts Carl von Clausewitz's dictum and asserts that politics is the continuation of war by other means.[118] In these lectures, Foucault praises attempts by historians at the end of the sixteenth and the beginning of the seventeenth centuries to study the struggles that have divided society even in times of relative peace.[119] Their histories no longer focussed exclusively on the victors and so-called great events. Instead, they revealed that the 'history of

---

115   Florence, 'Foucault', *Essential Works: Aesthetics*, p. 460; trans. mod.
116   David Weberman, 'Foucault's Reconception of Power', *The Philosophical Forum*, p. 205.
117   Adorno, *History and Freedom*, p. 92.
118   Foucault, *Society Must be Defended*, p. 48.
119   Ibid., p. 65.

some is not the history of others' and that the 'triumph of some means the submission of others'.[120]

So, where Adorno describes society as an antagonistic totality in which economic trends and tendencies invariably come into conflict with the individuals over whom they predominate, Foucault observes that our totalizing society is riven by power struggles. Given this shared interest in the antagonisms that rend society, it is not surprising that Adorno and Foucault also address Marx's claims about class conflict as the motor of history even as they try to settle their accounts with Hegel's dialectical conception of history. Since I shall discuss their views on class conflict in later chapters, I shall end with an examination of Adorno's and Foucault's criticisms of dialectics as an approach to the study of the present.

I have already noted that negative dialectics differs in significant ways from Hegel's dialectics. Stressing the nonidentity of particular objects and universal concepts, of individuals and society, Adorno refuses to subsume the nonidentical under an ostensibly 'higher' and more universal unity. He also questions whether the antagonistic relations between the individual and society will ever be overcome. Against Hegel, Adorno denies that the negation of the negative – whether negation takes the form of a critique of damaged life, or of struggles that aim to transform society – will necessarily lead to something positive. He also charges that Hegel's claim that the negation of negation necessarily results in something positive 'is the quintessence of identification' (ND 158). A claim like this, Adorno contends, could only be 'upheld by someone who presupposes positivity from the beginning' (ND 160).

Hegel postulated that spirit was progressing inexorably towards the identity of identity and difference. To this, Adorno objects that Hegel saw identity 'as a palliative for dialectical contradiction, for the expression of the insolubly nonidentical'. As a result, Hegel ignored what contradiction means (ND 160). In an illuminating interpretation of this aspect of Adorno's work, Bernstein writes that, for Adorno, contradiction means that 'there is an antagonism between the social system, rationalized society as formed through the demands of capital, and the particular objects and subjects formed'. Specifically, it 'points to the claim of the particular, the nonidentical, against its social identifications'.[121] Shierry Nicholsen and Jeremy Shapiro express this idea in a different but equally illuminating way when they note that 'Adorno sought to recuperate in Hegel the basis for a dialectic of resistance' to late capitalism precisely 'by concentrating on the nonidentical'.[122]

120   Ibid., pp. 69–70 *passim*.

121   Bernstein, 'Negative Dialectic as Fate', *The Cambridge Companion to Adorno*, p. 38.

122   Shierry Weber Nicholsen and Jeremy Shapiro, 'Introduction', in Adorno, *Hegel*, p. xii. In *Social Philosophy After Adorno*, Lambert Zuidervaart questions Adorno's 'presupposition' that 'somehow the nonidentical is there *in der Sache*, historically and societally available' (p. 72). One of the aims of this book is to demonstrate in what respects the nonidentical is indeed 'there'. Chapter Five will also argue that, while Adorno admits that the nonidentical is a 'thin basis' for hope, he thinks that it is the only ground on which hope can be based – and something similar can be said of Foucault.

For his part, Foucault objects that Hegel's dialectics is inadequate for under-standing concrete historical processes. Denying that power is an ultimate prin-ciple to which everything can be reduced, Foucault criticizes Hegel's idealism, complaining that, under the 'dialectical sovereignty of the same', alterity, differ-ence, persist only as 'nonbeing'.[123] He also questions the role that contradiction plays in Hegel's dialectics. Although the word 'contradiction' does have a mean-ing in logic, Foucault insists that real processes are devoid of contradictions like these. Even antagonistic processes 'do not constitute . . . a contradiction in the logical sense'. Struggles, conflicts and antagonisms, including class struggles, are not (as Foucault says Nietzsche also realized) dialectical processes.[124] To be sure, Foucault views his genealogies as part of a development in historiography that influenced Marx's dialectical account of history – a development in which history was reconceptualized as the history of struggles.[125] At the same time, however, he urges us 'to think struggle and its forms, objectives, means and processes in terms of a logic free of the sterilising constraints of the dialectic' and its 'meagre logic of contradiction'.[126]

Foucault recognizes that capitalism exploits individuals: 'that you have a job, and that the product . . . of your work belongs to someone else is a fact'. Still, our alienation from the products of our labour is not a contradiction but 'the object of a struggle, of a confrontation'.[127] In fact, Foucault worries that those who use the logic of contradiction 'as a principle of intelligibility and a rule of action in political struggle' will wrongly see 'everything that allows the contra-diction to be localised or narrowed down' as a 'break or a blockage'.[128] By exten-sion, they may believe that struggles have 'sense and legitimacy' only when they can 'act radically on the whole'. This belief 'terrorizes' those who struggle in specific sites with the following dilemma: 'either you attack on a local level, but you must be sure that it's at the weakest link, the one whose breakage will demol-ish the whole structure; or else, . . . the link wasn't the weakest one, the adver-sary needed only to re-organise his front, and a reform has reabsorbed your attack'.[129] For these reasons, Foucault abandons the notion of contradiction and scrutinizes concrete historical struggles in local sites.

Interestingly, Adorno's and Foucault's criticisms of Hegel appear to be based on similar concerns. Although Adorno retains the notion of contradiction, thereby emphasizing his links to the Hegelian and Marxist traditions, he radi-cally reconceptualizes it when he states that contradiction involves an antago-nism between the universal and the particular, or between concept and object

123   Foucault, 'Theatrum Philosophicum', Essential Works: Aesthetics, p. 358.
124   Foucault, 'Dialogue sur le Pouvoir', Dits et écrits III, p. 471.
125   Foucault, Society Must be Defended, pp. 65–6.
126   Foucault, 'Power and Strategies', Power/Knowledge, pp. 143–4 passim.
127   Foucault, 'Dialogue sur le Pouvoir', Dits et écrits III, p. 472.
128   Foucault, 'Power and Strategies', Power/Knowledge, p. 143.
129   Ibid., p. 144.

and between society and the individuals who comprise it. As for Foucault, given his interest in those who are excluded and marginalized from society, in those who are unwilling or unable to identify with and conform to prevailing norms and modes of conduct, he also seems to believe that the antagonisms that fragment society reveal a contradiction, in Adorno's equally nonlogical sense of that word, between individuals and society.

In fact, Adorno anticipates Foucault's arguments when he charges that Hegel 'spiritualized' the difference between concepts and things. When spiritualized, this difference 'assumes the logical form of contradiction because, measured by the ruling principle, whatever does not bow to its unity will appear, not as something different from and indifferent to the principle, but as a violation of logic' (ND 48). To return to Bernstein's interpretation of Adorno: contradictions are usually taken as 'signs that reason has failed'. Understood in this way, contradictions spur us to 'seek a better, more consistent, more unifying account'. Yet, for Adorno, and arguably for Foucault as well, the problem often lies in the very unity and consistency that are imposed upon individuals and things. In this case, a contradiction indicates that 'something has slipped through the unifying net'; it testifies 'to antagonisms in reality (between what is demanded of things and the things)'.[130]

Adorno and Foucault want to come to the aid of all those who are trying to slip through this unifying net. Again, I shall argue here that, in spite of the many differences between them that make it impossible to reduce one to the other, Adorno's and Foucault's critical theories converge when they examine the coercive shaping of our identities and evaluate the prospects for resisting it. Admittedly, the account of Adorno and Foucault that I am offering here is not definitive because their work remains open to a variety of readings. However, this book will try to make good on Foucault's claim that there are striking parallels between his analysis of our disciplinary society and Adorno's account of the totally administered world, parallels that open up new avenues for critique and contestation.

---

130   Bernstein, 'Negative Dialectic as Fate', *The Cambridge Companion to Adorno*, p. 37.

Chapter 2

Is Power Always Secondary to the Economy?

I have already observed that Adorno and Foucault appear to orient their critiques of the West around different, and possibly incompatible, poles.[1] In contrast to Adorno, who is interested in exchange relations and their effects on phenomena as diverse as artworks, individuals and interpersonal relations, Foucault is primarily interested in the effects of disciplinary power and biopower on individuals. In part, these distinct centres of interest reflect divergent perspectives on the work of Karl Marx: Adorno remains squarely within a Marxist paradigm, even as he attempts to revise and update it, and Foucault seems to abandon traditional Marxist concerns about economic exploitation and class conflict when he emphasizes the individual's subjection to power. Among other things, this chapter will try to determine whether Adorno's and Foucault's critical theories are as incompatible as their views about Marx may suggest.

Some of these views will be discussed in the first section of this chapter. At issue is whether Marx, with his powerful critique of capitalism, continues to offer a useful framework for understanding how Western societies function. By extension, of course, the theoretical foundations of critical theory are at issue as well. In the second section, Adorno's ideas about the relations between the economy and the state will be compared with Foucault's account of relations between disciplinary institutions, the biopolitical state and the capitalist economy. In this context, I shall look closely at *The Birth of Biopolitics*, where Foucault remarks that there has been a significant shift in relations between the economy and the state. The third section of this chapter will explore what seems to lie at the heart of the differences between their work, namely Adorno's claims about the pervasiveness of exchange relations in Western societies and Foucault's claims about the ubiquity of power relations. Here too, *The Birth of Biopolitics* will prove to be a valuable resource. Finally, on the basis of this assessment of the differences between Adorno and Foucault, I shall evaluate the compatibility of their critical theories.

WHITHER MARX?

Adorno was not an orthodox Marxist. Among other things, he supplemented his Marxist analysis of the economy with a Freudian account of the psychology

---

1   This chapter takes its title from a question that Foucault asks in *Society Must be Defended*, p. 14.

of individuals, arguing that capitalism affects the process of individuation when it turns individuals into commensurable and fungible units of value. Using psychoanalysis to explore some of the effects of exchange relations on individuals, Adorno also developed a Freudian account of why individuals seldom resist them. In addition, he was concerned that the psychotechnologies that were deployed in Nazi Germany to promote adherence to the fascist cause continue to be used to foster social integration in other Western countries. These technologies play a particularly important role in the economic sector that Adorno called the culture industry. As Martin Jay explains, 'what made it impossible to reject psychology was the unexpected rise of an irrationalist mass politics in fascism'. However, even after Nazi Germany collapsed, Adorno could not ignore the psychological impediments to emancipation that were posed by 'the manipulated society of mass consumption that seemed to follow in its wake'.[2]

Apart from supplementing his Marxist account of capitalism with a Freudian analysis of individuation and social integration in the West, Adorno thought that Marx's critique of capitalism had to be revised because capitalism had changed since the nineteenth century. Of course, Marx had predicted some of these changes. Among the predictions Marx made that proved to be correct, and that demanded revisions to his account of capitalism, was that capital would become increasingly concentrated and centralized in monopolies. Marx rightly foresaw that competition among capitalists would result in smaller enterprises being overtaken by larger, and more economically viable, concerns that would eventually monopolize the market. As a result of this change, liberal capitalism was transformed into monopoly, or late, capitalism.

Marx was also right when he predicted that Western countries would exhibit more trenchant class divisions. Given the increasing concentration and centralization of capital, Adorno contends that we find ourselves in a situation where 'a few owners' now confront and exploit 'the overwhelming mass of the expropriated'.[3] Unlike Marx, however, Adorno thought that this situation would likely persist for some time to come. Marx also postulated that there was a tendency for the general rate of profit from surplus value to fall, but Adorno countered that, even if this were correct, 'one would still have to concede that the capitalist system has been resilient enough to postpone the anticipated collapse indefinitely'. Capitalism continues to survive owing in part to 'an immense increase in technological development which enables the production of a plethora of consumer goods from which all members of the highly industrialized nations have benefited'.[4]

---

2   Jay, *Adorno*, p. 85.
3   Adorno, 'Reflections on Class Theory', *Can One Live After Auschwitz?*, p. 99.
4   Adorno, 'Late Capitalism or Industrial Society?' *Modern German Sociology*, pp. 232–3; trans. mod.

Other changes had taken place in the West that Marx did not predict, including the adoption of social welfare policies (under Franklin D. Roosevelt's New Deal, for example) after the 1929 stock market crash. On the one hand, the burgeoning welfare state had helped to raise the standard of living for many individuals. Measured against the nineteenth-century conditions that Marx described, individuals now benefit from shorter 'working hours, and better food, housing, and clothing'. They can also expect to live longer, and they often receive pensions in their old age. On the other hand, the welfare state masks the persistence of class stratification, making it far less likely that workers will revolt. Under the welfare state, it is not just the case that workers are no longer 'driven by hunger to join forces and make a revolution'.[5] For workers no longer experience themselves as members of a class. Marx's prognosis for capitalism 'finds itself verified in an unsuspected way' because, with the welfare state, the ruling class 'adopts as its own cause the idea that its fate is to feed the workers and to "secure for the slaves their existence within slavery" in order to secure its own'.[6]

But if Adorno remains close to Marx, even as he revises and supplements Marx's critique of capitalism in light of the changes that occurred in the West in the late nineteenth and early twentieth centuries, what complicates an account of his relation to Marx is the claim, made by a number of influential commentators, that Adorno adopted Friedrich Pollock's state capitalism thesis.[7] Briefly, Pollock's thesis postulates that there had been transition in the West 'from a predominantly economic to an essentially political era'.[8] Although Pollock qualified his thesis, he did try to demonstrate that the power motive was supplanting the profit motive in both command economies (Nazi Germany, for example) and mixed economies (such as the United States). For Pollock, then, and as Douglas Kellner observes, state capitalism was in the process of superseding market capitalism.[9]

When commentators assert that Adorno sided with Pollock on this issue, they also imply that Adorno no longer believed that the economy retains its primacy vis-à-vis the state. And if Adorno had adopted Pollock's state capitalism thesis, the compatibility of his critique with Foucault's might be easier to establish. Yet Adorno did not fully endorse this thesis. Instead, he continued to stress the primacy of the economy in Western states as well as the persistence of antagonistic class relations. Against the view that state intervention in the economy, which involves 'large-scale and long-term planning', demonstrates 'that

---

5   Adorno, 'Reflections on Class Theory', *Can One Live after Auschwitz?*, p. 103; trans. mod.

6   Ibid., p. 105; trans. mod.

7   See, for example, Helmut Dubiel, *Theory and Politics*, p. 81; David Held, *Introduction to Critical Theory*, pp. 63–4; William Scheuerman, *Between the Norm and the Exception*, p. 124; and Douglas Kellner, *Critical Theory, Marxism and Modernity*, pp. 62–3.

8   Friedrich Pollock, 'State Capitalism', *Studies in Philosophy and Social Research*, p. 207.

9   Kellner, *Critical Theory, Marxism and Modernity*, p. 59.

late capitalism can no longer be termed "capitalism", Adorno argued that economic forces remain paramount and that they continue to pose a considerable threat to individuals in the West.[10] Although he was prepared to accept the view that 'control of economic forces is increasingly becoming a function of political power', Adorno nonetheless insisted that there are 'compelling facts which cannot . . . be adequately interpreted *without* invoking the key concept of "capitalism"' because '[h]uman beings are, as much as ever, ruled and dominated by the economic process' – a process which 'produces and reproduces a class structure'.[11]

Recognizing that there is a tendency towards the predominance of state power in Western societies, Adorno also thought that this tendency itself was economically driven. In other words, state intervention only helped to buttress capitalism; it represented a form of self-defence.[12] Specifically, Adorno suggested that state intervention represented a limited defence against class conflict (both real and potential) after 1929 when he said that it served to neutralize the threats arising from 'unrevolutionized relations of production'.[13] Although he also conceded that state intervention could lead to the breakdown of capitalism in the sense that it could result in 'direct political domination independent of market mechanisms',[14] Adorno maintained that state intervention was intended to protect capitalism from collapse by enabling capitalism to contain its crisis tendencies. In short, the emergence of the welfare state also helps to explain why capitalism may survive indefinitely.

To be sure, Adorno realized that if the economically driven trend towards political domination were to continue, the West would 'steer directly towards forms which are no longer defined by the classical exchange mechanism'. At the same time, he denied that this had happened in most Western states – with the notable exception of Nazi Germany. Nazi Germany had proved Hegel right. In his *Philosophy of Right*, Hegel predicted with 'diabolical innocence' that, in order to avoid falling apart, civil society would end by evoking 'powers out of itself – the so-called corporations and the police'. And, though Hegel saw this development as something positive, Adorno remarked that 'we have learned most thoroughly from fascism . . . what a renewed transition to direct domination can mean'.[15]

Disagreeing with Pollock about the waning predominance of the capitalist economy in the West, Adorno continued to defend Marx. Correspondingly, Adorno believed that Western societies remain stratified in socio-economic

10   Adorno, 'Late Capitalism or Industrial Society', *Modern German Sociology*, p. 244.
11   Ibid., p. 237 *passim*; italics in the text.
12   Ibid., p. 244.
13   Ibid., p. 243.
14   Ibid., p. 245.
15   Adorno, 'Diskussionsbeitrag zu "Spätkapitalismus oder Industriegesellschaft?"' *Soziologische Schriften* I, p. 583. All translations of *Soziologische Schriften* I are my own.

classes, and he adopted Marx's criterion of ownership of, and control over, the means of production to appraise class membership.[16] Yet the economic position of the bourgeoisie had changed. Formerly comprised of relatively independent entrepreneurs, the bourgeoisie forfeited much of its economic power as capital was concentrated in monopolies. Now working as salaried employees or wage labourers, the economically disenfranchised bourgeoisie forms with the proletariat a new mass class. This class finds itself under the 'economic and political command of large capitalists [*der Großen*] who wield the same police threat against both their supporters and the workers'.[17]

Turning to Foucault's ideas about Marx and Marxism, it is important to note from the outset that Foucault shares Adorno's view that class stratification and struggle persist in the West. Although he formerly thought that 'the social struggle, the struggle between classes . . . was coming to an end', Foucault eventually realized that 'the class struggle still exists, it exists more intensely'.[18] However, since power permeates all social interaction, class struggle is only one of many agonistic relations in society, and Foucault also believes that it is no longer as important as it once was. Indeed, I remarked earlier that Foucault generalizes the notion of struggle. Struggles against power occur everywhere, and in diverse sites, to the point where 'we are all fighting each other' all the time. For Foucault, 'there is always within each of us something that fights something else'.[19] Moreover, since struggle is ubiquitous, Foucault contends that it needs to be rethought. No one, including Marx, for whom class struggle was paramount, has satisfactorily explained what struggle means.[20]

Foucault not only agrees that class struggle persists; he employs the concept of class in his genealogies. In a 1977 interview, he responds to the observation that he seldom makes use of the concept of class when he insists that the institutionalization of practices such as psychiatric internment (to give but one example) is not 'foreign to the existence of class in the Marxist sense of the term'. Although their relation to class is 'extremely complex', practices like these must 'be placed inside historical processes that are economic'.[21] In the first volume of *The History of Sexuality*, moreover, Foucault takes exception to the claim made by some Marxists that the controls on sex that began to proliferate in the nineteenth century originally targeted the proletariat. Against this claim, Foucault objects that these controls were first applied, 'with the greatest intensity, in the economically privileged and politically dominant classes'.[22]

---

16   Adorno, 'Late Capitalism or Industrial Society', *Modern German Sociology*, p. 233.
17   Adorno, 'Reflections on Class Theory', *Can One Live After Auschwitz?*, p. 99; trans. mod.
18   Foucault, 'Rituals of Exclusion', *Foucault Live*, p. 72.
19   Foucault, 'The Confession of the Flesh', *Power/Knowledge*, p. 208.
20   Foucault, 'Méthodologie pour la Connaissance du Monde', *Dits et écrits* III, p. 606.
21   Foucault, 'Pouvoir et Savoir', *Dits et écrits* III, p. 403.
22   Foucault, *The History of Sexuality*, Vol. 1, p. 120.

36

At the same time, Foucault historicizes the conception of history that sees it as driven by class struggle. In *Society Must be Defended*, for example, he argued that historians reconceptualized history as a war or struggle between races – originally understanding 'race' in an historical and political sense – at the turn of the seventeenth century. (To illustrate this new conception of history, Foucault discusses Henri de Boulainvillier's history of the struggles between the bourgeoisie and the nobility in France.) In this reconceptualization, historians rejected 'Roman' history, which lionized sovereigns while ignoring ordinary individuals, and they produced what Foucault calls 'counterhistories'; these highlighted the divisions that rent society when one or more groups struggled against other groups.[23] According to Foucault, Marx also inherited this conception of history, but he took it in a new direction when he characterized history as the history of class struggle. To support this claim, Foucault cites a letter in which Marx said that he had derived the idea of class struggle from French historians, such as Augustin Thierry, whose work focussed on struggles between races.[24]

Nevertheless, Foucault's historicization of the idea of class struggle by no means amounts to a repudiation of it. He recognizes that his own genealogies are products of the same trend in historiography that had such a profound influence on Marx: he and Marx are both interested in the history of struggles and they both produce counterhistories.[25] Still, Foucault shifts the focus away from class struggle and highlights the political character of many struggles in the West. He also diverges from Marx when he claims that economic domination is always also rooted in power relations. Although 'small power relations are often directed, induced from on high, by big state powers or by a large dominant class', Foucault contends that 'class domination or a state structure can only function if there are, at base, these small power relations'.[26] This helps to explain why Foucault denies that there is 'a massive and primal condition of domination, a binary structure with "dominators" on one side and "dominated" on the other'. Rather, we find a 'multiform production of relations of domination' (and, consequently, diverse kinds of struggle), and these relations are only 'partially susceptible of integration into overall strategies'. In some cases, class struggle may not be 'the "*ratio* for the exercise of power"', yet it may nonetheless 'be the "guarantee of intelligibility"' for certain grand strategies'.[27]

So, class struggle persists, but it is always also built up out of power struggles that take place in diverse sites. As Balibar remarks, Foucault tried to

---

23 Foucault, *Society Must be Defended*, pp. 65–6. In his gloss on the word 'race', Foucault explains that, in its earlier historical instantiation, 'the word "race" . . . is not pinned to a stable biological meaning. And yet the word is not completely free-floating. Ultimately, it designates a certain historico-political divide' (p. 77).
24 Ibid., p. 79.
25 Ibid., p. 65.
26 Foucault, 'Pouvoir et Savoir', *Dits et écrits* III, p. 406.
27 Foucault, 'Power and Strategies', *Power/Knowledge*, p. 142 *passim*.

incorporate into the definition of class 'the complexity of power relations and the multiplicity of the forms of conflict and resistance'.[28] Balibar also notes that Foucault made use of the Gramscian notion of hegemony in the first volume of *The History of Sexuality* when he ascribed what he called the 'major domina-tions' to 'hegemonic effects' that are sustained by all the power struggles that form and play themselves out in 'the machinery of production, in families, smaller groups, and institutions'. It is these struggles that serve as 'the basis for the wide-ranging effects of cleavage that run through the social body as a whole'.[29] According to Balibar, social hegemonies are simply the 'terminal forms' around which resistive struggles may crystallize.[30]

Foucault also believes that struggles that revolve around power are now more prevalent in Western societies than they once were. If, in the nineteenth century, it was true to say that 'the major problem was . . . economic exploita-tion, the formation of wealth, the wealth of capital, through the immiseration of the very people who produced it', Foucault thinks that struggles against subjec-tion have become at least as widespread as struggles against exploitation used to be. This is not to say that impoverishment no longer remains a problem in the West. However, Foucault claims that impoverishment lacks the 'urgency' that it once had because individuals in the West are now confronted with an equally serious problem, namely the problem of too much power, of 'the surplus produc-tion [*surproduction*] of power'.[31] In 'Western industrialized societies', Foucault argues, 'the questions "Who exercises power? How? On whom?" are . . . the questions that people feel most strongly about'.[32]

Western history has been marked by three types of struggles: struggles against ethnic, social and religious domination, struggles against 'forms of exploitation that separate individuals from what they produce', and struggles 'against that which ties the individual to himself and subjects him to others in this way (struggles against subjection, against forms of subjectivity and submis-sion)'. One type of struggle may appear in an isolated form during a particular historical period, but these types may also be mixed. Even when mixed, however, one type will usually predominate, and today, Foucault contends, it is struggles against subjection to power that prevail. The 'main objective' of contemporary struggles 'is to attack not so much such-or-such institution of power, or group, or elite, or class but, rather, a technique, a form of power' (SP 331).

To support the contention that economic exploitation has been, if not displaced, then at least compounded, by the subjection of individuals to power, Foucault points to the emergence of fascism and Stalinism in the twentieth century. Importantly, he also argues that fascism and Stalinism were made

---

28   Balibar, 'Foucault and Marx', *Michel Foucault Philosopher*, p. 52.
29   Foucault, *The History of Sexuality*, Vol. 1, p. 94 *passim*; trans. mod.
30   Balibar, 'Foucault and Marx', *Michel Foucault Philosopher*, p. 52.
31   Foucault, 'La Philosophie analytique de la Politique', *Dits et écrits* III, p. 536.
32   Foucault, 'On Power', *Politics, Philosophy, Culture*, p. 103.

38

possible by technologies and practices that were already widespread in the West. 'After all', Foucault remarks, 'the organization of big political parties, the development of police apparatuses, the existence of techniques of repression such as labour camps, all this is a legacy that was actually instituted in Western liberal societies, and that Stalinism and fascism only had to appropriate'. In fact, Foucault reveals that it was the twin threat posed by fascism and Stalinism that led him to study power in the first place.[33] He chose to study power relations in order to explore practices and technologies that were subsequently adopted and extended in the Soviet Union and Nazi Germany. Controversially, Foucault even ventures to claim that the goal of making the state wither away is all the more imperative today owing to the 'hypertrophy or excess of power in both socialist and capitalist countries'. It is the excess of power that 'justifies, from the strategic point of view of resistive struggle, the aim of making the state disappear'.[34]

Yet Foucault's interest in power by no means blinds him to the importance of an economic analysis of society. In a conversation with Gérard Raulet, Foucault said that he simply wanted to unburden and liberate Marx's work 'in relation to party dogma, which has constrained it, touted it and brandished it for so long'. When Raulet followed up this remark by asking Foucault whether Marx had influenced him, he replied: 'Yes, absolutely.'[35] Distinguishing between Marx and Marxism, Foucault asserts that we do not need to free ourselves from Marx – which he also claims is impossible in any case – but from party-political Marxism. We need to free ourselves from party-political Marxism because it has hemmed in our political imaginations with its scientific, or pseudo-scientific, prophecies; these continue to exercise 'a coercive force on a certain truth about the past and future of humanity'.[36] Secondly, since Marxism has often attached itself to political movements and parties, it also relies for its survival on the existence of states which make use of it for their own ends.[37] Third, Marxists and Marxist political parties fail to consider the important problems that now cluster around medicine, sexuality, reason and madness. When they do not actively try to weaken the social movements that deal with these problems, Marxists tend to ignore them. And the need to have done with party-political Marxism was all the more pressing given what had happened in the gulags and psychiatric institutions of the USSR.[38]

Adorno is also critical of party-political Marxism. He is especially concerned about its authoritarianism, as evidenced in its hierarchical, top-down

33 Foucault, 'La Philosophie analytique de la Politique', *Dits et écrits* III, pp. 535–6. See also Foucault, 'Pouvoir et Savoir', *Dits et écrits* III, p. 400, and 'Power and Sex', *Politics, Philosophy, Culture*, p. 119.
34 Foucault, 'Méthodologie pour la Connaissance du Monde', *Dits et écrits* III, p. 613.
35 Foucault, 'Critical Theory/Intellectual History', *Politics, Philosophy, Culture*, pp. 45–6.
36 Foucault, 'Méthodologie pour la Connaissance du Monde', *Dits et écrits* III, pp. 599–600.
37 Ibid., p. 601.
38 Ibid., pp. 602–3 *passim*.

organizational structures and its suppression of disagreement and dissent. Although he argues that individuals all over the world have been harnessed to collectives, Adorno also observes that collectivism is 'directly commanded' in countries that 'monopolize the name of socialism', but it is 'commanded as the individual's subordination to society'. This subordination 'belies the socialism of those countries and solidifies antagonism' (ND 284). In fact, Adorno calls Bertolt Brecht's claim that a thousand eyes see better than two 'a lie' because it turns collectivities into the fetishes that critical theory has the task of unmasking. In light of the serious problems that undermine collective action today, Adorno believes that 'the universal and rational hibernate better in the isolated individual than in the stronger battalions that obediently abandon the universality [*Allgemeinheit*] of reason'.[39]

Adorno's trenchant criticisms of Marxism and the USSR do not extend to Marx's claim about the primacy of the economy in the West; he endorses this claim even though he recognizes that, if the tendency towards state intervention were to persist and intensify, exchange relations would no longer predominate. By contrast, even as Foucault emphasizes the importance of Marx for his work on struggles (an influence that is especially apparent in some of his early lectures[40]), and he accepts key Marxist concepts (including the concept of class), he challenges Marx's insistence on the primacy of the economy when he argues that power relations are at least as important as economic relations and that social conflicts now revolve primarily around power. Responding to the question 'Is power always secondary to the economy?' Foucault states that power may be 'deeply involved in and with economic relations' without being functionally subordinate or formally isomorphic with respect to them. A relation of force, power is simply 'of a different order' than economic relations, and it is this order that Foucault proposes to investigate on its own terms.[41] Since Foucault denies that power, including the biopolitical state, is invariably subordinate to the economy, the following section of this chapter will take a closer look at Adorno's and Foucault's ideas about relations between the economy and the state.

THE ECONOMY AND THE STATE

Adopting Marx's view that society is trenchantly divided between an ever dwindling number of owners of the means of production and an ever growing

---

39   Adorno, 'Individuum und Organisation', *Soziologische Schriften* I, p. 455.

40   See, for example, Foucault, *The Punitive Society*. Stéphane Legrand remarks that, in *The Punitive Society*, Foucault took from Marx many concepts and themes that would reappear (often without reference to Marx) in *Discipline and Punish*. See Legrand, 'Le Marxisme oublié de Foucault', *Actuel Marx*. Apart from deploying Marx's notions of class and class struggle in *The Punitive Society*, Foucault compares what he calls the prison-form to the wage-form, arguing that they interpenetrate (see page 71). Moreover, Foucault insists that disciplinary power and biopower are linked very closely to the rise of capitalism, as I shall show here.

41   Foucault, *Society Must be Defended*, p. 14.

number of exploited workers, Adorno also contends that, once monopoly conditions developed at the end of the nineteenth and beginning of the twentieth centuries, the economy assumed an increasingly totalitarian character. As a result, the oligarchical ruling class had become largely faceless, anonymous. In another, albeit indirect, criticism of Pollock's state capitalism thesis, Adorno wrote that the ruling class now disappears 'behind the concentration of capital' – a concentration that has become so great that capitalism now appears to be 'an institution, . . . the expression of society as a whole'.[42] Since capitalism pervades every facet of society today, Adorno insists that 'the concept of a capitalist *society* is not a *flatus vocis*' (ND 50).[43]

Some commentators have charged that there is a 'political deficit' in Adorno's work.[44] Although I shall return to this criticism later, it could be argued in Adorno's defence that he focussed exclusively on exchange relations precisely because he saw the state as subordinate to the economy in most Western countries. Where totalitarianism in Nazi Germany and the Stalinist USSR prompted Foucault to study power relations, Adorno observed that the horrific excesses of power under the Third Reich and Stalinism had not occurred in other Western countries. To be sure, the 'concentration of economic and administrative power on one side and complete impotence on the other' – which Adorno deems 'the decisive cause of fascism' – had only 'progressed' during the post-war period.[45] The resurgence of fascism remains a real danger because 'the immense concentration of economical and administrative power leaves the individual no more room to maneuver'.[46] Yet, it is also the case that the traditions of militant nationalism that fuelled Adolf Hitler's rise to power have weakened in Germany. To this Adorno adds that, in the United States, 'the democratic rules have functioned so well up to now that the danger of fascism in America is, at the moment in any case, very slight'.[47]

Relations of production now pit relatively impotent individuals, not just against the owners of the means of production, but against what Adorno calls 'administration' as well. Under the rubric of administration, Adorno includes the state which, he claims, now plays the role of 'the general capitalist [*Gesamtkapitalist*]'.[48] Remaining subordinate to capitalism, the state simply aids and abets it. As Adorno complains in *Minima Moralia*, 'state power has shed even the appearance of independence from particular interests in profit; always

---

42   Adorno, 'Reflections on Class Theory', *Can One Live after Auschwitz?*, p. 99.
43   I am citing the footnote in *Negative Dialectics* that appears on pp. 49–50; the emphasis on the word 'society' is mine.
44   See, for example, Jay, *Adorno*, p. 86.
45   Adorno, 'Discussion of Professor Adorno's Lecture "The Meaning of Working Through the Past"', *Critical Models*, p. 305.
46   Ibid., p. 298.
47   Ibid., p. 305.
48   Adorno, 'Late Capitalism or Industrial Society', *Modern German Sociology*, p. 240.

in their service in fact, it now places itself there ideologically as well'.[49] The state aids capitalism with its police forces, as Adorno stresses when he remarks that the state often uses the threat of police force to keep everybody in line. But the state also aids capital with its welfare policies and with institutions such as schools and universities which provide captains of industry with skilled, educated workers.

Although Adorno suggests that John Maynard Keynes' welfare-state policies were adopted in the West with the aim of pacifying class conflict (both real and potential) during the depression of the 1930s, his view was challenged indirectly by economic historian Herman Van der Wee when he argued that Keynes' policy of 'full employment, social security, income redistribution, and mutual co-operation' was intended primarily as an instrument for economic growth. In other words, Van der Wee alleged that countries like Britain, the United States, France and Italy engaged in 'economic planning in order to be able to specify extra-high growth rates and ensure that they were achieved'.[50] However, no matter which explanation for the adoption of welfare policies is correct, Adorno and Van der Wee do agree on one point, namely that the welfare state largely served to bolster capitalism.

Also allied with capitalism is the culture industry, a significant economic sector in its own right which is also dominated by monopolies. Selling standardized, pseudo-individuated products, the culture industry encourages individuals to think in schematic and stereotypical ways, while promoting conformity to prevailing standards or norms. That this industry greatly influences the behaviour of individuals is due, in part, to the waning influence of the family. Once the bourgeoisie had been absorbed into the new mass class, the family forfeited its role as the primary agent of socialization. As 'Notes on Individuation' will show in more detail, parents now vie for authority, more or less impotently, with teachers, experts and specialists (such as public health officials and physicians); they no longer serve as the primary standard against which children measure their strength through rebellion or resistance. As a result, children are far more susceptible to extra-familial pressures to adapt and conform, including the pressures exerted by the mass media.

Along with his concerns about our conformity to prevailing norms, Adorno also offered an account of the abstract norms and procedures used by bureaucratic organizations and welfare-state agencies. His account shows that these procedures have had both positive and negative effects. On the one hand, the development of standardized procedures for classifying and processing individuals allows state bureaucracies to deal 'with every case automatically and "without consideration for the person"'. They promise 'an element of justice' to the extent that they guarantee that 'arbitrariness, accident, and nepotism do not

49   Adorno, *Minima Moralia: Reflections on Damaged Life*, p. 53; trans. mod. Cited hereafter in the text as MM.
50   Herman Van der Wee, *Prosperity and Upheaval*, p. 283.

rule people's fate'. On the other hand, the same procedures are responsible for 'depersonalization and reification'. Treating all individuals in a uniform way, regardless of their circumstances and their particular needs and concerns, ostensibly egalitarian procedures effectively oblige individuals to identify themselves with institutional and organizational categories and to orient their behaviour accordingly. Individuals have become mere 'appendages' of organizations; these now affect their behaviour, right down to 'their most private reactions'.[51]

Foucault also claims that Western societies are normalizing. Since his ideas about normalization will be examined in some detail in the following chapter, I shall confine myself here to remarking that Foucault links normalization to mechanisms and techniques that are deployed by disciplinary institutions and the biopolitical state. More to the point, he claims that disciplinary institutions, which came of age during the industrial revolution, facilitated the rise of capitalism by helping to produce an efficient labour force as they moulded and shaped the human body through exercise, training and supervision.[52] Disciplinary power makes the flesh stronger by increasing the forces of the body, turning bodies into ever more efficient instruments for the accumulation of capital, while simultaneously weakening the spirit by encouraging unquestioning submission to authority figures. For Foucault, modernity coincides (in part) with the development of institutions that target the most minute behaviours of individuals in order to make individuals productive workers and compliant citizens.[53]

Foucault often described the relation between power – with its colonization of the body – and the economy as both reciprocal and complex. To be sure, 'it is largely as a force of production that the body is invested with relations of power and domination', but Foucault also argues that the body could be constituted as labour power only after it had been 'caught up in a system of subjection'.[54] At one and the same time, then, disciplinary power served as an instrument of capitalist exploitation, and exploitation required the prior subjection of individuals to power. Capitalism needed bodies that would submit to the rigours of the assembly line, and bodies would function efficiently only after they had been disciplined. Foucault made this point throughout his work: capitalism would not have been possible if 'a continuous, atomistic, and individualizing power' had not developed so that, 'in place of global, mass controls, everyone, each individual, in its body and its gestures, could be controlled'.[55]

Where disciplinary power targeted individuals in a wide variety of institutions that eventually formed what Foucault calls the 'carceral archipelago', the power deployed by the state targets the population, which it treats both a species,

---

51   Adorno, 'Individuum und Organisation', *Soziologische Schriften* I, p. 447.
52   Foucault, *Discipline and Punish*, p. 297.
53   Ibid., p. 138.
54   Ibid., pp. 25–6.
55   Foucault, 'The Meshes of Power', *Space, Knowledge and Power*, pp. 158–9; trans. mod.

a biological entity, and as a public with manipulable opinions, mores, behaviours, prejudices, fears and the like (STP 75). Today, one of the biopolitical state's principal functions is to manage risks with the goal of ensuring the security of the population as a whole. To achieve this goal, the state attempts (*inter alia*) to regulate the population's birth and death rates, its levels of morbidity and life expectancy, its nutritional practices and its reproductive behaviour. Remarking on the signal role that medicine now plays in the West, Foucault states that the emergence of biopower marks the instantiation of 'a new right, a new morality, a new politics, and a new economy of the body'. Today, Western states are concerned primarily with the 'care of the body, bodily health, the relation between disease and health'.[56]

With the emergence of disciplinary power and biopower, then, 'the "body" appears as the bearer of new variables'.[57] As the power exercised on the body through the 'anatomo-politics' of disciplinary institutions was supplemented and amplified by the biopolitical regulation of the population in the nineteenth century, the state began to acquire 'power over life' and human biology 'came under state control'.[58] This control and regulation, undertaken in the name of ensuring the security of the state and managing perceived risks to the population, was gradually extended to 'a range of factors and elements that seem far removed from the population itself and its immediate behavior, fecundity and desire to reproduce'. Among the more distant factors on which biopolitical states work in order to achieve the 'right relationship between the population and the state's resources and possibilities' are currency flows, exports and imports.[59]

Like disciplinary power, biopower was 'an indispensable element in the development of capitalism'. Capitalism 'would not have been possible' without 'the adjustment of the phenomena of population to economic processes'. According to Foucault, then, '[t]he adjustment of the accumulation of men to that of capital, the joining of the growth of human groups to the expansion of productive forces and the differential allocation of profit, were made possible in part by the exercise of bio-power in its many forms and modes of application'. At the same time, biopower also operates within 'the sphere of economic processes, their development, and the forces working to sustain them'.[60] In fact, indirectly, and perhaps unwittingly, Foucault's account of the reciprocal and complex relations between capitalism, disciplinary power and biopower helps to explain why economic exploitation persists, even though he believes that exploitation is less problematic today than political subjection.

In *The Birth of Biopolitics*, however, where the emergence of biopolitical states is linked to the development of liberal and neoliberal arts of government,

---

56   Foucault, 'Crise de la Médicine ou Crise de l'Antimédicine?', *Dits et écrits* III, pp. 42–3.
57   Foucault, 'The Politics of Health in the Eighteenth Century', *Essential Works: Power*, p. 95.
58   Foucault, *Society Must be Defended*, pp. 239–40.
59   Foucault, *Security, Territory, Population*, p. 72. Cited hereafter in the text as STP.
60   Foucault, *The History of Sexuality*, Vol. 1, pp. 140–1.

Foucault's account of relations between the economy and the state undergoes an interesting shift. And, at first sight, this shift appears to bring Foucault closer to Adorno and his Marxist claims about the primacy of the economy. In this series of lectures, Foucault suggests that the state exercised considerable control over the economy until the mid-eighteenth century. From this point on, relations between the state and the economy began to alter as the influence of liberal arts of government on Western states gave rise to a 'dissymmetrical bipolarity' between the economy and the state.[61]

With liberalism, Foucault declares, we entered the age of the market economy because liberalism turned the economy into a 'site of veridiction', or a site of truth, for Western governments. Liberal economists encouraged Western states to adopt a principle of self-limitation – the famous principle of *laissez-faire* – which stipulated that the economy should be allowed to operate in accordance with its own 'natural' or spontaneous mechanisms (Adam Smith's invisible hand, for example). But once the market started to operate more independently of the state, it began to 'constitute a standard of truth' against which governmental practice could be judged. For liberalism, Foucault claims, 'it is the natural mechanism of the market and the formation of a natural price that enable us to falsify and verify governmental practice' (BB 32).

However, liberalism's principle of *laissez-faire* was altered in the mid-twentieth century as neoliberalism superseded liberalism in post-war Germany, the United States and other Western countries. For German neoliberals – Ordo-liberals – the Keynesian welfare state was a *bête noire*.[62] Indeed, Foucault believes that the 'negative theology of the state as the absolute evil' can be traced back to Ordo-liberals. Claiming that Keynesian policies were adopted and extended in Nazi Germany, Ordo-liberals also alleged that Nazi Germany effectively revealed that 'the defects and destructive effects [that were] traditionally attributed to the market economy should instead be attributed to the state and its intrinsic defects' (BB 115). To remedy these defects, Ordo-liberals began to demand 'even more from the market economy than was demanded from it in the eighteenth century' (BB 116). They would ask 'how the overall exercise of political power can be modeled on the principles of a market economy' (BB 131).

German neoliberals also wanted to ground the state's legitimacy in its capacity for creating 'a space of freedom for economic partners' (BB 106; trans. mod.). The market was to become the 'organizing and regulating principle of the state'; it would serve 'as the principle, form, and model for a state which, because

---

61   Foucault, *The Birth of Biopolitics*, p. 20. Cited hereafter in the text as BB.

62   Interestingly, Foucault views the welfare state as a response to the dangers posed by mass unemployment after 1929 (see BB 68). In addition, he believes that the welfare state is a means to the end of preserving the state's 'labour force, production capacity, and military power' (see 'Crise de la Médicine ou Crise de l'Antimédicine?', *Dits et écrits* III, p. 41). Finally, Foucault also claims that the welfare state responds to the political need to govern *omnes et singulatim*, as Chapter Four will explain.

of its defects, is mistrusted by everyone on both the right and the left, for one reason or another' (BB 117). Yet American neoliberals – including Gary Becker whose work Foucault cites extensively in *The Birth of Biopolitics* – went much further than their German counterparts. Although they also encouraged governments to generalize the economic form of the market, they wanted to generalize the market 'throughout the social body . . . including the whole of the social system not usually conducted through or sanctioned by monetary exchanges'. In other words, American neoliberals were more radical because they wanted to extend economic models to social relationships, the family and individual behaviour (BB 243). In addition, they proposed that the market could be used as an 'economic tribunal' to test governmental action and gauge its validity by subjecting the activities of government officials to cost-benefit analyses, among other things (BB 246).[63]

It is important to note in this context that Foucault tries to distinguish his genealogical account of the growing predominance of the economy from a causal analysis when he insists that he is not trying to explain *why* we entered the age of the market economy. In fact, he claims that the aim of allowing the market to function as a site of truth for governmental practice cannot be explained by the influence of the political economists whom Marx so severely criticized – an influence that, ironically perhaps, Foucault himself documents. According to Foucault, however, we cannot find '*the* cause of the constitution of the market as an agency of veridiction'. Instead, we simply need to 'establish the intelligibility of this process', or to show 'how it became possible' (BB 33).[64]

Still, it is unfortunate that Foucault fails to engage with Marx's account of liberalism. Nor does he engage with Marx on other key issues. So, for example, Foucault states, without critical commentary, that though neoliberals were concerned about monopoly conditions, they thought that these conditions had been fostered by the state, and not, as Marx believed, by tendencies intrinsic to

---

63   On page 4 of 'Becker on Ewald on Foucault on Becker' (the transcript of a conversation between Gary Becker, François Ewald and Bernard E. Harcourt that took place at the University of Chicago on 9 May 2012), Ewald describes Foucault as an apologist for neoliberalism (see University of Chicago Institute for Law and Economics, Olin Research Paper, no. 614; University of Chicago, Public Law, Working paper, no. 401). That Foucault was not a neoliberal apologist should be clear, among other things, from his criticism of neoliberal attempts to extend the model of *homo œconomicus* to domains that are not 'immediately economic', including forms of conduct that relate means to ends, and even to non-rational forms of conduct (BB 268–9). Indeed, Foucault also notes at the end of *The Birth of Biopolitics* that, under neoliberalism, *homo œconomicus* is eviscerated; it becomes an individual who is governable, a mere correlate of government technologies.

64   Usefully, Foucault remarks that to 'establish the intelligibility of the process' that turned the market into a principle of veridiction, we need to establish 'a polyhedral relationship between: the particular monetary situation of the eighteenth century, with a new influx of gold on the one hand, and a relative consistency of currencies on the other; a continuous economic and demographic growth . . .; an intensification of agricultural production; the access to governmental practice of a number of technicians who brought with them both methods and instruments of reflection; and finally a number of economic problems being given a theoretical form' (BB 33).

capitalism.[65] Arguably, Foucault's failure to assess the veracity of this neoliberal claim about the monopolization of capital (along with other neoliberal claims that contest Marx's critique of capitalism) reveals that he is not primarily interested in analyzing the capitalist economy in *The Birth of Biopolitics*. Instead, he focuses on neoliberal theories developed in Germany and the United States with the aim of examining what he calls their new rationality of self-limiting government.

I shall return to this criticism of Foucault later in this chapter. To end this section, however, I want to summarize its central points. Adorno adopts Marx's view that Western states are subordinate to the economy. For Adorno, even the trend towards state capitalism was economically generated. By contrast, Foucault suggests in *The Birth of Biopolitics* that the economy owes its dominant position in society to liberalism and neoliberalism. To the extent that Western states adopted neoliberal arts of government, they began to limit their intervention in the economy while intervening increasingly in the population. Here, of course, Foucault only underscores the idea that relations between the biopolitical state and the capitalist economy are reciprocal and complex. On his account of neoliberalism, Western governments were supposed to subordinate themselves to the capitalist economy – and in particular, to its need for a relatively free market – to bolster their own legitimacy, even as they modelled themselves on the market.

To conclude this section, I would like to consider a possible objection, namely that I am placing too much emphasis here on Foucault's ideas in *The Birth of Biopolitics* – ideas that some commentators believe are unique and experimental and so must be treated with 'extreme caution'.[66] To this objection, I shall respond that, to the extent that this lecture series plumbs the conditions that led to the neoliberal assault on the welfare state, Foucault is advancing the discussion of biopolitics and the welfare state that he had already broached in 'The Birth of Social Medicine', 'Crise de la Médecine ou Crise de l'Antimédicine', 'The Politics of Health in the Eighteenth Century' (among other essays and interviews), and that he will take up again in a 1983 interview, 'Social Security'.[67] (More tenuously, perhaps, *The Birth of the Clinic* can be read as an early precursor to this discussion.) Equally important for the purposes of this chapter, *The Birth of Biopolitics* is the only text that addresses directly claims (like Adorno's) about the pervasiveness of exchange relations in the West. So, while I am prepared to concede that the caveats regarding these lectures should be taken seriously, I believe that Foucault's comments about the market economy and the welfare state in *The Birth of Biopolitics* merit consideration because Foucault not

---

65   See BB 133–7.

66   Frédéric Gros, 'Is There a Biopolitical Subject?', *Biopower*, p. 259.

67   See Foucault, 'The Birth of Social Medicine', *Essential Works: Power*; 'Crise de la Médecine ou Crise de l'Antimédicine', *Dits et écrits* III; 'The Politics of Health in the Eighteenth Century', *Essential Works: Power*; and 'Social Security', *Politics, Philosophy, Culture*.

only takes issue with Marx's emphasis on exchange relations, he develops ideas that he had broached in earlier work and to which he will later return.

EXCHANGE RELATIONS AND POWER RELATIONS

Since Foucault believes that Western societies entered the age of the market economy with the advent of liberalism, the differences between his work and Adorno's may be less polarizing than a cursory view would suggest. In fact, it might seem as though Foucault makes a major concession in *The Birth of Biopolitics* when he charts the growing predominance of the capitalist economy vis-à-vis Western states. However, it is also important to examine Adorno's claims about the impact of exchange relations on virtually every aspect of human life and to compare them with Foucault's ideas about the ubiquity of power relations, because one of the major differences between their critiques of the West lies in these distinct targets.

Marx's critique of the commodity form in the first volume of *Capital* shaped Adorno's ideas about exchange relations under late capitalism. For Marx, once a thing is commodified, it changes 'into a thing that transcends sensuousness' because its use value is transformed into an abstract and commensurable unit of value.[68] Furthermore, the concrete human labour involved in the production of commodities is also commodified and turned into something abstract. Under capitalism, labour is objectified and transformed into socially necessary labour time, or the time 'required to produce any use value under the conditions of production normal for a given society and with the average degree of skill and intensity of labour prevalent in that society'.[69] As a result, the commodity form 'reflects the social characteristics of men's own labour as objective characteristics of the products of labour themselves, as the socio-natural properties of these things'.[70] Finally, relations between producers are themselves transformed into relations between things as exchange mechanisms turn the interaction of producers into a power that acts independently of them.

Adopting Marx's view that exchange relations preponderate over individuals, Adorno also agrees with Marx that 'the real movement of society' has become independent of the individuals who created society and [who] continue to sustain it. Citing Marx, Adorno says that our exchange-based society now operates over individuals' heads and 'through their heads' when it reduces individuals to agents of exchange, to producers and consumers (ND 304). Today, life can reproduce itself only when 'the metamorphosis of labour-power into a commodity has permeated individuals through and through and objectified each of their impulses into formally commensurable variations of the exchange relationship' (MM 229). As a result, late capitalism has become as 'extraneous

---

68   Marx, *Capital*, Vol. 1, p. 163.
69   Ibid., p. 129.
70   Ibid., pp. 164–5.

and therefore heteronomous to the individual as anything once said to have been ordained for him by demons' (ND 315).

Alluding to the reification of human life under capitalism, Simon Jarvis observes that, in *Minima Moralia* and other works, Adorno takes up a prominent theme in Marx, namely his distinction between the living and the nonliving. Like Marx, Adorno constantly appeals to 'the need to protect living experience from becoming "dead", "lifeless", "petrified"'.[71] For Adorno, late capitalism has turned individuals into lifeless objects that are in thrall to the anarchic exchange of equally lifeless commodities. Even when human labour is replaced by machines, Adorno argues that individuals continue to serve as 'means of production', as opposed to 'living purposes', because they remain 'partial moments in the network of material production' (MM 229). As individuals are turned into cogs in the wheels of capitalism, 'moments of naturalness' are assimilated as well. These 'moments' are 'incorporated into technology'; they are forced into 'the service of production'. For Adorno, then, 'it has long ceased to be a matter of the mere sale of the living' because the living are now obliged to transform themselves into 'a thing, a piece of equipment', or to become parts of the productive apparatus (MM 229–30; trans. mod.).

When it reifies labour by reducing it to 'the abstract universal concept of average working hours', exchange is 'fundamentally akin to the principle of identification'. Forced into the mould of exchange relations, 'nonidentical individuals and performances become commensurable and identical'. According to Adorno, exchange imposes 'on the whole world an obligation to become identical, to become total' (ND 146). In his commentary on this key aspect of Adorno's work, Fredric Jameson emphasizes the powerful effects of exchange relations on individuals when he notes that Adorno adopted Marx's view that the modes of abstraction that inform different types of value – from barter all the way to exchange relations – also affect 'the whole range of distinct human activities (from production to the law, from culture to political forms, and not excluding the psyche and the more obscure "equivalents" of unconscious desire)'.[72] As Adorno states in *Aesthetic Theory*, with more than a hint of irony, exchange relations have become the measure of all things.[73]

Adorno's claims about the ubiquity of exchange relations are matched by Foucault's equally insistent claims about the pervasiveness of power relations. Nevertheless, it is important to stress that Adorno conceives of exchange in relational terms and Foucault views power in much the same way. Where exchange relates diverse things and activities by equating them, reducing them to an abstract identity, power relations consist in a play of forces in which one force relates to another by attempting to bring it under its influence or control (from benign activities that involve teaching someone how to do something, to more

71   Jarvis, *Adorno*, p. 68.
72   Fredric Jameson, *Late Marxism*, p. 149.
73   Adorno, *Aesthetic Theory*, p. 310.

malign activities involving coercion). When one force surrenders, the victorious force will be able to 'direct, in a fairly constant manner and with reasonable certainty, the conduct of others' (SP 347). It will also help to shape the identities of those who come under its influence.

Since power is always present 'in human relationships, whether they involve verbal communication . . ., or amorous, institutional, or economic relationships', struggle too is ubiquitous.[74] Again, for Foucault, society consists in 'a perpetual and multiform struggle'. Individuals are 'everywhere in conflict' because 'power relations necessarily incite, constantly call for and open up the possibility of resistance'. Foucault's generalization of struggle to the point where it includes the child who picks his nose at the kitchen table to upset his parents – an example Foucault gives in a 1977 interview – may appear to trivialize it.[75] Yet the child's resistance is arguably less trivial when it is understood as a struggle against the normalizing incursions of disciplinary power.

Interestingly, given his focus on power relations, Foucault says that he 'refrains from seeing power everywhere'. When Pierre Boncenne pointed out in an interview that, like Marx, who was criticized for his exclusive focus on the economy, Foucault could be accused of reducing everything to power, Foucault rejected this criticism on the grounds that he constantly shows the 'economic or political origin' of power mechanisms.[76] On a charitable interpretation, Foucault was saying here that, despite their ubiquity, power relations by no means explain all social phenomena – even, perhaps, all aspects of the struggle in which the nose-picking child is engaged with its parents. To reiterate, for Foucault, power is not an ultimate explanatory principle. As Richard Lynch rightly notes, Foucault's assertion that power relations are omnipresent 'entails neither that power relations are the only omnipresent relation nor that power relations are the most important relations in social situations'.[77] Still, Foucault denied that disciplinary power could be reduced to an economic phenomenon; he did so on the grounds that disciplinary training techniques have their own specificity or logic; they 'obey a type of rationality, and are all based on one another to form a sort of specific stratum'.[78] And the same can be said, *mutatis mutandis*, about biopower.

Colin Gordon observes that, with his focus on power relations, Foucault 'brings Nietzsche to the aid of Marx'. According to Gordon, moreover, 'what *Capital* had done for the study of relations of production', Foucault proposes to do 'for relations of power – duly recognizing . . . the profoundly material

74   Foucault, 'The Ethics of the Concern for Self as a Practice of Freedom', *Essential Works: Ethics*, pp. 291–2.

75   Foucault, 'Pouvoir et Savoir', *Dits et écrits* III, p. 407.

76   Foucault, 'On Power', *Politics, Philosophy, Culture*, p. 105.

77   Richard Lynch, 'Is Power All There Is?', *Philosophy Today*, p. 65. Cited in Amy Allen, *The Politics of Our Selves*, p. 178.

78   Foucault, 'On Power', *Politics, Philosophy, Culture*, p. 105.

interconnection of the two factors'.[79] In fact, Foucault also believes that, by adopting a Nietzschean conception of power as an agonistic relation between forces, there is 'a much better chance' of grasping the connection 'between power and struggles, and especially the class struggle'.[80] Of course, Foucault's extended discussion of how struggle gradually became a model for understanding history in Society Must be Defended can be read as a significant contribution to his project of developing Marx's notion of struggle. So too can his notion of counterconduct – a notion that was introduced in Security, Territory, Population to refer to struggles in the Christian world (the struggles that accompanied the Reformation, for example), and to the political and revolutionary struggles that took place in the nineteenth century (STP 197–9).

One could also argue that Foucault brings Marx to the aid of Nietzsche when he cites Capital to explain why he thinks that Marx's analysis of power is exemplary. For Marx, Foucault writes, there is not just one power, but many different powers; these are localized in factories, armies and other sites, and then coordinated, juxtaposed and linked together hierarchically. Second, these powers are not derived from a monolithic central power. Instead, Marx shows how, 'from the initial and primitive existence of these small regions of power – such as property, slavery, the workshop and also the army – the grand apparatuses of State were able to form'. Third, Marx's 'superb' analyses of discipline in armies and workshops reveal that power produces efficiencies, aptitudes and skills – or that power is not only negative or repressive. Finally, by reading 'between the lines' in Capital, Foucault discovers a history of technologies of power, their invention, development and extension throughout society.[81]

Facilitating the rise of capitalism, disciplinary power and biopower shape the body: they target the physical body through exercise, training and constant surveillance, and they shape the biological and social body through state regulations and programmes. Sex is the point where these two forms of power intersect; it is their common target.[82] Importantly, Foucault also asserts that the measures taken by states to regulate sex would eventually become 'anchorage points for the different varieties of racism of the nineteenth and twentieth centuries'.[83] In fact, he contends that the historical counterpart to Marx's theory of class struggle, which was based on struggles between races in a historico-political sense, was racism 'in its modern, "biologizing", statist form'. Biological racism took shape when 'the thematics of blood' helped to revitalize biopower. Involving 'a whole politics of settlement, family, marriage, education, social

79   Colin Gordon, 'Introduction' in Essential Works: Power, p. xiv. Here Gordon is specifically comparing Capital to Discipline and Punish.
80   Foucault, 'The Confession of the Flesh', Power/Knowledge, p. 208.
81   I am paraphrasing and quoting Foucault in 'The Meshes of Power', Space, Knowledge and Power, pp. 156–8 passim; trans. mod.
82   Foucault, The History of Sexuality, Vol. 1, p. 145.
83   Ibid., p. 26.

hierarchization, and property, accompanied by a long series of permanent interventions at the level of the body, conduct, health, and everyday life', biological racism expressed 'the mystical concern with protecting the purity of the blood and ensuring the triumph of the race'.[84]

It is not just the case that racism characterized the exercise of biopower in Nazi Germany. For Foucault argues that racism is 'a mechanism that allows biopower to work' in all Western states. States are 'obliged to use race, the elimination of races and the purification of race' in order to exercise power.[85] According to Foucault, the 'reason [why] this mechanism can come into play is that the enemies who have to be done away with . . . are threats, either internal or external, to the population and for the population'.[86] Along with criminals, the mad and the sexually perverse, then, some races are also viewed as existential threats. As a result, Western states attempt either to neutralize or to eradicate these menacing 'deviants'.[87] The purification of the population may require murder, either directly or indirectly. It may involve 'exposing someone to death, increasing the risk of death for some people, or, quite simply, political death, expulsion, rejection, and so on'.[88]

Foucault's and Adorno's views about racism will be discussed in subsequent chapters as well, but I should mention briefly here that Adorno shares Foucault's view that prejudice – including racial prejudice – is pervasive in the West. Even individuals who are not overtly prejudiced against a particular race or races tend to distinguish between in-groups and out-groups, and these distinctions are often based on preconceptions about the out-group's behaviour, appearance, predilections, intentions, etc. Those who are discriminated against are frequently seen as more 'natural' than others in the sense that they are perceived as animal-like, inhuman or not fully human, instinctive and irrational. According to Adorno, one of the trademarks of totalitarian movements is that they monopolize 'all the so-called sublime and lofty concepts, while the terms they use for what they persecute and destroy – base, insect-like, filthy, subhuman and all the rest – they treat as anathema'.[89] Perceived as threats to in-groups, out-groups will be marginalized within, or excluded from, society, when they are not simply murdered. Once an individual or group is relegated to an out-group, there is no indignity that may not be perpetrated against it; torture, rape, segregation, confinement and enslavement are just some of the ways in which deviant out-groups have been brought to heel.

Unlike Foucault, however, Adorno blames the spread of exchange relations for discrimination. Briefly, by homogenizing and levelling individuals, exchange

---

84   Ibid., p. 149.
85   Foucault, *Society Must be Defended*, p. 258.
86   Ibid., p. 256.
87   Ibid., p. 258.
88   Ibid., p. 256.
89   Adorno, *Metaphysics: Concept and Problems*, p. 123.

relations also encourage individuals to think in stereotypical and schematic ways. In the culture industry, for example, stereotypical images and schematized themes rigidify experience, encouraging individuals to see themselves and others in fixed, standardized ways. This employment of stereotypes has a counterpart in the use of constantly repeated psychological and rhetorical devices – devices that were also deployed in the speeches and rituals of National Socialists, giving them a mechanically rigid pattern. Through stereotypes and clichés, the culture industry only reinforces the status quo while providing a narcissistic gain for individuals when they successfully recognize who or what is being depicted. But Nazi propaganda and cultural commodities offer another fillip to narcissists when they suggest that those who belong to a particular group are 'better, higher and purer' than members of other groups.[90]

To summarize, Adorno and Foucault make similar claims about the pervasiveness of racial prejudice and other forms of discrimination in the West, but their explanations obviously differ. In Foucault, the power that is wielded by Western states is inherently racist. Racism is biopower's 'basic mechanism.'[91] Racism is, as it were, built into biopower because, in its attempts to promote 'the physical vigor and the moral cleanliness of the social body', biopower ostracizes all those who deviate from prevailing norms.[92] In Adorno, by contrast, it is exchange – which ensures that things and individuals become commensurable and fungible – and identity thinking – which subsumes everything under fixed and rigid categories – that help to explain why discrimination has become so widespread.

I am discussing Adorno's and Foucault's distinct accounts of racism in order to highlight the more obvious differences between their approaches to the study of our present. In the rest of this section, I shall assess these differences more critically. To begin with Adorno, one could object that, with his focus on exchange relations, Adorno is too reductive, and on his own terms. Since he saw Nazi Germany as state capitalist, and recognized that other Western states exhibit state capitalist tendencies, Adorno should have included in his critique of domination a critique of state power. In conjunction with this, one could object that Adorno's claims about social conflict are also problematic. To the extent that Foucault succeeds in showing that many social conflicts today revolve around our subjection to disciplinary institutions and the biopolitical state, Adorno's insistence that these conflicts invariably find their 'objective basis in economic antagonisms' can be challenged.[93]

When Foucault interprets Marx as a theorist of power in 'The Meshes of Power', he remarks again that struggles against power now outstrip struggles against economic exploitation. Although he could be charged with minimizing the bloody

90   Adorno, 'Freudian Theory and the Pattern of Fascist Propaganda', *The Essential Frankfurt School Reader*, p. 130.
91   Foucault, *Society Must be Defended*, p. 254.
92   Foucault, *History of Sexuality*, Vol. 1, p. 54.
93   Adorno, 'Anmerkungen zum sozialen Konflikt heute', *Soziologische Schriften* I, p. 182.

conflicts that accompanied the establishment of trade unions in the late nineteenth and early twentieth centuries, for example, Foucault's claim about the pervasiveness of struggles against power today has more than a little plausibility. For the war against Nazi Germany, which mobilized hundreds of millions of people, along with the institution of gulags and the psychiatrization of political prisoners in the USSR, obviously involved power struggles. However, since Foucault also insisted that the power wielded by states and institutions maintains reciprocal but complex relations with the economy, he also recognized that his critique of power needed to be supplemented with a critique of the capitalist economy.

Nevertheless, there are problems with Foucault's account as well. Without naming Adorno, Foucault implicitly criticizes his exclusive focus on exchange relations in his discussion of neoliberalism when he begins to analyze what it meant to 'introduce market regulation as a regulatory principle of society'. Making direct reference to Marx, Foucault asks whether the introduction of the market as a regulatory principle effectively amounted to 'establishing a market society, that is to say, a society of commodities, of consumption, in which exchange value will be at the same time the general measure and criterion of the elements, the principle of communication between individuals, and the principle of the circulation of things' (BB 146). To this question, Foucault responds emphatically in the negative.

According to Foucault, neoliberal societies are regulated, not by the exchange of commodities, but by 'mechanisms of competition'. A neoliberal society is not 'a supermarket society, but an enterprise society'. What neoliberals seek is not 'a society subject to the commodity-effect, but a society subject to the dynamic of competition'. Or again, the neoliberal model for government, *homo œconomicus*, 'is not the man of exchange or man the consumer, he is the man of enterprise and production'. For these reasons, Foucault denies that neoliberalism represents 'a return to the kind of market society that Marx denounced in *Capital*'. Rather, neoliberalism marks 'an attempt to return to a sort of social ethic of the enterprise, of which Weber, Sombart, and Schumpeter tried to write the political, cultural, and economic history' (BB 147).

Importantly, Foucault concedes that, with their critique of the commodity form, theorists were 'criticizing something that was certainly on the explicit or implicit horizon, willed or not, of . . . arts of government' from the 1920s to the 1960s. However, he also insists that 'we have gone beyond that stage'. We 'are no longer there' because the neoliberal art of government 'absolutely does not seek the constitution of that type of society'. Foucault makes this point repeatedly: neoliberalism 'is not orientated towards the commodity and the uniformity of the commodity, but towards the multiplicity and differentiation of enterprises'. Consequently, critics, including Adorno, who denounce our 'standardizing, mass society of consumption and spectacle, etcetera, are mistaken when they think they are criticizing the current objective of governmental policy' (BB 149). At best, Adorno and others may have been correct about the early twentieth century, but Foucault implies that Adorno's analysis was rendered irrelevant by neoliberalism.

Yet one problem with Foucault's own analysis is its failure to assess the extent to which neoliberalism successfully steered the West away from a market society based on exchange towards an enterprise society based on competition. Indeed, Adorno was not criticizing economic theories. Rather, he was criticizing what he saw as really existing tendencies within society: the material forces that shape society and orient its trajectory (forces that are analogous to disciplinary power and biopower themselves). Furthermore, Foucault problematically asserts both that neoliberal policies were not strictly applied (BB 144) and that they had a growing impact on government policy as governments 'increasingly aligned' themselves with neoliberalism (BB 145). Interested almost exclusively in the economic programmes that helped to shape the 'government's consciousness of itself' (BB 2), Foucault never evaluates their impact on the actual functioning of Western economies (with the exception, perhaps, of France's economy under Valéry Giscard d'Estaing[94]).

Furthermore, even if the impact of these policies on governments in the West has been considerable, Foucault never explains why the enterprise society championed by neoliberal economists is incompatible with a market society. Contra Foucault, it could be argued, in support of Adorno (and, of course, Marx), that the commodity form now absorbs and transforms more phenomena than it did in the past, even and especially in states that have implemented neoliberal policies oriented towards competition. So, for example, one effect of the university-as-enterprise model (which is especially pervasive in North America) has been the commodification of students. Students, who are targeted by advertising, are seen as consumers of an education that has been reduced to, and is sold to them as, a commodity.

Against neoliberalism, then, one could argue that exchange remains one of the major activities of any enterprise. Yet, on Foucault's account of Becker, consumption does not involve exchange. Instead, consumption is an 'enterprise activity by which the individual, . . . on the basis of the capital he has at his disposal, will produce something that will be his own satisfaction'. To be sure, Foucault concedes that Becker's view of consumption differs substantially from the classical one. Nevertheless, on the basis of this novel view of consumption, Becker concludes – and Foucault appears to agree with him – that 'the classical conception of consumption in terms of exchange, along with all the sociological analyses . . . of mass consumption, of consumer society', do not 'hold up', that they 'have no value' (BB 226). To this, however, one could object that it is Becker's conclusion that does not hold up because Becker by no means demonstrates that exchange has become obsolete.

Interestingly, Foucault appears indirectly to contradict his own claims about exchange when he observes that American neoliberalism is far more

---

94   See BB Lecture of 7 March 1979.

radical than its German counterpart because it seeks to generalize the economic form of the market 'throughout the social body . . . including the whole of the social system not usually conducted through or sanctioned by monetary exchanges' (BB 243). Here, Foucault seems to adopt Adorno's view that exchange has become the measure of all things. As Foucault remarks in his discussion of Becker, neoliberal economists encourage states to turn phenomena that were not formerly treated as economic – including education, marriage, parenting, health and genetics – into instances of human capital. As instances of capital, however, these phenomena are also commodified and exchanged.

Finally, Foucault's choice of Becker to exemplify American neoliberalism is problematic: it could be objected that Becker's more famous – and arguably more influential – counterparts in the Chicago School, including Milton Friedman, would have provided better examples. As Melinda Cooper notes (though largely uncritically), Becker is a somewhat anomalous figure; he not only stands 'alone among the Chicago School economists', he is 'unorthodox by the general standards of the discipline'. In fact, Cooper believes that what drew Foucault to Becker was his focus on 'precisely those domains of social power which Foucault had studied through the lens of "normalization"'.[95] Cooper may well be right about the reasons for Foucault's interest in Becker's work. However, since Becker is a relatively minor figure in the neoliberal pantheon, Foucault's choice of Becker to represent American neoliberalism tends to skew his analysis precisely because it enables him to focus almost exclusively on neoliberalism's biopolitical dimensions, while ignoring other important features.

INITIATING A DIALOGUE

So where does this critical comparison leave us? On the surface, the issue of the compatibility of Adorno's and Foucault's critiques of the West is only made more difficult in *The Birth of Biopolitics* when Foucault flatly denies that exchange relations predominate today. However, to determine the complementarity of these critiques, it will not be necessary to show that power relations infiltrate exchange relations, or conversely, that exchange infiltrates power. It will not be necessary, in other words, to reduce one theory to the other. Foucault makes this point himself when he insists on the need for an independent, noneconomic analysis of power on the grounds that power is a force *sui generis*, albeit a force that is 'deeply involved in and with economic relations'.[96] Rather than reducing one theory to the other, then, one must answer the question that Foucault poses in *Society Must be Defended*: is power *always* secondary to the economy?

To begin, it should be noted once again that *The Birth of Biopolitics* is largely concerned with liberal and neoliberal theory. Interestingly, Foucault stated in

---

95   Melinda Cooper, 'The Law of the Household', *The Government of Life*, p. 40.
96   Foucault, *Society Must be Defended*, p. 14.

his first lecture that he did not want to study 'the way in which governors really governed'. Instead, he wanted to examine governments' 'reflection on the best way of governing', or how governments conceptualized the practice of government (BB 2). For this reason, it is unclear that his objections to exchange-based models of society succeed; these objections are filtered through an analysis of neoliberal theories whose implementation by states and whose practical effects Foucault never assessed. With respect to the neoliberal critique of monopoly conditions, for example, neoliberal theorists may have ascribed these conditions to state intervention in the economy but, whatever their origin or cause, it could be argued that the persistence and spread of these conditions undermine competition to the point where they fatally compromise the enterprise society that neoliberals seek to establish. In other words, with its focus on competition, neoliberalism is reactionary; it is engaging in a rearguard action against well-entrenched monopoly conditions. Foucault should have addressed issues like these in order to respond adequately to critics, as well as to Adorno's own claims about the centrality of exchange relations in the West.

Serge Audier has argued in *Néolibéralisme(s)* that *The Birth of Biopolitics* must be seen in a polemical context because Foucault was trying to position himself against the critique of the society of consumption that had been advanced by thinkers as diverse as Jean Baudrillard, Herbert Marcuse, Guy Debord and Henri Lefebvre. In connection with this observation, Audier criticizes Foucault. He not only alleges that Foucault was not really interested in consumption in *The Birth of Biopolitics*, he objects that it is not possible to think seriously about neoliberalism without acknowledging that neoliberal governments have allowed wealth and power to be concentrated increasingly in the hands of an ever smaller number of people. Since Foucault does not acknowledge this, Audier charges that *The Birth of Biopolitics* is dogmatic and rigid.[97]

To return to another point that was made earlier, Foucault also expressed concern, early in *The Birth of Biopolitics*, that his study of liberalism would be misinterpreted because readers might believe that he was only describing what was going on in the heads of economists (BB 30). As I have argued here, however, *The Birth of Biopolitics* encourages this 'misinterpretation' precisely because it focuses almost exclusively, and largely uncritically, on neoliberalism's theoretical move away from exchange and towards competition. Of course, the pervasiveness of exchange relations is the central tenet in Adorno's critique of late capitalist societies, but Foucault has not shown that neoliberalism invalidates it. He has not shown convincingly that Adorno was right about the pervasiveness of exchange relations before the emergence of neoliberalism but that his view was later falsified by the encroachment of neoliberal theory on Western governments' consciousness of themselves in the mid-twentieth century.

---

97   Serge Audier, *Néolibéralisme(s)*. Cited by Michael Behrent in 'La Querelle du Néolibéralisme', *Sciences Humaines*, p. 51.

Indeed, Foucault's assessment of neoliberal states in *The Birth of Biopolitics* is problematic for yet another reason. For if he is correct, and neoliberal econo-mists, with their 'anti-state suspicion', their 'state phobia' (BB 188), succeeded in encouraging states to diminish their direct intervention in the market economy and to intervene instead in the population (by medicalizing it and influencing its opinions and beliefs), then states actually retained much of their power, even if they only used it to ensure that the market effectively counterbalanced it.[98] More to the point, since Foucault contends that liberalism marked the birth of a dissymmetry between the economy and the state – a dissymmetry that ushered in the age of the market economy – he recognizes that the market economy does predominate, if only at the instigation of the state itself. And if the economy is the predominant force in the West, then on Foucault's own account, there are good reasons why it should remain the primary focus of a critical theory.

Still, on a more positive reading, Foucault does challenge successfully the exclusive focus on the economy that characterizes Adorno's work when he stresses the historical links between the rise of liberal capitalism and the emer-gence of disciplinary power and biopower. Indeed, I shall argue throughout this book that Foucault's critique of power can supplement Adorno's critique of late capitalism, especially since they both focus on our historical present with a view to alerting us to the possibility of a resurgence of fascism.[99] On his account of Nazism as a form of state capitalism, Adorno maintains that, where the state predominates, domination becomes more 'direct' – and perhaps even in some of the ways that Foucault describes when he discusses the biopolitical state's secu-rity apparatus along with its extensive interventions in the population.[100] Backed

---

98   Todd May and Ladelle McWhorter point out that states intervene indirectly in the economy by increasing their biopolitical regulation of the population and by promoting policies that concern 'agriculture . . ., monopoly regulation, taxes, welfare, and trade'. See May and McWhorter, 'Who's Being Disciplined Now?', *Biopower*, p. 251. With respect to the biopolitical regulation of the population, Frédéric Gros notes in the same volume of essays that the 'biopolitical operation consists in depoliticizing the subject and addressing only her demand for personal satisfaction. By stimulating the subject's egoist appetite as a priority, by appealing only to the level of her private desires, we effectively end up by extracting from polymorphous, vital potentialities a pure consumer subject who will calculate her usefulness and . . . pursue her egoist satisfaction, but . . . remain blind to all other appeals.' See Gros, 'Is There a Biopolitical Subject?', *Biopower*, p. 269; trans. mod.

99   In *The Birth of Biopolitics*, Foucault suggests that it is precisely the neoliberal attempt to reduce the power wielded by the state that could lead to a resurgence of fascism: 'we should not delude ourselves by attributing to the state itself a process of becoming fascist which is actually exogenous, and due much more to the state's reduction and dislocation' (BB 192). Unfortunately, Foucault did not elaborate on this remark – a remark that seems to conflict with claims he made in other work to the effect that Nazism represented a malignant excrescence of state power. See, for example, Foucault, 'La Philosophie analytique de la Politique', *Dits et écrits* III, p. 536. This point will be revisited in 'Critique'.

100   See, for example, STP 45. In contrast to disciplinary mechanisms, 'apparatuses of security . . . have the constant tendency to expand; they are centrifugal. New elements are constantly being integrated: psychology, behavior, the ways of doing things of producers, buyers, consumers, importers and exporters, and the world market. Security therefore involves organizing, or . . . allowing the development of, ever-wider circuits.'

58

in part by police intimidation, which always threatens to erupt into more extreme forms of oppression, state capitalist societies will use physical force to maintain themselves in power. In fact, Adorno recognizes that political domination has often proved to be far more malign than its economic counterpart.[101] Wherever the power motive supersedes the profit motive, direct physical and psychological control over citizens may be the option of first resort by many states – as it was in Nazi Germany.

Again, Adorno's almost exclusive interest in the economy and exchange relations (along with their psychological effects on individuals) is too reductive. The centrality of the economy in his work is all the more surprising given that Adorno accused Friedrich Engels of 'doctrinal intransigence' on the grounds that Engels believed that the economic process 'produces the conditions of political rule and keeps overturning them until the inevitable deliverance from the compulsion of economics'. Equally important, Adorno charged that Engels' intransigence on this point 'was precisely political'. Engels and Marx did not want to extend the revolution to 'society's political form', to 'the rules of the game of domination', because they had the political aim of holding anarchists in check. Believing that the revolution was 'directly imminent', they wanted to break up anarchist movements, which would, 'they had to fear, have to be crushed like Spartacus long ago, or like the peasant uprisings' (ND 323).

In this context, Adorno also criticizes Marx's claim that domination 'must not be deduced otherwise than economically'. Countering Marx, Adorno suggests that economic domination may have originated in political domination when he speculates that domination could have evolved 'contingently from arbitrary archaic acts of seizing power'. Yet, even as he concedes that it is not 'idle' to speculate about the origin of domination, Adorno believes that this issue will never be resolved because the relevant facts have faded away 'in the mists of primitive history' (ND 322). In a less speculative vein, however, Adorno argues that the former Soviet Union revealed that the economic revolution could fail 'even where it succeeded'. Indeed, Marx and Engels did not foresee 'that domination could outlast a planned economy' (ND 323). Here Adorno himself acknowledges that domination may well have a political dimension, if not a political origin. As a result, it could be argued that Adorno's exclusive interest in the economy and exchange relations is problematic.

When Foucault approvingly cites *Capital* in 'The Meshes of Power', he effectively shows that a Marxist account of Western societies can accommodate a study of power relations because he suggests that Marx himself demonstrated that the political and economic dimensions of critique are compatible. Furthermore, I have argued here that Foucault's interest in power relations by no means invalidates or calls into question an economic analysis of society.

101   Adorno, 'Diskussionsbeitrag zu"Spätkapitalismus oder Industriegesellschaft?"', *Soziologische Schriften* I, p. 584.

Although he rejected exchange-based models of society in *The Birth of Biopolitics*, Foucault also insisted throughout his work that his problem 'was not to replace an economic explanation with an explanation in terms of power'.[102] Again, his own genealogies confirm that economic analyses are at least as important as political ones, and sometimes more important. Constantly stressing the links between disciplinary power, biopower and the rise of liberal capitalism, Foucault only underscores the need to take economic phenomena into account in any critique of the West. Indeed, his claims about the predominance of the economy in *The Birth of Biopolitics* arguably make an economic analysis of society all the more imperative.

It is less clear that Adorno would accept that the economy and the state are coeval and coequal as Foucault suggests when he remarks that the economy and the state maintain reciprocal and complex relations with one another. Indeed, since Foucault fails to refute Adorno's claims about the predominance of exchange relations, it could be argued that power relations will remain subordinate to exchange relations in many, if not most, cases. At the same time, however, it must be emphasized again that, even when it can be shown that power is subordinate to the economy, this would not justify reducing power relations to exchange mechanisms. Rather, it would simply mean that a noneconomic analysis of Western society is almost always incomplete.

In short, Foucault underscores the need for an independent analysis of power, but the need for such an analysis is frequently belied, not just because Foucault constantly observes that disciplinary power and biopower were tied to the rise of capitalism, but because he accepts that we have entered the age of the market economy. Conversely, when Adorno insists on tracing all phenomena, including social conflicts, back to the economy and exchange relations, his insistence is not always justified, and on his own terms. Still, a comprehensive analysis of power relations can seldom be made in complete abstraction from economic factors; it must ultimately be placed within the larger historical context of liberal and neoliberal capitalism (rather than in the context of liberal and neoliberal theories). Power may not *always* be subordinate to the economy, but it will *often* be.

On the one hand, then, Adorno is right: we continue to live in a society that is based on exchange, a society in which an ever dwindling number of individuals controls the vast majority of the wealth. Indeed, Adorno usefully reminds readers of the continued importance of a critique of capitalism for critical theory, and Foucault agrees with him even though he does not engage in this critique himself. On the other hand, I would argue that Adorno's critique of economic domination under late capitalism needs to be supplemented with a critique of our subjection to power. Foucault makes a convincing case – based in part on his sympathetic reading of Marx – for the claim that some conflicts

---

102   Foucault, 'Interview with Michel Foucault', *Essential Works: Power*, p. 284.

are primarily rooted in power. And, since power is not always secondary to the economy, Foucault demonstrates that critical theory should not be limited to a critique of capitalism.

To be sure, other issues must be addressed in order to make a complete and balanced assessment of Adorno's and Foucault's critical theories. For example, their ostensibly conflicting views on emancipation should be compared – a comparison that will be made in 'Resistance'– and this will require an assessment of their positions on Marx's call for a revolution. The problem of determining the compatibility of their analyses also demands an assessment of their ideas about the plight of individuals in the West. This assessment, which will be undertaken in the next chapter, will involve a more extensive discussion of Adorno's and Foucault's views about psychoanalysis. However, in this chapter, I have tried to correct some of the more egregious misunderstandings of their work, particularly with respect to their positions on Marx, misunderstandings that may have obscured some of the more significant ways in which Foucault's work complements Adorno's.

Chapter 3

Notes on Individuation

A central theme in critical theory, the social construction of individuals is discussed throughout Adorno's and Foucault's work. Of course, Adorno believes that we are the products of societies that force virtually all things, people, processes and activities into the homogenizing and levelling mould of exchange relations, and Foucault claims that we have been shaped by mechanisms of disciplinary power and biopower that penetrate deeply into the fabric of our lives. Nevertheless, Adorno and Foucault share the view that individuals do not pre-exist their formation in Western societies. There is no pristine inner core in individuals that is subsequently entangled in society and invested by exchange relations or overlaid by power relations. As individuals, we are just the effects of forces of which we are largely unaware and over which, for that very reason, we exercise little or no control.

In order better to understand the process of individuation under late capitalism, Adorno employs Freudian theory, with its postulate of dynamic relations between ego, id and superego. However, since commentators frequently allege that Foucault repudiated psychoanalysis, this chapter will begin with an account of Adorno's and Foucault's positions on Freudian theory, placing particular emphasis on Freud's instinct theory and his so-called repressive hypothesis. Following this discussion, I shall compare Adorno's claims about the individual as a precipitate of exchange relations with Foucault's conception of the individual as an effect of disciplinary power and biopower. This analysis will issue in a consideration of precisely *what* is being shaped into individuals. For, if individuals are the products of extensive social conditioning, it is important to ask about the 'stuff' that is being conditioned and individuated. In fact, some critics have charged that Foucauldian individuals are effectively created *ex nihilo* and I shall answer these critics here. On the basis of this account of the process of individuation in Adorno and Foucault, the final section of this chapter will discuss their claims about the predominant character traits of individuals in the West.

ADORNO, FOUCAULT, FREUD

Adorno was neither an orthodox Marxist nor an orthodox Freudian. In fact, he had serious reservations about key aspects of Freudian theory. For example, he criticized Freud's conception of the ego, claiming that Freud conceived of the ego as both conscious – to the extent that it engages in reality-testing – and unconscious, when it acts as the agent of repression. Since Freud failed to investigate the dialectical character of the ego, Adorno charged that many of his observations about the ego 'involuntarily contradict one another'. By extension, Freud lacked 'adequate criteria for distinguishing "positive" from "negative" ego-functions', thereby undermining, inter alia, his distinction between repression and sublimation.[1] More damningly still, Adorno described Freud as a conservative thinker who vacillated between denouncing the renunciation of instinct as repressive and applauding it as a beneficial form of sublimation (MM 60). In conjunction with this, Adorno objected that Freud was hostile to both reason and pleasure: he saw pleasure solely as a means to the end of preserving the species, while treating reason as epiphenomenal, a mere superstructure (MM 61).

Adorno only underscores Freud's conservatism when he argues that psychoanalysis serves the end of normalization because its therapeutic techniques encourage adaptation to existing states of affairs. Against Freud, Adorno contends that a therapeutic method that had 'a standard other than successful adaptation and economic success would have to aim at bringing people to a consciousness of unhappiness both general and . . . personal, and at depriving them of the illusory gratifications by which the abominable order keeps a second hold on life inside them' (MM 62). In 'Sociology and Psychology', Adorno also objects that Freud tried to turn psychoanalysis into a seamless system that explains everything. His 'psychological insight was combined with a systematic trait which was permeated by monolithic, authoritarian elements'. Turning 'individual findings' into 'total theses', Freud's systematizing was largely responsible for the 'untruths of psychoanalytic theory'.[2]

Notwithstanding these criticisms, Adorno borrows a great deal from psychoanalysis, including Freud's theory of instincts and many of Freud's ideas about repression. Adorno's defence of Freudian theory appears, among other places, in 'Die Revidierte Psychoanalyse', a paper that he presented to the Psychoanalytic Society in San Francisco in 1946. Criticizing the revisionism of Karen Horney and other psychologists in this paper, Adorno charges that their rejection of Freud's instinct theory amounts to a repudiation of Freud's view that society gives rise to discontent and unhappiness because it demands the repression of many instincts. In addition, Adorno argues that, when they separate the ego from its 'genetic connection with the id', revisionists do with character traits what they allege Freud did with instincts: they hypostatize them and turn them into absolutes.[3]

If Adorno makes extensive use of psychoanalysis in spite of his criticisms of it, James Bernauer suggests that Foucault does the opposite. Although

---

1   Adorno, 'Sociology and Psychology', New Left Review 47, pp. 86–7.
2   Adorno, 'Sociology and Psychology', New Left Review 46, p. 74.
3   Adorno, 'Die Revidierte Psychoanalyse', Soziologische Schriften I, p. 22.

Foucault acknowledged Freud's considerable achievements, Bernauer believes that 'Freud and psychoanalysis remain exemplary of the system from which Foucault sought to escape.'[4] On Bernauer's reading, Foucault wanted to escape psychoanalysis for a number of reasons. First, he thought that Freud had adopted uncritically the major themes of modern knowledge: death, desire and the law. Second, he charged that sexuality plays too prominent a role in psychoanalysis. Third, Freud allegedly saw power as completely repressive. Fourth, 'Freud cooperates in constituting the family as a privileged target for political governance in that it is transformed into the "germ of all the misfortunes of sex".' Finally, Bernauer claims that Foucault criticizes Freud for adopting 'the techniques of confessional practice', thereby placing 'the individual under the obligation to manifest truth to another in a situation of dependence and through the action of speech, which is invested with a special virtue of verification'.[5]

It was this last criticism in particular that prompted some psychoanalysts to cast Foucault as virulently anti-Freudian. Nevertheless, in a vigorous response to these objections (and, indirectly, to Bernauer's account of Foucault's position on Freudian theory as well), Foucault observed that, unlike physicists who took no offence when Albert Einstein said that physics could be traced back to demonology, Freudian analysts reacted so strongly to his genealogy of psychoanalysis owing to their concerns about the precarious scientific status of their discipline. Foucault said that he would have greater confidence in the scientific truth of psychoanalysis if analysts were able to take a more sanguine view of the history of psychoanalysis.[6] Throughout his work, Foucault distinguishes between genesis and validity: the validity of Freudian theory is no more compromised by its genesis than the validity of physics is.

In fact, Foucault was by no means as anti-Freudian as many of his critics (and even sympathetic commentators, including Bernauer) claim. In the opening chapter, for example, I mentioned Foucault's positive appraisal of Freud's conception of the subject. In conjunction with this, Foucault praised Freud's postulate of the unconscious on the grounds that it had prompted a re-evaluation of individual autonomy. Claiming that the subject is an outgrowth of the unconscious forces of the id, Freud recognized that the subject is something fabricated, not an unchanging given.[7] Equally important, Foucault commended Freud for opposing the racism that was implicit in the nineteenth-century theory of degeneracy when he refused to link sexual pathologies to heredity. Although he agreed with Adorno that there is a normalizing impulse in Freud, Foucault nonetheless observed that, 'of all those institutions that set out . . . to

4   James Bernauer, 'Michel Foucault's Ecstatic Thinking', *The Final Foucault*, p. 56.
5   Ibid., pp. 57–8.
6   Foucault, 'Interview de Michel Foucault', *Dits et écrits* IV, p. 666. All translations of *Dits et écrits* IV are my own.
7   Foucault, 'Truth and Juridical Forms', *Essential Works: Power*, p. 3.

medicalize sex', psychoanalysis alone 'rigorously opposed the political and institutional effects of the perversion-heredity-degeneracy system'.[8]

Foucault also attributed to Freud the erosion of the Church's influence on
our understanding of sexuality. In an interview he gave at the end of the 1970s,
Foucault noted approvingly that Freud transferred confession 'from the rigid
baroque rhetoric of the Church to the reclining couch of the psychoanalyst'. As
a result, understanding the behaviour of individuals was no longer 'something
that one could obtain in five minutes from someone who declared himself superior because he was in the service of a higher power'. Foucault prefaces this
largely positive assessment of psychoanalysis with the observation that, while
Freud's theories are not entirely correct, there is nonetheless 'some truth in each
of them'. Hence, Foucault cautions that Freud should not be 'underestimated'.[9]

To be sure, Foucault and Adorno do appear to disagree about Freud's theory
of instincts. Claiming that instincts account for much of our behaviour, this
theory also postulates that instincts have somatic sources even as it concedes
that these sources are difficult to locate because instincts only make their presence known in mental life in the form of their ends or aims. To cite Freud in
'Instincts and their Vicissitudes', instinct (*Trieb*) is 'the psychical representative
of the stimuli originating from within the organism and reaching the mind, as a
measure of the demand made upon the mind for work in consequence of its
connection with the body'.[10] In this essay, Freud also adopted the working
hypothesis (which he would later revise) that a distinction must be made
between ego instincts (such as hunger and thirst) which aim at self-
preservation, and sexual instincts whose primary aim is pleasure. At the same
time, he maintained that some sexual instincts are permanently linked to ego
instincts, furnishing self-preserving ego instincts with libidinal components.

Taking up many of Freud's ideas, Adorno was especially interested in the
impact of self-preserving ego drives on our thought and behaviour. Agreeing
with Freud, Adorno remarked that the ego first 'came into being . . . as an instrument of self-preservation, that of reality-testing'.[11] Even today, the ego, with its
highly developed capacities for speech and logical thought, remains an organ of
adaptation to the environing world. But if the ego continues to devote much of
its energy to mastering the environing world in the interest of ensuring its
survival, it adopts an antagonistic relationship to its own internal nature as well.
Adorno argued that *homo sapiens* developed an ego – 'the self of self-
preservation' (ND 217) – only after it had banished many other instincts to 'the
zone of unfree bondage to nature' (ND 222). As Joel Whitebook explains, the
unity of the self or ego is ultimately 'achieved by dragooning all the diffuse and

8   Foucault, *The History of Sexuality*, Vol. 1, p. 119; trans. mod. See also p. 150.
9   Foucault, 'M. Foucault. Conversation sans Complexes avec le Philosophe qui analyse les
"Structures du Pouvoir" ', *Dits et écrits* III, p. 675 *passim*.
10   Sigmund Freud, 'Instincts and their Vicissitudes', *The Standard Edition*, p. 122.
11   Adorno, 'Marginalia to Theory and Praxis', *Critical Models*, p. 272.

conflicting forces of inner nature into its service and regimenting them according to the external demands of the ego principle'.[12]

Although the ego and its rational faculties have evolved and changed, they remain linked to self-preservation. Motivated by survival instincts, even science and philosophy sublimate what Adorno calls the 'anthropological schema' that is rooted in human prehistory. Just as our forebears stalked, pounced on and devoured their prey, Adorno observes (with Nietzsche) that scientists try to bring both internal and external nature under their conceptual yoke in explanatory systems with a view to dominating and controlling nature (ND 22). This is why Adorno denounces our belief 'in the supremacy of nature-controlling reason'; this belief is a delusion because the 'suppression of nature for human ends is a mere natural relationship' (ND 179). Our ceaseless attempts to dominate nature reveal that we are as imprisoned in nature as all other animals.

Adorno also stresses the historical character of the self-preserving instincts – and indeed of all other instincts as well. Although Freud himself tended to view instincts as ahistorical, Adorno defends Freud when he argues that Freud did not preclude the possibility that 'the concrete manifestation of instincts might undergo the most sweeping variations and modifications'.[13] Adorno makes a related point when he coins the term 'addendum' (*das Hinzutretende*) to refer to instinct. Describing the addendum in much the same way that Freud defined instinct, namely as 'intramental and somatic in one', Adorno rejects an exclusively biological conception of instinct – a conception that risks turning instincts into historically invariant drives (ND 228–9). In fact, instincts are socially mediated to such an extent that whatever appears to be natural in them is really only 'something that has been produced by society'.[14]

If Adorno accepts (with qualifications) Freud's instinct theory, while constantly emphasizing the pernicious effects of untrammelled survival instincts on our thought and behaviour, Foucault may appear to question the existence of instincts when he offers a genealogy of the concept of instinct in *Abnormal*. Perplexed and fascinated in turns by ostensibly motiveless murders, nineteenth-century psychiatrists attempted to account for them by postulating the existence of overpowering energies or passions which they called instincts. With the concept of instinct, they began to refer to a new domain of objects – a domain that comprised 'impulses, drives, tendencies, inclinations, and automatisms'.[15] This concept not only helped to explain seemingly inexplicable behaviour, it enabled psychiatrists to reconceptualize pathologies and to 'organize the whole problematic of the abnormal at the level of the most elementary and everyday

---

12   Joel Whitebook, *Perversion and Utopia*, p. 68.

13   Adorno, 'Die Revidierte Psychoanalyse', *Soziologische Schriften* I, p. 21. Adorno also argues that Freud saw instincts as ahistorical only because their development had been arrested; see Adorno, 'Sociology and Psychology', *New Left Review* 47, p. 80.

14   Adorno, 'Theses on Need', *Adorno Studies*, p. 102; trans. mod.

15   Foucault, *Abnormal*, p. 131.

conduct'. Equally important, the concept of instinct allowed psychiatry to insert itself into a 'biological problematic', thereby improving its scientific credentials.[16]

Foucault's genealogy of instinct certainly indicates, to borrow Nietzsche's phrase, its *pudenda origo*, its lowly beginnings. Yet Foucault never questions the validity of the concept of instinct. Moreover, he does not deny that the word refers to something material, physical. So, for example, when he was asked why he described sex in so much of his work, Foucault replied (perhaps too glibly) that sex is not just a constant preoccupation for the majority of individuals but the most powerful human drive, stronger in some respects than hunger and thirst.[17] More to the point, Foucault not only acknowledges the existence of phenomena that we call instincts, he stresses their historical character. We may believe 'in the dull constancy of instinctual life', but genealogy 'easily seizes the slow elaboration of instincts'.[18] In fact, Foucault agrees with Adorno and Freud that instinct 'should not be interpreted as a simple natural given, a natural biological mechanism'.[19] For all three thinkers, it is also the case that knowledge has 'instincts as its foundation, basis, and starting point'. Knowledge is based on 'instincts in their confrontation'.[20] Like Nietzsche, moreover, Foucault links the will to know to the will to power.[21]

I shall return to a discussion of Adorno's and Foucault's ideas about instinct later in this chapter and in subsequent chapters as well. At this juncture, however, I want to discuss another Freudian issue on which Adorno and Foucault might be thought to disagree. For Adorno also appears to diverge from Foucault when he endorses Freud's theory of repression. According to Adorno, who was particularly impressed by Freud's *Civilization and its Discontents*, human beings succeeded in mastering nature, other individuals and themselves only by repressing many of their instincts or by delaying their satisfaction. In fact, Adorno contends that no clear distinction can be made today between 'a need that is proper to humanity and one that would be a consequence of repression' because all our instincts have been socially conditioned. As the products of society, our instincts and needs have been monopolized.[22]

For Adorno, moreover, the entire course of human history can be traced in the displacement, distortion and repression of our instincts and passions. Calling this our underground history, Adorno endorses Freud's claim that 'it is impossible to overlook the extent to which civilization is built up upon a renunciation of instinct, how much it presupposes precisely the non-satisfaction (by

16   Ibid., pp. 132–3 *passim*.
17   Foucault, 'M. Foucault', *Dits et écrits* III, p. 673.
18   Foucault, 'Nietzsche, Genealogy, History', *Essential Works: Aesthetics*, pp. 379–80.
19   Foucault, 'The Meshes of Power', *Space, Knowledge and Power*, p. 153.
20   Foucault, 'Truth and Juridical Forms', *Essential Works: Power*, p. 8.
21   Foucault, *Lectures on the Will to Know*, p. 198.
22   Adorno, 'Theses on Need', *Adorno Studies*, p. 103.

suppression, repression, or some other means?) of powerful instincts'.[23] But if society requires renunciation in order to function, individuals rarely benefit from it. Individuals do not benefit because 'there is no real equivalence between renunciation of instincts in the present and compensation in the future'. Society is organized irrationally because 'the equivalent reward it always promises never arrives'.[24]

Again, it might be thought that Adorno's adherence to Freud's theory of repression distinguishes his work from Foucault's because, on one highly influential interpretation of Foucault's work, commentators allege that he simply rejected Freud's so-called 'repressive hypothesis'. Nevertheless, this interpretation (which Bernauer also adopts in the article cited above) cannot be sustained. It is highly problematic because Foucault explicitly stated on several occasions that he did not reject the repressive hypothesis. In fact, he protested that 'critics . . . reproached me for denying that sexuality had been repressed. But I certainly never claimed that there had been no repression of sexuality'.[25] Rather than denying the reality of repression, Foucault merely asks whether relations between power, knowledge and instinct in the modern age can be understood exclusively in terms of repression. Furthermore, he argues that repressive mechanisms may be incorporated into more complex and global strategies in which repression is not always the primary objective.

Although Foucault is also interested in our underground history, and he does not deny that instincts may be repressed, he does question Freud's view (and, by extension, Adorno's) that human history as a whole can be characterized as the history of repression. Foucault challenges this view of human history on the grounds that power is not simply negative or prohibitive, but always also productive. Acknowledging that sexual drives may be repressed, Foucault nonetheless contends that power also helps to construct sex owing, *inter alia*, to the persistent 'institutional incitement to speak about it'.[26] This incitement to speak about sex in detail and in depth manifested itself in the publication of countless books, articles and essays that dealt with sex in a variety of disciplines in the nineteenth and twentieth centuries. It also led to the invention of a panoply of therapies and treatments for sexual behaviours that were considered to be

---

23 Freud, *Civilization and its Discontents*, in *The Standard Edition*, p. 97.

24 Adorno, *Problems of Moral Philosophy*, p. 139.

25 This passage appears in Foucault's preface to the German translation of the first volume of *The History of Sexuality: Sexualität und Wahrheit*. It is cited by Eribon in *Michel Foucault*, pp. 275–6. See also Foucault, 'The Minimalist Self', *Politics, Philosophy, Culture*, p. 9: 'it is not a question of denying the existence of repression. It's one of showing that repression is always part of a much more complex political strategy regarding sexuality. Things are not merely repressed.' See also Foucault, *Wrong-doing, Truth-telling*, p. 245: 'The repression of sexuality is interesting only to the extent that it makes a certain number of people suffer, still today. It is also interesting because it has taken diverse forms but has always existed. What I think it is important to ask is how and why this relation to our sexual behaviors poses a problem, and under what forms . . . it poses a problem' (trans. mod.).

26 Foucault, *The History of Sexuality*, Vol. 1, p. 18.

pathological, and even to architectural arrangements that were designed to disclose or to conceal sexual behaviours and activities. Applied to 'the body, sexual organs, pleasures, kinship relations, interpersonal relations, and so forth', the burgeoning discourse on sexuality eventually forced this 'heterogeneous ensemble' to congeal, producing ideas about sex that deeply inform both our understanding and our experience of it.[27]

Foucault highlights the productive aspects of power throughout his work. Importantly, however, David Weberman cautions against making a hard and fast distinction between the productive dimensions of power and power's negative effects. Although Weberman mistakenly thinks – along with some other commentators – that Foucault rejected the repressive hypothesis only surreptitiously to make use of it, he makes a point that is worth emphasizing when he remarks that, in Foucault, 'negative and positive effects always entail one another'. For when power encourages a particular course of action, it will simultaneously prohibit or discourage other courses of action. Conversely, the prohibition of actions – especially when it is accompanied by sanctions – may encourage the adoption of more socially acceptable actions. In other words, the positive and the negative effects of power are 'flip sides of the same coin'. On this basis, Weberman concludes that 'if power's positive and negative effects go hand in hand, then the effects of power, even on Foucault's construal, are always repressive as well'. This means that 'Foucault is best understood not as an opponent of the repressive hypothesis, but as one of its more subtle spokesmen, thanks to his recognition of the repressiveness of normalization.'[28]

At the risk of courting even more controversy, I would argue that Foucault adopts a view of repression that is comparable in important respects to Freud's.[29] In *Discipline and Punish*, for example, Foucault claims that those who are subjected to the gaze of teachers, doctors, psychologists, social workers and other experts end by internalizing the norms against which they are judged, and they subsequently adapt their behaviour to these norms. Constantly observed, supervised, examined and tested in disciplinary institutions, we become individuals when we impose upon ourselves the normative constraints of power, or when we inscribe in ourselves power relations in which we simultaneously play the role of judging subject and judged object.[30]

Commenting on Jeremy Bentham's panopticon – which serves as a cipher for our carceral society in *Discipline and Punish* – Foucault insists in 'The Eye of Power' that 'we are talking about two things here: the gaze and interiorisation.'[31] In this interview, he also explains that disciplinary mechanisms involve 'a gaze

---

27   Foucault, 'The Confession of the Flesh', *Power/Knowledge*, p. 210.
28   Weberman, 'Foucault's Reconception of Power', *The Philosophical Forum*, pp. 194–5 *passim*.
29   I first argued that Foucault adopts a Freudian view of repression in 'Foucault, Freud, and the Repressive Hypothesis', *The Journal of the British Society for Phenomenology*.
30   Foucault, *Discipline and Punish*, pp. 202–3.
31   Foucault, 'The Eye of Power', *Power/Knowledge*, p. 154.

which each individual under its weight will end by interiorising to the point that he is his own overseer, each individual thus exercising this surveillance over, and against, himself'.[32] Furthermore, Freud observed that internalization allows society 'to dispense with external measures of coercion'.[33] And for Foucault as well, once individuals make the constraints of power 'play spontaneously' upon themselves, 'external power may throw off its physical weight; it tends to the non-corporal'.[34]

By extension, it could be argued that the Foucauldian gaze produces something analogous to the Freudian superego. For Freud and Foucault – not to mention Nietzsche, who also influenced Freud[35] – the individual (or the ego, in Freud) comes into being when social norms are internalized and a moral 'conscience' is formed. For both, these norms promote conformity: when internalized, they encourage the suppression of impulses and inclinations that are deemed abnormal or deviant as the individual attempts to conform to socially acceptable behaviour. In addition, Freud and Foucault stress the harsh and punitive character of our socially engendered conscience. Finally, to his Freudian assessment of the coercive character of the internalized gaze, Foucault adds another critical note – a note that is sounded frequently in Adorno as well: once norms are internalized, individuals effectively become 'the principle of their own subjection'.[36]

Of course, in contrast to Foucault, whose Freudian account of internalization is only implicit, Adorno openly adopts Freud's ideas about the internalization of norms and the formation of the superego. Although he objects that Freud later endorsed repression because he thought that civilization would not be possible without it, Adorno notes approvingly that Freud originally started out as a critic of the superego.[37] In early work, Freud argued that the superego is 'heteronomous and alien to the ego' on the grounds that the superego represents 'blindly, unconsciously internalized social coercion' (ND 272). Agreeing with these claims about the coercive character of the superego, Adorno

---

32   Ibid., p. 155.
33   Freud, *The Future of an Illusion*, in *The Standard Edition*, p. 11.
34   Foucault, *Discipline and Punish*, pp. 202–3.
35   Nietzsche observed that we develop our 'souls' by turning instincts back against ourselves. He called this 'internalization'. See Nietzsche, *On The Genealogy of Morals*, p. 84. Freud comments on Nietzsche's influence in 'On the History of the Psycho-analytic Movement', *The Standard Edition*, pp. 15–16: 'In later years I have denied myself the very great pleasure of reading the work of Nietzsche with the deliberate object of not being hampered in working out the impressions received in psycho-analysis by any sort of anticipatory ideas. I had therefore to be prepared . . . to forgo all claims to priority in the many instances in which laborious psycho-analytic investigation can merely confirm the truths which the philosopher recognized by intuition.' Indeed, Freud also compares instincts to the will to power in 'A Difficulty in the Path of Psycho-analysis', *The Standard Edition*, p. 298: 'The force by which the sexual instinct is represented in the mind we call "libido" – sexual desire – and we regard it as something analogous to hunger, the will to power, and so on, where the ego-instincts are concerned.'
36   Foucault, *Discipline and Punish*, p. 203.
37   Adorno, *Problems of Moral Philosophy*, p. 137.

maintains that a more substantive form of individual autonomy would emerge only if the superego were sublated because the superego allows society to extend repressively into our psyches.[38] Controversially, he also declares that, in a 'state of universally rational actuality [*ein Zustand allseitiger rationaler Aktualität*] . . . no superego would come into being' (ND 273).

Adorno's ideas about the superego will be discussed again in the next section of this chapter. However, to end this account of Adorno's and Foucault's positions on Freudian theory, I shall simply reiterate that Adorno's critique of the superego has a counterpart in Foucault's critique of the coercive internalized gaze and the normalizing effects of power. Furthermore, they both acknowledge the importance of instinct in human life, even as they underscore the historicity of instincts. For both, knowledge itself is based on instinct: Foucault adopts Nietzsche's view of knowledge as rooted in conflicts between instincts, and Adorno sees reason, including its more sophisticated instantiations in science and philosophy, as an outgrowth of the instinctually driven struggle to survive. Still, these broad agreements must not be allowed to obscure the differences between Adorno and Foucault, especially since Foucault fails to note the parallels between his discussion of the internalization of the panoptic gaze and Freud's account of internalization. These parallels extend to Foucault's account of the process of individuation, as the next section will show.

INDIVIDUATION

Foucault's claim that power relations are always also positive and productive applies to exchange relations in Adorno as well. If, to quote Weberman, power relations ' "have" us and are exercised through us', if they can be said to '"produce" us',[39] the same can be said about exchange relations. In fact, Adorno argues throughout his work that we are shaped profoundly by our exchange-based society. On his view, 'the thesis that individuality and individuals alone are the true reality' is completely 'incompatible with Marx's . . . theory of the law of value' (ND 199). It is incompatible with Marx's theory because Marx claimed that individuals have been reduced to 'involuntary executors' of that law (ND 262). Of course, Foucault obviously differs from Adorno when he says that 'we should equally see the real constitution of the individual on the basis of a certain technology of power'.[40] Nevertheless, since he recognizes that economic factors are involved in the process of individuation, Foucault sees the individual as the product of both power and the economy.

Exchange relations and power relations are forces that constitute individuals by subjecting them to various forms of constraint. Yet as powerful as exchange relations are, I have already suggested that Adorno distinguishes integration

38   Adorno, 'Sociology and Psychology', *New Left Review* 47, p. 79.
39   Weberman, 'Foucault's Reconception of Power', *The Philosophical Forum*, p. 199.
40   Foucault, *Psychiatric Power*, p. 57.

through exchange from direct physical and psychological control when he rejects Friedrich Pollock's state capitalism thesis. Although Western states do exhibit tendencies that could culminate in the political domination that was exercised under the Third Reich – with all the police, military and paramilitary violence that this would entail – Adorno denies that we have reached, or will necessarily reach, the point where Western societies resort to the overt physical force that was applied to the Jewish people, homosexuals, communists and others in Nazi Germany.

Distinguishing exchange from direct physical force, Adorno nonetheless insists that exchange has 'real objectivity' (ND 190). He makes this point again when he cites Marx's *Grundrisse*: exchange stands above individuals as '"an *alien* social power"', and it regulates their '"mutual interaction as a process and power independent of them"'.[41] For both Marx and Adorno, the 'universal development of the exchange system . . . happens independently of the qualitative attitudes of producer and consumer, of the mode of production, even of need'.[42] Hovering over individuals, exchange relations not only shape the instinctual energy that drives *homo œconomicus*,[43] they affect everyone else as well. Even those who are not motivated by profit are in thrall to the law of exchange; they must respect this law if they want to survive.[44]

The predominance of exchange relations over individuals and things results in reification. And, to cite Martin Jay, Adorno broadly defines reification as 'the suppression of heterogeneity in the name of identity'.[45] Stressing the homogenizing force of exchange relations, Adorno argues that all things and people have been affected profoundly by the process that transforms use value into exchange value to the extent that this process abstracts from their concrete, sensuous characteristics and qualities. One effect of this process is that individuals begin to measure their self-worth equally abstractly in terms of the value of the goods they possess and the positions that they occupy in the economic system; these serve as social markers that both position them within groups and distinguish them from others.

Exchange relations also affect the ego. In fact, Adorno contends that 'the social power structure hardly needs the mediating agencies of ego and individuality any longer'. Rather than fostering strong egos, as it did in the competitive liberal phase of capitalism, our 'brutal, total, standardizing society arrests all

---

41   Marx, *Grundrisse*, pp. 196–7. Cited in Adorno, 'Extorted Reconciliation', *Notes to Literature*, Vol. 2, p. 220; italics in the text.

42   Adorno, 'Society', *Salmagundi*, p. 148.

43   Adorno, 'Sociology and Psychology', *New Left Review* 46, p. 71.

44   Adorno, 'Society', *Salmagundi*, p. 149.

45   Jay, *Adorno*, p. 68. However, Jay's claim (on the same page) that 'reification in Adorno is not equivalent to the alienated objectification of subjectivity' is problematic because reification can be said to suppress heterogeneity in the name of identity precisely by abstracting from living human beings and their activities and objectifying them, or by turning them into fungible and commensurable things.

differentiation, and to this end it exploits the primitive core of the unconscious'.[46] This exploitation of the unconscious makes the ego weak and narcissistic. To be sure, ego formation was always a precarious achievement but, under late capitalism, the ego fails to 'develop its intrinsic potential for self-differentiation' and it regresses 'towards what Freud called ego libido'. As a result, '[w]hat actually wanted to get beyond the unconscious . . . re-enters the service of the unconscious and may . . . even strengthen its force'.[47] Since the ego's defences against the instinctual energies of the id and the superego are now extremely weak, the 'triumphant archaic impulses, the victory of id over ego, harmonize with the triumph of society over the individual'.[48]

Adorno claims that the individual is not just 'entwined' with our exchange-based society, but that it is constituted by society 'in the most literal sense' because 'its content comes from society' (MM 154). As in Foucault, moreover, this 'content' largely consists in internalized social norms. However, where subjection to power relations involves direct subjection to norms (the coercive force of disciplinary power and biopower is just the force of normalization), domination by exchange involves a more indirect subjection to norms. For the growing power of the norm-bearing superego over the ego – a power so harsh that Adorno advocates the complete dissolution of the superego – is due, in large measure, to the fact that late capitalism arrested the process of individuation when it assumed many of the ego's self-preserving functions on the largely specious grounds that its assumption of these functions would benefit society as a whole.

Now that domination has been internalized in the superego, Adorno observes that individuals tend to conform with and adapt to whatever society demands of them. Similarly, Foucault maintains that, once norms are internalized and begin to regulate behaviour, they turn individuals into politically docile citizens and economically useful subjects. Moreover, Foucault also underscores the material objectivity of power relations. Where Adorno sees exchange as a powerful force that affects virtually every aspect of our lives, Foucault argues that all power is physical and that its targets are physical as well.[49] In 'The Meshes of Power', Foucault baldly declares: 'Power has become materialist.' It is not just the case that disciplinary power and biopower are material forces; they fasten on 'real things, which are the body, life'.[50]

In *The Punitive Society*, Foucault says that capitalism put in place 'something like a *coercive* element'; this element linked morality to penality as capitalism developed 'a range of everyday constraints that focus on behaviors, customs,

46   Adorno, 'Sociology and Psychology', *New Left Review* 47, p. 95.
47   Ibid., p. 87.
48   Ibid., p. 95.
49   See Foucault, *Psychiatric Power*, p. 14: 'what is essential in all power is that ultimately its point of application is always the body. All power is physical, and there is a direct connection between the body and political power.'
50   Foucault, 'The Meshes of Power', *Space, Knowledge and Power*, p. 161.

and habits' with the aim of morally transforming and correcting individuals.[51] Still, Foucault only stresses the reciprocal and complex relations between power and the economy when he observes that disciplinary power facilitated the rise of capitalism by turning the 'explosive energy' of our pleasures, needs, festivals and leisure time into a constant and cohesive labour force.[52] And, if disciplinary power turns inchoate bodies into regimented workers and obedient citizens, biopower also targets the body. With disciplinary power, 'numerous and diverse techniques for achieving the subjugation of bodies' began to proliferate.[53] The biopolitical state supplemented these with techniques that seek to regulate, manage and control the population, from its 'biological rootedness through the species up to the surface that gives one a hold provided by the public'. *Inter alia*, biopower regulates our biological lives through medical observation and intervention, and it controls our social lives 'through education, campaigns, and beliefs' (STP 75; trans. mod.).

I have already argued that Foucault's claims about the internalization of norms accord with Adorno's view that individuals perpetuate their own subjection as 'society extends repressively into psychology in the form of censorship and superego'.[54] Just as Adorno claims that the internalization of norms gives rise to a superego that, in Freud's words, constitutes the individual as 'a moral being and a social being' who will serve society's interests,[55] internalization in Foucault can be said to be equally productive. By pinning the body to social norms, internalization produces something positive to the extent that it constitutes subjectivity or consciousness. In other words, as the body is subjected to norms, it is subjectified, turned into a subject – a two-pronged process that Foucault captures in the word '*assujettissement*'.[56] Individuation occurs as power subjectifies the body, fixing the 'subject-function' on it when the gaze is internalized. According to Foucault, then, the individual does not pre-exist 'the subject function, the projection of a psyche, or the normalizing agency'.[57]

Like the narcissistic ego in Adorno, the Foucauldian individual is extremely weak. Not only is the individual a product of disciplinary power and biopower, it is produced by power to be as submissive as possible. Nevertheless, it is important to stress that Adorno and Foucault have very distinct historical accounts of the processes that led to the formation of weak and submissive individuals.

51   Foucault, *The Punitive Society*, p. 110; trans. mod. Foucault often uses the adjective 'coercive' to describe disciplinary power in *Discipline and Punish*, but Gros notes that, in *The Punitive Society* (lectures that he gave prior to the publication of *Discipline and Punish*), Foucault used the word 'le coercitif' – the coercive – to refer to disciplinary power. See Gros, 'Is There a Biopolitical Subject?', *Biopower*, p. 263.
52   Ibid., p. 232.
53   Foucault, *The History of Sexuality*, Vol. 1, p. 140.
54   Adorno, 'Sociology and Psychology', *New Left Review* 47, p. 79.
55   Freud, *The Future of an Illusion*, in *The Standard Edition*, p. 11.
56   As Gilles Deleuze puts it, the interior is a 'fold' that is made by what is exterior. See Deleuze, *Foucault*, p. 81. The translator uses the words 'inside' for 'interior' and 'outside' for 'exterior'.
57   Foucault, *Psychiatric Power*, p. 56.

Where Adorno thinks that ego weakness is a relatively recent phenomenon that is tied to the development of monopoly capitalism and our growing dependence on the economy and the welfare state, Foucault traces the inculcation of self-abnegation and self-renunciation by modern power relations all the way back to an earlier modality of power that he calls pastoral power. The power that is wielded in modern institutions and the state is rooted historically in the power that the Christian Church began to exercise early in its history. In fact, Foucault argues that 'the history of the pastorate involves . . . the entire history of procedures of human individualization in the West'; it 'involves the history of the subject' (STP 184).

The pastoral power deployed by the Christian Church aimed to govern individuals. One of its more important techniques was the examination of conscience or confession. Much like their modern counterparts (psychoanalysts, social scientists and others), priests and pastors used confession to diagnose the state of the individual's soul. Indeed, Foucault compares the pastor to 'a doctor who has to take responsibility for each soul and for the sickness of each soul' (STP 174). As spiritual directors, moreover, priests and pastors demanded obedience, and it is in this respect that the examination of conscience in confession was 'absolutely innovative'. Confession is a practice 'by which a certain secret inner truth of the hidden soul becomes the element through which the pastor's power is exercised, by which obedience is practiced, by which the relationship of complete obedience is assured, and through which . . . the economy of merits and faults passes' (STP 183).

We have not freed ourselves from pastoral power. Pastoral power 'has not yet experienced the process of profound revolution that would have definitively dispelled it from history' (STP 150). Pastoral power persists because disciplinary power and biopower inherited and further developed the 'absolutely specific modes of individualization' that the Christian Church invented (STP 184). This is why Foucault contends that the pastorate is 'one of the decisive moments in the history of power in Western societies' (STP 185). Emphasizing the innovative character of pastoral power, Foucault claims that it was the first form of power to constitute a subject 'who is subjected in continuous networks of obedience, and . . . subjectified [subjectivé] through the compulsory extraction of truth' (STP 184–5).

In his genealogy of pastoral power and its successors, Foucault also observes that the locus of authority moved from the family to institutions and the state as pastoral power was displaced by disciplinary power and biopower. As a result, the influence of the family on the process of normalization diminished. On this point, Adorno agrees: given our dependence on the welfare state and the capitalist economy, institutional authorities play a greater role in the normalization of children than the family once did. Of course, others have made this point as well. For example, Christopher Lasch commented on the displacement of parental authority by institutional authorities, arguing that it led to the 'socialization of reproduction'. According to Lasch, when capitalists 'took production out of the household and collectivized it . . . in the factory', they appropriated 'workers' skills and technical knowledge, by means of "scientific management"', bringing them under 'managerial direction'. Furthermore, capitalists extended their 'control over the worker's private life when doctors, psychiatrists, teachers, child guidance experts, officers of the juvenile courts, and other specialists began to supervise child-rearing, formerly the business of the family'.[58]

Foucault acknowledges that the family continues to play a crucial role in the process of individuation by fixing 'individuals to their disciplinary apparatuses'.[59] Yet he also recognizes that the family itself has come under the sway of the institutional authorities (including educators and physicians) who now 'supervise and dominate' it.[60] But if Foucault and Adorno agree that there has been a shift in the locus of authority in the modern age – a shift that helps to account for the prevalence of authoritarian tendencies and traits in the West – they have different historical accounts of this shift as well. Foucault traces it back to the displacement of pastoral power by disciplinary power from the sixteenth century to the late eighteenth and early nineteenth centuries. By contrast, Adorno thinks that this shift is linked to monopoly capitalism's economic disenfranchisement of bourgeois entrepreneurs in the late nineteenth and early twentieth centuries.

Adorno's and Foucault's accounts of the norms that individuals internalize also differ. Unlike Adorno, who speaks very broadly about social norms (highlighting, in some of his work, the norm of equality), Foucault offers a more detailed account of disciplinary and biopolitical norms. He also emphasizes their medical provenance. Following Nietzsche when he observes that religious truths were gradually displaced by scientific truths, Foucault had already remarked in *The Birth of the Clinic* that the norms to which discipline subjects bodies are often borrowed, 'through transference, importation, and metaphorical turns of phrase', from medicine.[61] In a 1977 interview, Foucault adds that medical thought 'organizes things around a norm . . . that distinguishes the normal from the abnormal'. With its quasi-medical norms, discipline constitutes 'a kind of hierarchy of more or less able individuals, a hierarchy of those who obey a certain norm and those who deviate from it, of those who can be corrected and those who cannot, of those whom one can correct with a certain technique and those for whom other means of correction must be used'.[62]

---

58   Christopher Lasch, *Haven in a Heartless World*, pp. xx–xxi.
59   Foucault, *Psychiatric Power*, p. 81.
60   Foucault, *Abnormal*, p. 255. Freud certainly recognized that not all the norms internalized in the superego come from our parents. For example, in 'An Outline of Psycho-analysis', *The Standard Edition*, p. 146, Freud remarked that influences on the superego extend beyond the parents to other family members, as well as to teachers and public figures who serve as models for admired social ideals.
61   Foucault, *The Birth of the Clinic*, p. 36; trans. mod.
62   Foucault, 'Le Pouvoir, une Bête magnifique', *Dits et écrits* III, pp. 374–5 *passim*.

In disciplinary institutions, norms may originate as statistical averages that define what is 'normal' for a person of a certain age, or with a certain level of training. These averages are subsequently treated as prescriptions stating what ought to be the case. Flouting the is/ought distinction, disciplinary norms distribute individuals around 'a positive pole and a negative pole' or, as Foucault puts it, around 'the opposed values of good and evil'.[63] Depending on the institution, the axis of normality will revolve primarily around the norms of sanity (the asylum), docility (the school), industriousness (the factory) and obedience (the army). Sanity, docility, industriousness and obedience are just some of the norms on which the judgement of individuals is based in a disciplinary society.

Biopolitical norms are linked even more closely to medicine. Again, once governments 'perceived that they were dealing with a population', they made concerted attempts to regulate and control 'its specific phenomena and its peculiar variables: birth and death rates, life expectancy, fertility, state of health, frequency of illnesses, patterns of diet and habitation'.[64] However, since sex lies at 'the heart of this economic and political problem of the population', governments tend to focus on reproductive concerns. These concerns include 'the age of marriage, the legitimate and illegitimate births, the precocity and frequency of sexual relations, the ways of making them fertile or sterile, the effects of celibacy or of prohibitions, [and] the impact of contraceptive practices'.[65] With respect to each of these factors, statisticians plot 'different curves of normality' and establish an interplay between them in order 'to bring the most unfavorable in line with the more favorable', the latter serving as the norm (STP 63).

For his part, Adorno agreed with Nietzsche that 'modern morality has been nurtured on faded theological ideas', but he never elaborated on this claim.[66] Nevertheless, he did comment extensively on an important corollary to the internalization of norms: the development of our capacity for self-reflection. With the rise of capitalism, Adorno argued, the individual was constituted as a 'unit [*Einheit*] by its own self-reflection' (ND 218). Requiring a degree of autonomy from the bourgeoisie in its capacity as an economically active subject, liberal capitalism fostered a reflective turn (ND 262). At the same time, however, self-reflection was largely confined to identifying the individual's

---

63   Foucault, *Discipline and Punish*, p. 180.

64   Foucault, *The History of Sexuality*, Vol. 1, p. 25. In STP 57, Foucault complicates his account of norms when he introduces a further distinction between disciplinary power and biopower, claiming that the former involves normation, whereas the latter could more properly be said to involve normalization. In an important gloss on this distinction, Todd May and Ladelle McWhorter explain: 'Normation sets a norm and then seeks to develop practices that induce conformity to that norm. The practices of visibility, hierarchical organization, and examination … are classic examples of normation. By contrast, normalization requires one to understand the normal curve of a given phenomenon (behavior, disease, economic activity), and then to arrange things at the level of the population … to maximize … the promotion or diminishing of the phenomenon.' See May and McWhorter, 'Who's Being Disciplined Now?', *Biopower*, p. 249.

65   Ibid., pp. 25–6; trans. mod.

66   Adorno, *Problems of Moral Philosophy*, p. 15.

interests and defending them against the interests of others (ND 348). As Raymond Geuss remarks, the 'modern individual is a product of the market: each individual is essentially defined and constituted by his or her own "self-interest", which is the form the impulse toward self-preservation takes in a market society'.[67] To survive under the fiercely competitive conditions that characterized liberal capitalism, the bourgeoisie was thrown back on itself and compelled to become self-reliant and self-regarding to a degree that was unparalleled in human history.

For Adorno, then, the concept of the individual is a 'reflective concept'. Individuation entails that 'subjects become conscious of their individuality and singularity, in contrast to the totality, and only define themselves as individuals . . . in the consciousness of this opposition'.[68] However, given that reflexivity was made possible by the formation of the superego against whose norms individuals judge themselves, Adorno stresses the paradoxical character of the process of individuation. On the one hand, since it is defined over and against society, individuality connotes a degree of autonomy with respect to society. On the other hand, the 'bourgeois concept of individuality contained the call for its socialization, that is to say, its adaptation to social norms'. As a result, this concept had a 'shadow side' as well because it contained in germ 'the *crisis* of individuality'.[69] Under monopoly conditions, and the concomitant decline in competition, individuals lost the little autonomy they had once enjoyed – an autonomy that was always only a functional requirement of capitalism anyway. Social integration triumphed over autonomy as individuals began to identify themselves 'in their innermost behavior patterns with their fate in modern society'.[70]

Tracing the emergence of the modern individual back to the sixteenth century, Adorno finds its historical prototypes in literary figures (especially Hamlet), and in philosophers such as Descartes and Montaigne. Agreeing with the historian Jacob Burckhardt that individuality was not unknown in antiquity, Adorno also supports his claim that individuality in the Hellenistic age existed only for a privileged few who remained largely separate from society. If the Hellenistic period marked 'the true age of individualism in Greek society', Adorno contends that the Hellenistic individual was relatively weak owing precisely to its separation 'from the political and social reality'. For Adorno, the concept of the individual really only 'becomes radical in the modern world, the bourgeois world, . . . when the form of the economy . . . began to be determined by initiative, by labour, a sense of responsibility, the autonomy of individuals standing in a relationship based on exchange'.[71]

---

67   Raymond Geuss, 'Suffering and Knowledge in Adorno', *Constellations*, p. 12.
68   Adorno, *History and Freedom*, pp. 70–1.
69   Ibid., pp. 86–7; italics in the text.
70   Adorno, 'Society', *Salmagundi*, p.152.
71   Adorno, *History and Freedom*, p. 86. Adorno is citing Jacob Burckhardt's *The Greeks and*

For Foucault as well, the modern individual emerged in the sixteenth century. Like Adorno, moreover, Foucault links individuation to self-reflection; he believes that individuals have always constituted themselves on the basis of relations that they establish with themselves (*le rapport à soi*). Still, Foucault claims that robust relations to self had already been formed in the Hellenistic period. He also examines the profound transformation that occurred as the Hellenistic relation to self was succeeded by a self-relation that drew on knowledge of the self – a knowledge that only the Christian Church and its representatives were thought to possess. Indeed, Foucault only underscores the relative autonomy of the individual in the Hellenistic period when he remarks that, once the pastorate began to supervise the relation of the self to itself, individuals were obliged to renounce their wills and to take direction exclusively from priests. With the advent of Christianity, Foucault argues, Western individuals were 'constituted through practices of subjection', rather than 'in a more autonomous way, through practices of liberation, of liberty, as in Antiquity'.[72]

Adorno and Foucault are interested in the historical vicissitudes of self-reflection because they value its critical potential. As I shall argue later in this book, they both associate self-reflection with greater autonomy. However, their historical accounts of the rise and fall of the individual obviously differ. To reiterate, where Adorno thinks that individuation under liberal capitalism produced strong individuals with a more highly developed capacity for self-reflection – a capacity that monopoly capitalism would later undermine – Foucault believes that modern individuals forfeited the autonomy that their forebears had enjoyed when the Christian Church effectively undermined their capacity for self-reflection by regulating and controlling their relations to themselves in practices that included confession. The autonomy of individuals only diminished further when the state and its institutional accomplices assumed the Church's pastoral functions and became 'responsible for, entrusted with, and assigned new tasks of conducting souls' (STP 231).

To this, Adorno might object that Foucault failed to consider some of the beneficial effects of competitive economic conditions on our capacity for self-reflection. Under liberal capitalism, the individual was able, not just to distinguish itself from society, but to oppose itself to it. Adorno also links this

---

Greek Civilization. Interestingly, Foucault also cites Burckhardt. In *The History of Sexuality*, Vol. 2, p. 11, he praises Burckhardt's study of the Renaissance for stressing the importance of 'arts of existence' or 'technologies of the self'. Foucault also notes that, in his work on Charles Baudelaire, Adorno's colleague Walter Benjamin adopted Burckhardt's view of technologies of the self, thereby indicating that these technologies persisted long after the Renaissance. See also Benjamin, *Charles Baudelaire: A Lyric Poet in the Era of High Capitalism*. (Parenthetically, in his important historical account of the 'invention' of the individual, Larry Siedentop contests Burckhardt's view when he locates the origin of the individual, not in the Renaissance, but in the early Christian conception of the moral equality of each and every soul. See Siedentop, *Inventing the Individual*, pp. 334ff.)

72   Foucault, 'An Aesthetics of Existence', *Politics, Philosophy, Culture*, p. 50.

opposition to society to the influential role that parents (in particular, the father[73]) formerly played in initiating internalization. A relatively autonomous entrepreneur under liberal capitalism, the father was a powerful figure who was not just emulated but resisted: his children would internalize his values, but they might also assert their newly minted individuality by rebelling against them. In fact, Adorno speculates that this rebellion may even have helped to produce the individual. Under monopoly capital, however, most of the bourgeoisie became salaried workers or wage labourers. As they grew increasingly dependent on the fortunes of the owners of the means of production, reproduction was socialized and the 'forces of opposition' within society were paralysed (MM 23).

However, Adorno deals exclusively with the economic factors that are involved in individuation, and he neglects to consider the impact of Christianity on this process. He seems to believe that Mammon definitively displaced God with the advent of enlightenment, or the general trend towards demythologiza-tion which accompanied the influential critique of anthropomorphism in the West.[74] Tracing the history of the concept of the individual in *History and Freedom*, Adorno does observe (without elaborating on this point) that 'Christianity, with its doctrine of the absolute value of the individual soul as immortal and created in the image of God, did ... bring about a world-historical change of incalculable proportions'. Nevertheless, he thinks that Christianity effected this change, not by inventing techniques and practices that coercively shape our bodies, as in Foucault, but on the ideational level alone, in terms of how individuals think about themselves.[75] In *Problems of Moral Philosophy*, moreover, Adorno suggests that even this influence has waned: the 'positive morality' that is now imposed on individuals and that makes them what they are has 'escaped from its transparent theological underpinnings'.[76]

Foucault does not say that Protestant ethics influenced the *ethos* or spirit of capitalism, but he follows a path analogous to Max Weber's to the extent that he links the growth of capitalism to practices that first developed in Catholic institu-tions, including ascetic practices.[77] In fact, Foucault claims that we remain more Christian than we believe ourselves to be. Of course, Christianity's anthropo-morphic world vanished when pastoral power was superseded by disciplinary

---

73   In defence of Adorno's claims about the importance of the father, Andrew Bowie remarks that, 'given the changing roles in the family', it may no longer be 'apposite' to refer exclusively to the father's role in internalization. Nevertheless, 'the point about the internalization of norms does not depend on what may be something historically relative'. See Bowie, *Adorno and the Ends of Philosophy*, p. 194 n. 9.

74   This is how Adorno defines 'enlightenment' in *Kant's 'Critique of Pure Reason'*, p. 65.

75   Adorno, *History and Freedom*, p. 85.

76   Adorno, *Problems of Moral Philosophy*, p. 170.

77   Although Weber observed in *The Protestant Ethic and the Spirit of Capitalism* that the Puritan sects that helped to make modern capitalism possible rejected the practice of confession, he too stressed the continuity between Catholicism and Protestantism when he argued that Protestantism inherited the ascetic practices that had developed in Catholic monasteries. For his part, of course, Foucault recognized that the practice of confession was transformed as it was adopted by medical professionals and others.

power and biopower.[78] Yet Bernauer rightly notes that Foucault 'refused the topography of a religious era yielding to a secular age'.[79] Foucault refused this topography precisely because he thought that power relations in the modern age were rooted in the practices and techniques that were deployed by the Christian Church in its government of souls. Again, one of the more salient differences between Adorno and Foucault lies in Foucault's emphasis on the impact that Christian practices continue to have on the process of individuation.

Nevertheless, Adorno and Foucault share the view that individuation relies on the internalization of norms. Individuation takes place behind our backs, so to speak, because internalization has already occurred before we become conscious of ourselves as individuals. Socially preformed by the norms we have internalized, we simply adapt our behaviour to them. Indeed, Adorno only stresses the extent to which we are unknown to ourselves when he writes that 'countless moments of external – notably social – reality invade the decisions that are designated by the words "will" and "freedom"' (ND 213). Even in the rare cases where individuals consciously try to resist the immense internal and external pressure to conform, they may capitulate to it despite their better intentions. Alternatively, their interest in survival may persuade them that it is more prudent to adapt than to resist.

THE SOCIAL CONSTRUCTION OF *WHAT*?

Foucault implicitly referred to the historical links between pastoral power and disciplinary power when he described the fabrication of the modern 'soul' in *Discipline and Punish*.[80] Unlike the Christian soul, however, the modern soul 'is not born in sin and subject to punishment'. Rather, it 'is born . . . out of methods of punishment, supervision and constraint' that target the body. Inverting the Christian conception of the body as the prison of the soul, Foucault famously remarked that the soul has become the prison of the body. The soul can be said to imprison the body because, as the body is subjected to disciplinary norms, these norms are internalized and they subsequently have a significant impact on the individual's behaviour and self-understanding. For Foucault, our understanding of ourselves as having minds and personalities, or as subjects with the attribute of consciousness, is just an effect of the imposition of disciplinary constraints on the body and it ties us to a particular conception of ourselves *qua* individual. Immured in disciplinary and biopolitical norms, the individual is 'the effect of a subjection much more profound than himself'.[81]

Foucault's account of individuation invites readers to ask precisely what is being shaped by power relations, and the same question can be asked about

---

78   See STP 236f.
79   Bernauer, 'Secular Self-Sacrifice', *Foucault's Legacy*, p. 151.
80   Foucault, *Discipline and Punish*, p. 29.
81   Ibid., p. 30.

exchange relations in Adorno. As Adorno stated repeatedly, the reduction of individuals to agents and bearers of exchange value is not just 'an "influence" from outside'. Individuation does not affect a pre-existing substratum of interiority because there is 'no ontic interior on which social mechanisms merely act externally' (MM 229). Rather, social mechanisms effectively hollow out the space that is subsequently occupied by what we call consciousness or the ego. Although 'Critique' will offer a more general account of Adorno's and Foucault's ontologies, I shall take up here a question that was raised by Ian Hacking and ask precisely *what* is being subjected to power relations in Foucault and to exchange relations in Adorno.[82] Out of what is the modern individual 'constructed'?

To begin with Adorno, exchange relations target something material, and it is this material that is fashioned into individuals. And, among the 'stuff' that is targeted by exchange relations are instincts, along with the needs that are based on them. (Parenthetically, the fact that instincts are affected by exchange relations also implies that instincts are not static or invariant.) Indeed, Adorno warns that domination now 'migrates into individuals' through their monopolized needs. Yet he also refuses to distinguish between the natural and social dimensions of need, or between basic needs and superficial needs. Adorno rejects the former distinction when he argues that the instincts on which needs are based are always already socially mediated; he rejects the latter distinction on the grounds that monopoly capitalism has conditioned both basic needs and superficial ones for quite some time.[83]

Today, the satisfaction of virtually all needs is fulfilled 'by way of exchange value', or by way of the consumption of commodities, and individuals have been turned into a vast network of consumers. At the same time, the needs of individuals are extensively moulded and shaped by the educational system and advertising (among other agencies) to satisfy 'the requirements of the social apparatus'.[84] Still, it is also the case that the satisfaction of some needs and instincts will be displaced or delayed. Other needs will never be satisfied; they will simply be repressed. Referring again to *Civilization and its Discontents*, Adorno notes that 'the illusory and distorted aspects of the satisfaction of needs are undoubtedly registered at the subconscious level, and this contributes to the discontent with civilization'.[85]

Now that the satisfaction of needs is channelled almost exclusively into activities involving consumption, 'spirit' has been 'overcome by the fetishism of commodities'.[86] The need to go shopping, to touch, to buy and to own commodities, the need to have fun and to be part of the crowd, are among the needs

82   See Ian Hacking, *The Social Construction of What?*.
83   Adorno, 'Theses on Need', *Adorno Studies*, pp. 102–3 *passim*.
84   Adorno, 'Late Capitalism or Industrial Society?', *Modern German Sociology*, p. 238.
85   Ibid., p. 242.
86   Adorno, 'Theory of Pseudo-Culture', *Telos*, p. 28.

fostered by late capitalism and its powerful ally, the culture industry. Since our needs have been monopolized in these ways, domination obviously affects our psychological make-up as well. Even where we think that we have 'escaped the primacy of economics' – all the way into our psychology, 'the *maison tolérée* of uncomprehended individuality' – we are simply reacting 'under the compulsion of the universal' (ND 311). In fact, Adorno believes that, if we realized the extent to which society preponderates over us, we would despair because we would have been robbed of the 'faith' implanted in us by our 'individualistic society' that we are the very substance of society *qua* individuals (ND 312).

Among the instincts shaped by exchange are survival instincts. Now that our exchange-based society has taken upon itself the task of ensuring our survival, we have become completely dependent on its profit-seeking ventures and we must subordinate ourselves to exchange relations if we want to stay alive. Stressing the paradoxical character of the situation in which we now find ourselves, Adorno observes that '[t]he will to live finds itself dependent on the denial of the will to live: self-preservation annuls all life in subjectivity' (MM 229). On Jarvis' reading of this paradox, the more developed the means of production and the division of labour, 'the less living labour can set its own goals: the less, indeed, living labour is living'.[87] Survival requires that individuals spend their entire lives in the service of late capitalism, self-destructively strengthening the very forces that make a mockery of their individuality.

Of course, Adorno believes that survival instincts have always played a significant role in human behaviour. Reason itself was just an outgrowth of self-preservation: reason and its agent, the ego, only extricated themselves from other instincts for the purpose of self-preservation. Even today, the ego's establishment of 'a boundary between itself and internal nature as "its inner foreign territory"' is driven by survival instincts.[88] Since these instincts call for 'something more than conditioned reflexes', the ego remains under their sway (ND 217). Indeed, Adorno claims that the 'present condition' is destructive because it requires the 'loss of identity for the sake of abstract identity, of naked self-preservation' (ND 279). Rather than promoting solidarity, Western societies needlessly confine us to the lifelong struggle to procure the necessities of life. In so doing, they tie us all the more firmly to the 'obduracy' of our particular interests (ND 349).

On Adorno's view, then, instincts and needs are among the primary targets of exchange relations. Interestingly, Foucault says something similar about the targets of power relations. In *Psychiatric Power*, he states, very generally, that disciplinary power takes direct aim at bodies, or 'somatic singularities'.[89] However, Foucault expands on the range of material that is targeted by power in *Society Must be Defended* when he claims that it is 'bodies, forces, energies,

---

87 Jarvis, *Adorno*, p. 71.
88 Whitebook, 'Weighty Objects', *The Cambridge Companion to Adorno*, p. 66.
89 Foucault, *Psychiatric Power*, p. 54.

matters, desires, thoughts, and so on, [that] are gradually, progressively, actually and materially constituted as subjects, or as the subject'.[90] In the first volume of *The History of Sexuality*, where he repeats the claim that 'deployments of power are directly connected to the body', Foucault adds that power targets 'functions, physiological processes, sensations, and pleasures'.[91] Making a similar point in an interview, Foucault observes that the individual 'with his identity and characteristics, is the product of a relation of power exercised over bodies, multiplicities, movements, desires, forces'.[92]

By including forces, energies, desires and physiological processes among the targets of disciplinary power, Foucault implies that at least some of the material that is shaped in the process of individuation – possibly even, following Jacques Lacan, by repressive mechanisms themselves – are what we now call instincts. Among other commentators, John Ransom adopts this interpretation: Foucault has a Nietzschean account of individuation because he believes that power relations fashion individuals from 'a multiplicity of drives, tensions, instincts, and capacities'.[93] Mark Kelly interprets Foucault in much the same way: the individual 'is made from . . . drives that precede the existence of the individual'. As a result, the body should not be conceived as a monadic basis for the self. Rather, as in Nietzsche, the body is 'itself *already plural*'; it consists in 'sub-individual . . . drives and forces'. Kelly also complains about the 'baroque views' on this issue that have proliferated in the secondary literature. As Kelly sees it, 'the material body is straightforwardly marked by power: the body . . . does not depend on the existence of power *per se*, but nevertheless power is responsible for making it what it is'.[94]

To this, critics have objected that Foucault is inconsistent because they allege that he denies the existence of instincts altogether, or because they believe that power creates something out of nothing (or both). Since I already addressed the first criticism here, I shall briefly discuss the second, a version of which appears in Axel Honneth's early reading of Foucault. Commenting on Foucault's genealogy of the modern soul in *Discipline and Punish*, Honneth believes that Foucault deduces 'from social influences (which are themselves presented as merely external coercive practices that produce subjects) the formation of a sort of psychic life of humans, and then [he] connects the representation of the "human soul" directly to this'.[95] Here, however, Honneth is simply mistaken. He fails to recognize that, for Foucault, concepts such as psyche, soul and consciousness do refer to something material, but this material can only be grasped

90   Foucault, *Society Must be Defended*, p. 28.
91   Foucault, *The History of Sexuality*, Vol. 1, pp. 151–2.
92   Foucault, 'Questions on Geography', *Power/Knowledge*, p. 74.
93   Ransom, *Foucault's Discipline*, p. 120.
94   Mark G. E. Kelly, *The Political Philosophy of Michel Foucault*, pp. 96–7 *passim*; italics in the text.
95   Honneth, 'Foucault's Theory of Society', *Critique and Power*, p. 169.

obliquely through the prism of disciplinary practices and social scientific concepts. I shall elaborate on this point in 'Critique'.

Targeting the body's forces and drives, disciplinary power and biopower also help to shape them. And, to return to an earlier point, the moulding of instincts by power relations has an economic aim as well: disciplinary power must 'gain access to the bodies of individuals, to their acts, attitudes and modes of everyday behavior' in order to obtain 'productive service from individuals in their concrete lives'.[96] Allied to capitalism, disciplinary institutions train and exercise bodies with the aim of making them perform in economically useful ways. For their part, social scientific disciplines aid capitalism by analyzing the body and its forces, what they do, what can be done with them, where they can be used, and where they can be placed among other bodies.[97] Meticulously assessing the body's aptitudes and abilities, the social sciences construct norms with the aim of judging, correcting and training individuals.

When pastoral power shed its strictly religious form and was institutionalized in schools, hospitals, armies, workshops and prisons (among other sites), it was also transformed by the modern state which needed to administer, control and direct the accumulation of human beings in order to foster the accumulation of capital. It was at this point that medicine and biology were pressed into the service of the state and began to work 'on the level of life itself and its fundamental events', including birth, death and disease.[98] Again, since biopower enabled the state to acquire control over the biological and social body of the population, it too was an indispensable aid to capitalism. For capitalism, Foucault remarks, 'it was biopolitics, the biological, the somatic, the corporeal, that mattered more than anything else'.[99] This helps to explain why Foucault calls Western societies 'somatocracies'.[100]

Arguably, then, there is also an analogue in Foucault to Adorno's concerns about capitalism's assumption of the task of self-preservation. Where Adorno notes that self-preservation has been taken in charge by late capitalist societies (ND 318), Foucault observes that the biopolitical state 'has . . . taken control of life in general – with the body at one pole and the population at the other'.[101] To reiterate, when it assumes responsibility for the preservation of our biological lives, the modern state is concerned with our reproductive capacities and behaviours. Its interest in reproduction manifests itself in policies and programmes that run the gamut from sex education and family-planning clinics to subsidies for day care, benefits for dependent children, and so on. And, by taking charge

---

96 Foucault, 'Truth and Power', *Essential Works: Power*, p. 125 *passim*.

97 I am paraphrasing Foucault in 'La Philosophie analytique de la Politique', *Dits et écrits* III, p. 551.

98 Foucault, 'Crise de la Médicine ou Crise de l'Antimédicine', *Dits et écrits* III, p. 47.

99 Foucault, 'The Birth of Social Medicine', *Essential Works: Power*, p. 137.

100 Foucault, 'Crise de la Médicine ou Crise de l'Antimédicine', *Dits et écrits* III, p. 43.

101 Foucault, *Society Must be Defended*, p. 253.

of the reproductive health of individuals, and encouraging them to reproduce or discouraging reproduction, the state also manages and regulates their instincts or drives – if only indirectly. With biopower, Foucault claims, society tied its 'future and its fortune . . . to the manner in which each individual made use of his sex'.[102]

Foucault is also concerned that the state's very attempt to preserve life may result in the destruction of life. Warning about the threats that biopower poses to the survival of the population, Foucault says that medicine can be dangerous, not just 'because of its ignorance, but because of its knowledge'. Medicine now disposes of instruments that, 'precisely because of their efficacy, provoke certain effects – some simply noxious and others uncontrollable – that oblige the human species to traverse a hazardous history in a field of probabilities and risks whose amplitude cannot be measured precisely'. In this context, Foucault mentions the widespread use (or misuse) of antibiotics which risks making individuals more vulnerable to viruses.[103] More worrying still is 'the excess of biopower . . . when it becomes technologically and politically possible for man not only to manage life but to make it proliferate, to create living matter, to build the monster, and, ultimately, to build viruses that cannot be controlled and that are universally destructive'.[104]

However, in contrast to Foucault's concerns about our future prospects, Adorno's concerns are based explicitly on his ideas about the pernicious role that self-preservation now plays in human life. Since the economic machinery has dissociated itself from the individuals who sustain it, even as it exploits their untrammelled survival instincts for its own benefit, it has become destructive and self-destructive.[105] Ostensibly geared towards the preservation of individuals, late capitalism now risks destroying its living human substratum in its relentless pursuit of profit. It is working against itself by compressing individuals 'like a torture instrument' until they 'splinter', thereby threatening 'the life of the species' as well. Stressing the gravity of our current predicament, Adorno warns that the primacy of exchange relations 'has its vanishing point in the death of all' (ND 320).

WHO ARE WE?

Foucault believes that the individual existed long before the advent of the modern age, but he does recognize that the modern individual is historically unique. To be sure, he would reject Adorno's claim that 'individuals and even the category of the individual' are relatively recent phenomena.[106] Yet he would

---

102   Foucault, *The History of Sexuality*, Vol. 1, p. 26.
103   Foucault, 'Crise de la Médicine ou Crise de l'Antimédicine', *Dits et écrits* III, pp. 45–6 *passim*.
104   Foucault, *Society Must be Defended*, p. 254.
105   As Horkheimer put it in *Eclipse of Reason*, p. 128, 'the machine has dropped the driver'.
106   Adorno, *History and Freedom*, p. 70.

accept Adorno's view that, as the word is currently used, 'the individual itself . . . scarcely goes back much further than Montaigne or Hamlet, at most to the early Italian Renaissance'. Moreover, Adorno notes that a new typology was invented to refer to the newly minted individual: '[o]nce the free market economy had displaced the feudal system, it required entrepreneurs and free wage labourers, and these were formed not simply as professional, but as anthropological types'. At this time, 'concepts arose – such as those of personal responsibility, foresight, the self-sufficient individual, the fulfilment of duty, but also of rigid moral constraint, an internalized bond with authority'.[107]

For his part, Foucault argues that disciplinary power and biopower made possible new forms of knowledge – in particular, the knowledge of the social sciences, including criminology, sociology and psychology – as they targeted and moulded the body, along with its energies, forces and desires. Working in tandem, power and knowledge effectively produced the individual; the individual is 'a power-effect' or 'relay' precisely because 'power passes through the individuals it has constituted'.[108] But since Foucault recognizes that economic factors play an equally important role in forming individuals, socialization in his work is even more extensive and far-reaching than it is in Adorno. In a remark that may surprise some, Foucault asserts that, with its reciprocal and complex relations to power, the capitalist economy 'penetrates much more deeply into our existence' than even Marxists believe.[109]

Claiming that individuation largely consists in making the dominant norms of society our own as our instincts are 'domesticated' (so to speak), Adorno and Foucault also accentuate the coercive character of the process of individuation: we become what we are from the moment that we are compelled to adapt our bodies, instincts and desires to prevailing standards of good and evil. But individuation is problematic for another reason: it produces individuals who are blindly obedient and submissive to authority figures. In fact, obedience and submission are two characteristics that Adorno associates with authoritarian personalities in his empirical study of personality traits in Americans, *The Authoritarian Personality*.[110] Chapter Five will also argue that these traits are

---

107   Adorno, 'Individuum und Organisation', *Soziologische Schriften* I, p. 450.

108   Foucault, 'Society must be Defended', *Essential Works: Ethics*, pp. 29–30.

109   Foucault, 'Truth and Juridical Forms', *Essential Works: Power*, p. 86.

110   See Adorno et al., *The Authoritarian Personality*, p. 157, where the authors associate the following traits with authoritarianism: conventionalism, or a 'rigid adherence to conventional middle class values'; a 'submissive uncritical attitude toward idealized moral authorities of the ingroup'; aggression that manifests itself in the condemnation, rejection and desire to punish those who 'violate conventional values'; superstition and stereotypy (a 'belief in mystical determinants of the individual's fate', and 'the disposition to think in rigid categories'); a preoccupation with 'dominance-submission, strong-weak, leader-follower' and 'identification with power figures'; destructiveness and cynicism which take the form of 'generalized hostility'; projectivity (the 'projection outward of unconscious emotional impulses'); and an exaggerated concern with sex. These are the traits targeted by the F-scale (fascist scale) which Adorno and his co-authors devised to measure fascist tendencies in Americans and to determine how widespread these tendencies

only exacerbated by the immaturity – in the Kantian sense – of individuals. But Adorno and Foucault add other authoritarian traits to their depictions of the modern individual: individuals are not just weak, they have become conformists who reject those they perceive to be different, and they exhibit racist tendencies. To end this chapter, I shall examine these traits in more detail.

In *History and Freedom*, Adorno described the superego as 'the decisive layer of individuality'.[111] He repeated this point in *Negative Dialectics*: our conscience is derived 'from the objectivity of society, from the objectivity in and by which individuals live and which extends to the core of their individualization' (ND 282). If the stronger egos produced under liberal capitalism might have challenged these norms, the weak egos produced under monopoly capitalism tend simply to acquiesce to them. In another empirical study of the American character, *The Lonely Crowd* – a book that Adorno cites – David Riesman observed that individuals are no longer inner-directed, but outer-directed.[112] Indeed, for Adorno as well, what 'has been going on in recent times . . . is an externalization of the super-ego into unconditional adjustment' (ND 275). Adorno also complains that 'making-oneself-the-same, becoming civilized, fitting in, uses up all the energy that might be used to do things differently'.[113]

In Foucault too, the internalization of the gaze of institutional authorities tends to produce individuals who are largely compliant and weak. Ironically, however, it is also the case that authorities and experts in the West often adopted practices that were originally created to promote autonomy through self-government. To cite Edward McGushin's important study of Foucault's later work, Christianity transformed the practices of autonomous self-government that originated in the Hellenistic age when it began to use these practices as 'tools for submitting individuals to different and more profound forms of control'.[114] Today, the aim of control remains, but the task of controlling individuals – which was once the prerogative of priests and pastors – has been assumed by social scientists and institutional authorities who are thought to hold the truth about individuals and to understand them better than they understand themselves.

Although Foucault highlights the important role of pastoral power and its successors in the process of individuation, both he and Adorno adopt Nietzsche's views about the sheep-like character of individuals. Like Foucault, who points to the paradoxical nature of Western society when he notes that, for all its destructiveness and violence, society encourages individuals to see themselves

---

had become in the United States.

111   Adorno, *History and Freedom*, p. 263.
112   See David Riesman et al., *The Lonely Crowd*. Among other places, Adorno cites Riesman's book in 'Education after Auschwitz', *Critical Models*, p. 201.
113   Adorno, 'Reflections on Class Theory', *Can One Live After Auschwitz?*, p. 109; trans. mod.
114   Edward F. McGushin, *Foucault's Askesis*, p. 98.

as sheep in a herd, Adorno criticizes our herd mentality.[115] Again, the process of individuation encourages rank conformity. Moreover, since Western individuals tend blindly to follow the norms that they have internalized, they are largely unaware that they have become the vehicles for norms that bolster the very forces that subjugate them. To be sure, individuals in the West have developed the capacity for self-reflection – and, in this sense too, exchange relations and power relations produced something positive – but their internalization of norms, on which their capacity for self-reflection was honed, means that they are unlikely to resist.

In 'The Health unto Death' (a section of *Minima Moralia* whose title parodies Søren Kierkegaard's *The Sickness unto Death*), Adorno remarks that a study of the psychology of individuals today would reveal that the sickness of our time consists 'precisely in normality'. Since the 'libidinal achievements demanded of an individual behaving as healthy in body and mind are such as can be performed only at the cost of the profoundest mutilation', what society considers normal is, in fact, pathological (MM 60). Adorno even ventures to compare the prevailing idea of health to death: 'All the movements of health resemble the reflex movements of beings whose hearts have stopped beating' because so-called healthy individuals are simply those who comply, like unthinking automatons, with whatever is expected of them (MM 61). As for those who are deemed sick, they too 'usually only present, in a different way, the same disastrous pattern' (MM 62).

The individual who is said to be healthy in body and mind has simply yielded to the coercive force of prevailing norms. For his part, however, Foucault believes that the 'sick' – those who are recalcitrant, or who find it difficult to adapt to norms – are more fully individuated than those considered healthy. Although the norm represents the 'constraint of a conformity that must be achieved' for the healthy and the sick alike,[116] the latter are subjected to a more extensive and rigorous exercise of power (with its techniques of examination and surveillance, regulation and control) to ensure their compliance. Under a disciplinary regime, Foucault observes, 'the child is more individualized than the adult, the patient more than the healthy man, the madman and the

---

115   See STP 130: 'Of all civilizations, the Christian West has undoubtedly been . . . the most creative, the most conquering, the most arrogant, and doubtless the most bloody . . . But, at the same time, and this is the paradox I would like to stress: over millennia, Western man has learned to see himself as a sheep in a flock . . . Over millennia he has learned to ask for his salvation from a shepherd . . . who sacrifices himself for him. The strangest form of power that is most typical of the West, and that will have the greatest and most durable fortune . . . was born, or at least took its model from the fold, from politics seen as a matter of the sheep-fold.' As for Adorno, apart from his remarks about the sheep-like character of individuals in *Problems of Moral Philosophy*, see also 'Late Capitalism or Industrial Society?', *Modern German Sociology*, p. 237: 'Now, as much as ever, the societal process produces and reproduces a class structure which – even if it is not the one depicted in Zola's *Germinal* – is at the very least a structure which the anti-socialist Nietzsche anticipated with the formula "no shepherd and one herd".'

116   Foucault, *Discipline and Punish*, p. 183.

delinquent more than the normal and the non-delinquent'. It is towards the 'first of these pairs that all the individualizing mechanisms are turned in our civilization'.[117]

Even as disciplinary power singles out, surveils, corrects and punishes those who do not conform, biopower stigmatizes and casts out the degenerate and the perverse, along with other perceived threats to the population. For Foucault, of course, the biopolitical state promotes racism, a 'racism against the abnormal, against individuals who, as carriers of a condition, a stigmata, or any defect whatsoever, may more or less randomly transmit to their heirs the unpredictable consequences of the evil, or rather of the non-normal, that they carry within them'.[118] Here too, Foucault's claims about the effects of power find a counterpart in Adorno's views about the effects of exchange: whether individuals are subjected to norms with a medical provenance, or reduced, under the norm of equality, to lifeless equivalents who think and behave in much the same ways, they assume an identity *qua* normal that they oppose – often violently, in the case of racism – to whatever they perceive as other, different, abnormal.

Adorno only expands on his ideas about conformist tendencies under late capitalism in his criticisms of identity thinking. Like the exchange relations on which it is modelled, identity thinking relates 'all phenomena, everything we encounter, to a unified reference point'; it subsumes them 'under a self-identical, rigid unity', thereby removing them from their 'dynamic context'.[119] Since thought is now characterized by 'compartmentalism, rigid categorization and stereotypes coming from above', individuals tend to spurn what is different.[120] They single out and shun those who do not conform to approved models of behaviour. But individuals also experience an 'atavistic and often exaggerated social fear' of being cast out of society themselves. Fearing differences in other people, individuals also fear that others may see them as deviant. This fear of standing out from the crowd is pervasive; it has become 'second nature'.[121]

In Adorno and Foucault, deviance – or, in Adorno's terms, the nonidentity of the individual with respect to society – has become anathema in the West. According to Adorno, actual or imagined differences are perceived as 'stigmas indicating that not enough has yet been done, that something has still been left outside' the machinery of society, 'not quite determined by its totality' (MM 103). In fact, Adorno remarks that late capitalism effectively expunges individuality, and he criticizes the pseudo-individualism that results from our attempts to model ourselves on stereotypes and conform to prevailing norms. As for Foucault, he observes that we inherited from Christianity 'a mode of individualization that not only does not take place by way of affirmation of the self, but

---

117 Ibid., p. 193.
118 Foucault, *Abnormal*, p. 316.
119 Adorno, *Kant's 'Critique of Pure Reason'*, p. 114.
120 Adorno, *History and Freedom*, p. 56.
121 Adorno, 'Sociology and Psychology', *New Left Review* 46, p. 71.

one that entails destruction of the self' (STP 180). Individuals who fail to submit to the norms advocated by experts, or who will not allow authorities to do their thinking for them, set the disciplinary wheels in motion: a constant round of examinations, training and supervision that ends only when 'normality' is achieved. The cure for deviance is to join Nietzsche's herd, blend into an anonymous mass, to adapt and fit in.

As I mentioned earlier, Adorno argues that individuals now display status symbols and other social markers in their attempts to signal their identity with a particular group (and simultaneously distinguishing themselves from individuals in other groups). However, Foucault contends that 'the marks that once indicated status, privilege and affiliation' have increasingly been replaced – 'or at least supplemented – by a whole range of degrees of normality indicating membership of a homogeneous social body'. In conjunction with this, Foucault notes that, even as normalization 'imposes homogeneity', it indicates what society considers to be heterogeneous 'by making it possible to measure gaps, to determine levels, to fix specialties and to render the differences useful by fitting them one to another'. By extension, markers of normality subtend our legal system as well. According to Foucault, it is 'easy to understand how the power of the norm functions within a system of formal equality, since within a homogeneity that is the rule, the norm introduces, as a useful imperative and as a result of measurement, all the shading of individual differences'.[122]

Adorno also notes that Western societies are premised on the formal equality of individuals. However, he believes that our legal system has turned the 'formal principle of equivalence' – which is based on exchange – into a norm that governs our behaviour. To this, Adorno objects that, under late capitalism, the norm of equality simply reflects and reinforces social homogeneity. He also argues that an 'equality in which differences perish secretly serves to promote inequality' because 'legal norms cut short what is not covered, every specific experience that has not been shaped in advance' (ND 309). Obvious differences in the circumstances and needs of individuals are often ignored. Other differences may be more actively suppressed. Emphatically rejecting the claim that all people are equal, or 'the same', Adorno counters that it 'lays itself open to the simple refutation of the senses' (MM 102).[123]

In short, Adorno and Foucault contend that the homogeneity and conformity that are inculcated in individuals today have as their corollary the rejection

---

122 Foucault, *Discipline and Punish*, p. 184.
123 To avoid misunderstanding, I shall reiterate a point made in Chapter Two: Adorno does recognize that there is a positive dimension to the standard of equality. See Adorno, 'Individuum und Organisation', *Soziologische Schriften* I, p. 447: 'The depersonalization and reification that are tangible to the individual in the bureaucrat . . . express both the alienation of the whole from its human purpose, and are thus negative, but conversely, also evince the reason that might benefit everyone and which alone prevents something even worse.'

and exclusion of difference. The following chapters will demonstrate that their work is also devoted to finding solutions to these problems. In fact, they criticize the process of individuation in the West with the aim of strengthening individuals by making them more self-aware. Since Adorno believes that the norms internalized in the harsh, punitive superego are generally 'incompatible with the justified and legitimate interests of the individual', he also hopes to find less repressive ways to reconcile the individual's interests with those of society.[124] For his part, Foucault seeks to make individuals aware of the practices that foster self-renunciation, submission and conformity even as he explores (in later work) practices that may enable individuals to govern themselves. If we are ever to make freedom our foundation, as Foucault puts it,[125] we must first acquire a better understanding of the degree to which we are unfree as the creatures of social forces of which we are largely ignorant.

---

124   See, for example, Adorno, *History and Freedom*, p. 264; trans. mod.: Kant's claim 'that the freedom of each human being need be curtailed only in so far as it restricts someone else's freedom encodes a reconciled condition that rises above both the bad universal, the coercive machinery of society, and the obdurate individual who is a copy in miniature of that machinery'.

125   Foucault, 'The Ethics of the Concern for Self as a Practice of Freedom', *Essential Works: Ethics*, p. 301. Commenting on philosophy's critical function, Foucault recasts the injunction 'Take care of yourself' when he states that caring for oneself means: '"Make freedom your foundation, through the mastery of yourself"'.

Chapter 4

Resistance

Adorno is sometimes seen as an elitist mandarin who refused to engage in resistance to the socio-economic conditions that he criticized for more than four decades. By contrast, commentators often note that Foucault was an active participant in struggles that took place in France and elsewhere; he was also a staunch champion of those who resist coercive power relations. However, this contrast between the politically withdrawn theorist and the engaged activist will not withstand scrutiny. To be sure, Adorno problematizes collective action when he argues that resistance is compromised, *inter alia*, by the weakness of individuals' narcissistic egos and by their concomitant tendency to succumb to the blandishments of authoritarian leaders. Yet Adorno also encourages resistance to late capitalism, and he views his own critique of the West as a resistive act to the 'spell' that exchange relations have cast over individuals.

In the first section of this chapter, I shall explore Adorno's and Foucault's ideas about the agents and the targets of resistance. Very generally, of course, resistance in Adorno is directed against the reduction of all things, activities and individuals to fungible and expendable equivalents, and Foucauldian resistance targets the coercive techniques used by the biopolitical state and disciplinary institutions, along with their effects on individuals. At the same time, it is important to reiterate that Foucault is also concerned about the economic conditions that perpetuate poverty in the West. And, since Adorno fears that the power motive might supplant the profit motive, he would endorse resistance to the political tendencies that threaten to culminate in the direct physical and psychological control of the state over its citizens.

After providing an account of Adorno's and Foucault's ideas about resistance, I shall examine their ideas about freedom because freedom of some sort would seem to be needed to resist exchange relations and power relations. Although some critics have alleged that Adorno's and Foucault's diagnoses of our current predicament are so bleak that they depict Western society as a Weberian iron cage from which there is no escape, this chapter will show that Adorno and Foucault both reject determinism. In addition, they link freedom to the activity of self-reflection, or to the ability to look critically at the social, political and economic conditions that adversely affect the thought and behaviour even of those who resist, because the selves on which they enjoin us to reflect are just what these conditions have made of them. Following this discussion of freedom, I shall end the chapter with an account of Adorno's and Foucault's ideas about the ends or goals of resistance.

RESISTANCE

As I remarked in Chapter Two, Foucault argued that the impoverishment that blighted the nineteenth century during the industrial revolution was compounded, if not displaced, by another problem in the twentieth century. For the twentieth century also witnessed 'two great maladies of power, two great fevers': Stalinism and Nazism. To the problem of impoverishment was added the problem of the 'surplus production of power that Stalinism and fascism undoubtedly manifested in a naked and monstrous way'.[1] Nevertheless, the disciplinary and biopolitical techniques that Stalinism and Nazism inherited were also rooted in the need of the 'industrial class, the class of owners', for more effective forms of social control.[2] Again, Foucault recognized that these techniques 'cannot be studied outside their relation to mechanisms of exploitation and domination' (SP 332).

For Adorno as well, the problem of poverty is no longer as important as it once was. However, Adorno claims that impoverishment has diminished owing in part to the establishment of the welfare state. Revisions to Marx's theory of impoverishment (which predicts that the exploitation of labour, and the poverty to which it gives rise, will increase to the point where they become so unbearable that workers rise up and overthrow capitalism) are necessary because workers in the West now have far more to lose than their chains owing, *inter alia*, to the benefits provided by the welfare state, to improvements in labour law and to higher standards of living.[3] Under these conditions (which Marx could not have foreseen), impoverishment takes on a political cast: it also refers to the impotence of the vast majority of individuals who have been reduced to 'mere administrative objects of monopolies and their states'.[4] Equalizing the unequal, Western democracies vaunt an equality that abstracts from blatant differences in the life chances and opportunities of individuals, even as they mask the fact that power by no means lies in the hands of the people and that people do not make decisions for themselves.[5]

David Owen argues persuasively that a concern for autonomy animates Foucault's extensive critique of power in the West.[6] Adorno certainly shares

---

1   Foucault, 'La Philosophie analytique de la Politique', *Dits et écrits* III, p. 536.
2   Foucault, 'Truth and Juridical Forms', *Essential Works: Power*, p. 69.
3   Adorno, 'Reflections on Class Theory', *Can One Live After Auschwitz?*, p. 103.
4   Ibid., p. 105.
5   Adorno, 'Discussion of Professor Adorno's Lecture "The Meaning of Working through the Past"', *Critical Models*, p. 296.
6   David Owen, *Maturity and Modernity*, p. 161. Chapter Five will examine more closely Adorno's and Foucault's views on autonomy. (Parenthetically, I also discuss the importance of autonomy for Adorno in *Adorno on Nature*. In *Autonomy after Auschwitz*, Martin Shuster traces Adorno's concern for autonomy from *Dialectic of Enlightenment* to later work.)

this concern. Now that individuals have been relegated to 'the sphere of private existence and . . . mere consumption', Adorno complains that life under late capitalism is simply 'dragged along as an appendage of the process of material production, without autonomy or substance of its own' (MM 15). To survive under inherently unstable and unpredictable economic conditions, individuals must adapt to these conditions to the point where they end by negating 'precisely that autonomous subjectivity to which the idea of democracy appeals'. And it is this situation, which demands adaptation to and identification with the *status quo*, that threatens to culminate once more in totalitarianism.[7]

In Foucault, of course, servility and conformity are effects of the coercive technologies, instruments and practices of disciplinary power and biopower. Claiming that power now 'reaches into the very grain of individuals, touches their bodies and inserts itself into their actions and attitudes, their discourses, learning processes and everyday lives',[8] Foucault also stresses our 'in-depth Christianization' when he traces disciplinary power and biopower back to pastoral power.[9] To return to a point made in the previous chapter, Foucault notes that, once the Catholic Church assumed the task of caring for individual souls, 'the classical care of the self . . . was integrated, and lost a large part of its autonomy'.[10] Since Western states and institutions remain tied to 'the tradition of Christian morality which makes self-renunciation the condition for salvation',[11] they continue to encourage obedience for the sake of obedience. If obedience does have an ulterior goal, that goal is 'defined by the definitive and complete renunciation of one's own will' (STP 177–8).

To his account of the effects of power on individuals, Foucault adds another that has an important analogue in Adorno's critique of exchange relations. Today, individuals face a 'political "double bind" which is the simultaneous individualization and totalization of modern power structures' (SP 336). Modern states simply gave the individualizing and totalizing power that was formerly wielded by the Christian Church 'a new political shape' (SP 332). At the same time, it extended and intensified the Church's attempts to take charge of all and each from the cradle to the grave. If the Christian pastor can be compared to a shepherd who must keep his eyes on the whole flock while ministering to each sheep, the problem of governing *omnes et singulatim* remains one of the primary concerns of Western states. On Foucault's view, moreover, this problem also helps to account for the emergence of the welfare state: the welfare state is 'one

---

7   Adorno, 'The Meaning of Working Through the Past', *Critical Models*, p. 98 *passim*.
8   Foucault, 'Prison Talk', *Power/Knowledge*, p. 39.
9   Foucault, *Abnormal*, p. 177.
10   Foucault, 'On the Genealogy of Ethics: An Overview of Work in Progress', *Essential Works: Ethics*, p. 278.
11   Foucault, 'Technologies of the Self', *Essential Works: Ethics*, p. 228.

of the extremely numerous reappearances of the tricky adjustment between political power wielded over legal subjects and pastoral power wielded over live individuals'.[12]

Once people in the seventeenth and eighteenth centuries had been subsumed under the population as speaking, labouring and living beings, they were 'totalized' (STP 79). They were totalized in the sense that the state turned the population into a new 'political subject', or a new 'collective subject' (STP 42). Totalization was accompanied by individualization as disciplinary institutions targeted bodies and behaviours, regulating the conduct of individuals and shaping their identities. Disciplinary institutions ensure that individuals will submit to the ministrations of experts and professionals who are given the task of normalizing their behaviour and rooting out the deviant or abnormal. For Foucault, then, the 'integration of the individual in a community or in a totality results from a constant correlation between an increasing individualization and the reinforcement of this totality'.[13]

Foucault's critique of our individualizing and totalizing society finds a counterpart in Adorno's charge that, under late capitalism, individualism and collectivism 'complement each other in the wrong direction' (ND 284). As in Foucault, Adorno's critique of individualism points to the profound effects of socialization and integration on individuals. But if his critique of collectivism also reveals that Western societies are totalizing, Adorno has different reasons for making this claim. In Foucault, the biopolitical state totalizes individuals *qua* members of a population, aggregating and tabulating phenomena that run the gamut from the population's opinions and desires to the state of its health and reproductive capacities in order to manage and regulate it. By contrast, Adorno argues that society's totalizing character stems from the 'universal extension of the market system' – a system that demands that the individual 'respect the law of exchange if he does not wish to be destroyed'.[14]

With his critique of collectivism, moreover, Adorno was not just criticizing our obeisance to the culture of expertise and the dictates of the state. He was also concerned about the tendency of individuals to submerge themselves in larger collectivities and, more generally, to identify themselves with their fate in society. He observed that groups and organizations in the West (including socialist groups and organizations) are often top-down hierarchical formations whose leaders silence dissent and demand submission. Individualism and collectivism complement each other in the wrong direction because, even as individuals are confined to the atomistic pursuit of keeping themselves alive under monopoly conditions, conformist tendencies promote a follow-the-leader mentality and

12   Foucault, '"*Omnes et Singulatim*": Toward a Critique of Political Reason', *Essential Works: Power*, p. 307.
13   Foucault, 'The Political Technology of Individuals', *Essential Works: Power*, p. 417.
14   Adorno, 'Society', *Salmagundi*, p. 149.

what some have called 'group think'.[15] In fact, it is relatively easy to foster ersatz collectivities among individuals whose primary goal is survival because their survival instincts can be manipulated by the media, politicians and demagogues.

A strident critic of collective action in the twentieth century, Adorno described the 'objective spirit' of the modern age as a spirit of 'postindividual collectivism' (ND 307). He frequently compared groups and organizations in formally democratic countries to authoritarian organizations in Nazi Germany and the USSR. By contrast (and despite his often acerbic remarks about the authoritarianism of the *Parti communiste français*), Foucault did not direct his critique of totalization to the formation of hierarchically structured groups led by authoritarian leaders. However, his critique can arguably be extended to include some aspects of collectivism in Adorno's sense of that term, especially since Foucault's account of pastoral government reveals that Western individuals have become so many sheep in a herd. Moreover, when Foucault remarks that biopolitical states are racist, that they stigmatize and ostracize all those who deviate from the herd, his critique of totalization also converges with Adorno's critique of collectivism.

Although collectivism and totalization are distinct phenomena, they both help to explain the atrocities that occurred in Nazi Germany, the Soviet Union and elsewhere. Furthermore, since Foucault shares Adorno's view that the conditions that made the Third Reich and Stalinism possible were just more extreme versions of conditions that persist in Western countries, he joins Adorno in promoting resistance to the forces that prevent individuals from thinking for themselves and fashioning themselves more autonomously. Like Adorno, who criticizes 'the subject's self-concealed imprisonment within itself', adding that the individual is 'no less imprisoned within itself than it is within the universal, within society',[16] Foucault claims that we have become 'prisoners of certain conceptions of ourselves and of our conduct'.[17]

Resistance is meant to effect a prison break. Foucauldian resistance involves refusing what the state and institutions have made of us, and in Adorno, resistance involves seeing through the effects of exchange mechanisms even as we rebel against them.[18] To elaborate on an idea that was discussed in opening chapter, Adorno argues that, despite its integration of individuals, late capitalist

---

15   See, for example, Adorno's evocative description of committees in ND 308. It is unfortunate that Adorno's extensive account of the problems that undermine collective action has so often been ignored, or simply dismissed without argument. For one could object to Adorno's critics that, if collective action today were as unproblematic as they seem to believe, change would be a more constant feature of social life.

16   Adorno, 'On Subject and Object', *Critical Models*, p. 252; trans. mod.

17   Foucault, 'Foucault étudie la Raison d'Etat', trans. F. Durand-Bogaert, *Dits et écrits* III, pp. 801–2.

18   Adorno, 'Discussion of Professor Adorno's Lecture "The Meaning of Working through the Past"', *Critical Models*, p. 297.

society remains antagonistic to them because, the more it tries to 'totalize' itself by integrating individuals, 'the deeper its tendency to dissociation'. It is, in part, this very dissociation that 'disavows the spell cast over the whole, the false identity of subject and object' (ND 346). Hence, Adorno believes that late capitalism 'cannot extort that complete identity with human beings that is relished in negative utopias'.[19]

It is the suffering of individuals – often experienced as painful maladjustment or in neuroses, for example – which reveals that individuals have not been integrated completely. Moreover, suffering often motivates resistance. Citing Nietzsche's *Thus Spoke Zarathustra*, Adorno declares: 'Woe speaks: "Go". It is the 'physical moment' that 'tells our knowledge that suffering ought not to be, that things should be different' (ND 203).[20] Foucault has a similar view: the identities that modern societies have constructed are experienced by many as unbearable, and their suffering has prompted them to resist. Struggles are waged by 'all those on whom power is exercised to their detriment, all who find it intolerable'.[21]

Resistance has an instinctive component. Adorno illustrates this when he recounts a conversation he had with Fabian von Schlabrendorff, a former Nazi officer who was involved in the 1944 plot to assassinate Adolf Hitler. Resisting a situation that he could not tolerate, von Schlabrendorff was undoubtedly motivated to act on the basis of what he knew about what was taking place in Nazi Germany. Yet he was also driven to act by an instinctive revulsion to that horror.[22] His resistance provides an especially clear example of how instinct works together with reflective mental processes to drive our behaviour. Indeed, action would not be possible without the intervention of something physical or somatic. Criticizing Kant, who claimed that reason alone motivates action, Adorno countered that 'if the motor form of reaction were liquidated altogether, if the hand no longer twitched, there would be no will' (ND 230).

Foucault also suggests that there is an instinctive component to resistance. Although instincts are always also 'constructed', or shaped by historical forces, resistance would not occur if something in individuals did not kick against the pricks, so to speak. Foucault's account of convulsions in *Abnormal* is a case in point: once they were obliged to divulge the most intimate details of their lives in confession, some nuns began to experience convulsions. Even as the bodies of these women were 'penetrated by the right of examination and subject to the obligation of exhaustive confession', they opposed 'silence or the scream to the rule of complete discourse'. On Foucault's interpretation of convulsions, then,

---

19   Adorno, 'Progress', *Critical Models*, p. 156.
20   See the song 'Once More', in Nietzsche, *Thus Spoke Zarathustra*, pp. 339 and 436.
21   Foucault, 'Intellectuals and Power', *Language, Counter-Memory, Practice*, p. 216. The title of the first leaflet that was issued by the Groupe d'Information sur les Prisons (which was signed and 'written mostly by Foucault') was 'Intolerable'. The leaflet lists as intolerable: courts, cops, hospitals, asylums, schools, military service, the press, television, the state. The leaflet is cited in Eribon, *Michel Foucault*, p. 214.
22   Adorno, *Problems of Moral Philosophy*, p. 8.

these represent 'the resistance effect of Christianization at the level of individual bodies'.[23] Foucault offers another example of how instincts drive resistance in *Psychiatric Power* when he interprets the simulations of hysterics as involuntary acts of resistance against their psychiatric confessors.[24]

Foucauldian resistance can be cast in a Nietzschean mould (as Gilles Deleuze did in his influential reading of Foucault):[25] resistance involves forces and energies in the individual that attempt to transform, evade, deflect or defeat countervailing forces and energies, especially when these are experienced as insufferable. In fact, there is no power without resistance: resistance, in the form of struggles against subjection, always accompanies the incursions of power. Although resistance may well be undermined by the disciplinary and biopolitical norms from which we derive our self-understanding (whence also our subjection), disciplinary power and biopower presuppose resistance, without which they would have no reason for being. For if power were irresistible, it would be 'equivalent to a physical determination' that had conditioned individuals so thoroughly that it would no longer need to be exercised. In other words, where there is no resistance, and individuals simply acquiesce to whatever is demanded of them, the exercise of power is superfluous (SP 342).

In sharp contrast to Foucault, however, Adorno denies that resistance is widespread. On Adorno's view, resistance to the wide-ranging effects of exchange relations is relatively infrequent. Furthermore, it is usually ineffective when it does occur. There are a number of reasons for this. First, individuals who are confined to the solitary struggle for survival (to finding a job, and feeding, clothing and housing themselves under precarious economic conditions) tend to adapt to their confinement rather than resist it. As Simon Jarvis remarks, '[t]he more obvious it becomes that the economic basis of any individual's life is liable to annihilation, and the more real economic initiative is concentrated with the concentration of capital, the more the individual seeks to identify with and adapt to capital'.[26] Second, with the establishment of the welfare state, individuals do have more to lose than their chains, and they are less likely to resist. Third, working-class revolt is unlikely because the working class no longer experiences itself subjectively as a class.[27] Finally, the decline of the family – a decline that accompanied the rise of what Adorno calls our new 'collectivist order' – also explains why resistance has waned (MM 23). Always a pillar of capitalism, the bourgeois family would occasionally (and unwittingly) foster resistance. Yet once reproduction was socialized – taken in charge by teachers, doctors, psychologists and others – resistance diminished.

---

23 Foucault, *Abnormal*, p. 213.
24 Foucault, *Psychiatric Power*, p. 137.
25 See Deleuze, *Foucault*.
26 Jarvis, *Adorno*, p. 83.
27 Adorno, 'Reflections on Class Theory', *Can One Live After Auschwitz?*, p. 97.

In short, it could be said, with some caveats, that where Adorno *prescribes* resistance – but only after we have acquired a deeper understanding of the forces that hold us captive – Foucault devotes much of his work to *describing* resistance to subjection. To be sure, Adorno did conduct empirical studies that revealed some of the (frequently pathological) ways in which individuals resist.[28] However, all Foucault's work, beginning with his study of incarceration in psychiatric institutions, and ending with his lectures on the militant lives of the Cynics, represents an attempt better to understand the battles that individuals and groups have waged against power in the West. Recasting Nietzsche's 'solemn and mysterious' idea of the will to power, Foucault hopes to elucidate the nature of the struggles against subjection that he claims have become widespread.[29]

But if, on Foucault's account, struggles against subjection have become widespread, it by no means follows that they are always successful. On the one hand, Foucault does suggest at times that resistance has allowed some individuals to counter the practices that helped to consolidate their identities, thereby enabling them to create new identities for themselves.[30] Some individuals have been able to 'cease being submissive' by evading, or even transforming, power relations.[31] On the other hand, Foucault only underscores the difficulties that face those who try to resist individualizing and totalizing power when he warns that struggles that seek to oppose the individual and its interests to the state are 'just as hazardous' as struggles that oppose the community and its requirements to the state.[32] On John Ransom's reading, these oppositional strategies are risky because power 'is specifically geared to accommodating and co-opting resistance that centers either on the individual or the community'. Resistance is easily co-opted because the individual and the community are 'complementary terms' that are always already constituted by power.[33]

Foucault also problematized resistance in his later work. Citing Foucault, Frédéric Gros notes that, since 'the individual and the community, their interests and their rights, are complementary opposites', Foucault opposed to them 'what he calls "modes of life", "choices of existence", "styles of life" and "cultural forms"'.[34] When he studied practices in ancient Greece and Hellenistic Rome that turned the self back on itself, promoting a culture of the self and an art of

---

28   See, for example, Adorno, 'Free Time', *Critical Models*, and 'Anmerkungen zum sozialen Konflikt heute', *Soziologische Schriften* I.

29   Foucault, 'Méthodologie pour la Connaissance du Monde', *Dits et écrits* III, pp. 605–6 *passim*.

30   See, for example, Foucault, 'Interview with *Actes*', *Essential Works: Power*, p. 399.

31   Foucault, 'Interview with Michel Foucault', *Essential Works: Power*, p. 294.

32   Foucault, '"Omnes et Singulatim"', *Essential Works: Power*, p. 325. In 'Foucault's Technologies of the Self', *The Journal of the British Society for Phenomenology*, Katrina Mitcheson advances good arguments to show that more autonomous modes of self-creation are possible. However, she never assesses the prospects for subverting the effects of totalization.

33   Ransom, *Foucault's Discipline*, p. 90.

34   Gros, 'Course Context', in Foucault, *The Hermeneutics of the Subject*, p. 544.

living that were meant to strengthen the autonomy of the individual with respect to the historical conditions in which it was situated, Foucault was seeking effective counters to the 'art', rooted in pastoral power, 'of conducting, directing, leading, guiding, taking in hand, and manipulating people, an art of monitoring them and urging them on step by step, an art with the function of taking charge of people collectively and individually throughout their lives and at every moment of their existence' (STP 165; trans. mod). Still, it is important to stress that Foucault did not propose that these practices should be adopted *telles quelles*; he simply showed that practices that promoted autonomy had been devised in the past, while suggesting that new practices might be invented that would enable individuals to govern themselves.

What Adorno would have thought of practices like these is moot, and I shall attempt to answer this question later in this chapter. Yet Adorno believes that what is needed, for the time being at least, is not resistance in the form of political activism – an activism that Foucault champions in spite of his concerns about its efficacy – but resistance in the form of a more trenchant critique of late capitalism. In fact, Adorno believes that collective action should be deferred for the time being. Collective action should be deferred, not just because we need to find less authoritarian and more democratic ways to organize ourselves, but because those who struggle today can do nothing 'that will not threaten to turn out for the worse even if meant for the best' (ND 245). For motives of self-preservation compel even 'conscious individuals, capable of criticizing the whole, to do things and to take attitudes that blindly help to maintain the universal even though their consciousness is opposed to it' (ND 311). It is this very situation that makes critique imperative: critics have the indispensable task of revealing the forces that now undermine collective action itself.

In this context, it is also important to note that Adorno and Foucault reject the stringent distinction between theory and practice. Like Adorno, who asserts that critical thought is already 'a comportment, a form of praxis',[35] Foucault maintains that theory 'does not express, translate, or serve to apply practice: it is practice'.[36] Nevertheless, since Adorno believed that critical social theory is 'more akin to transformative praxis than a comportment that is compliant for the sake of praxis', critique is virtually the only type of practice that he was prepared to endorse given the factors that currently compromise resistance.[37] Questioning Marx's dictum that the point is to change the world rather than to interpret it, Adorno quipped that '*one* reason why the world was not changed was probably the fact that it was too little interpreted'.[38]

Although Foucault also stresses the need for critique, he denies that there is 'a time for criticism and a time for transformation' because 'the work of deep

35   Adorno, 'Resignation', *Critical Models*, p. 293.
36   Foucault, 'Intellectuals and Power', *Language, Counter-Memory, Practice*, p. 208.
37   Adorno, 'Resignation', *Critical Models*, p. 293.
38   Adorno, *Lectures on 'Negative Dialectics'*, p. 58; italics in the text.

transformation can be done in the open and always turbulent atmosphere of a continuous criticism'.[39] Furthermore, Foucault seems at times to disagree with Adorno about both the agents of social change and the kind of change that is desirable. For notwithstanding his serious concerns about collective action today, Adorno ultimately champions sweeping and radical change. Since 'humanity's own global societal constitution threatens its life', Adorno argues that 'a self-conscious global subject [*ein seiner selbst bewußtes Gesamtsubjekt*]' must develop and intervene to thwart it.[40] In the face of the increasingly totalitarian expansion of capital, only a global subject can counter the existential threats that the ruthless pursuit of profit under late capitalism now poses.

By 'global subject', Adorno does not mean 'an all-embracing terrestrial organization' such as the United Nations. Rather, he is referring to 'a human race that possesses genuine control of its own destiny right down to the concrete details'.[41] To be sure, this claim may appear to be contradictory: Espen Hammer objects that Adorno's advocacy of global resistance seems to contradict his suspicion of 'large-scale, unitary collectivities'.[42] Nevertheless, *pace* Hammer, it is important to recognize that Adorno's very critique of existing forms of collective action is meant to prompt critics to envisage more effective forms of collective action. Concerned about our narcissistic tendency to submerge ourselves in organizations or groups that are led by authoritarian leaders, Adorno appears to flout Marx when he says that we need to find an Archimedean point to ground a non-repressive praxis, a praxis that would allow individuals to flourish within groups rather than being suppressed by them. Without presuming to have located this point, Adorno maintains that, if it exists, only theory can find it.[43]

Foucault did not seem to view our current predicament in quite as bleak a light as Adorno did. Unlike Adorno, he was also more interested in struggles that take place in specific (often institutional) sites. He studied and supported local struggles against power, including struggles against 'the power of men over women, of parents over children, of psychiatry over the mentally ill, of medicine over the population, of administration over the ways people live' (SP 329). Of course, these struggles may be entangled in class conflicts.[44] And those who resist may confront the same 'adversary as the proletariat, namely multinational corporations, judicial and police apparatuses, property speculators, and so on'.[45] Nevertheless, Foucault said that he preferred 'partial transformations . . . to the

39   Foucault, 'So is it Important to Think?', *EssentialWorks: Power*, p. 457.
40   Adorno, 'Progress', *Critical Models*, p. 144.
41   Adorno, *History and Freedom*, p. 143.
42   Espen Hammer, *Adorno and the Political*, p. 133.
43   Adorno, 'Marginalia to Theory and Praxis', *Critical Models*, p. 274.
44   Foucault, 'Pouvoir et Savoir', *Dits et écrits* III, p. 403.
45   Foucault, 'Truth and Power', *Essential Works: Power*, pp. 126–7; trans. mod. In 'Intellectuals and Power', *Language, Counter-Memory, Practice*, p. 216, Foucault not only states that those who participate in local struggles are the 'natural allies of the proletariat', but that they are engaged 'in a revolutionary project'.

programs for a new man that the worst political systems . . . repeated throughout the twentieth century'.[46]

On this point too, however, Foucault was not always consistent. For example, I mentioned earlier that Foucault championed the abolition of the state in one interview when he argued that the 'hypertrophy or excess of power in both socialist and capitalist countries . . . justifies . . . the aim of making the state disappear'.[47] Moreover, Foucault appeared to endorse global resistance to power in a statement that was published in the French newspaper *Libération* shortly after his death. There he referred to an 'international citizenship' whose rights and duties include the obligation to speak out against 'every abuse of power, whoever its author, whoever its victims'. We not only have the right to 'intervene in the sphere of international policy and strategy'; we should will to make a place for ourselves in a reality that our governments try to monopolize, a 'monopoly which we need to wrest from them little by little and day by day'.[48]

Parenthetically, just as Foucault sometimes supported more sweeping and radical struggles, and recognized that local struggles against subjection may also be entangled in class struggles, Adorno did not ignore the plight of women, homosexuals and other marginalized or stigmatized groups. To give only two examples, Adorno spoke out against anti-sodomy laws in Germany, and he criticized the inferior status that has traditionally been accorded to women in the West throughout his work.[49] Again, his critique of identity thinking extends to the stereotyping and compartmentalization of individuals and groups, to their subsumption under a set of characteristics or attributes that ties them to particular roles, activities and behaviours. Nevertheless, since identity thinking is linked to the spread of reifying exchange relations, Adorno argues that exchange relations must first be superseded if substantive change is to occur.

Adorno's belief that radical change is needed to bring about a qualitative transformation of our individual and collective lives also helps to explain why he questions the effectiveness of struggles today and insists that critique, which has the task of revealing the pitfalls and problems that collective action now faces, must precede practice. At the same time, Adorno is under no illusions about the prospects for a revolution precisely because class consciousness has evaporated and individuals are now largely powerless in the face of capitalism

---

46   Foucault, 'What is Enlightenment?', *Essential Works: Ethics*, p. 316.

47   Foucault, 'Méthodologie pour la Connaissance du Monde', *Dits et écrits* III, p. 613.

48   Foucault, 'Confronting Governments: Human Rights', *Essential Works: Power*, pp. 474–5 *passim*. Although I dispute her claim that Foucault is a champion of *liberal* democracy, Amy Allen acknowledges the radical nature of some of Foucault's ideas about social change when she compares Foucault's idea of progress with Adorno's in *The End of Progress*.

49   See, for example, Adorno's criticism of anti-sodomy laws in Germany in 'Sexual Taboos and Law Today', *Critical Models*, pp. 79–80. (Paragraph 175 was repealed in West Germany in 1969.) See also his criticisms of the plight of women in MM 95: 'The feminine character, and the ideal of femininity on which it is modelled, are products of masculine society . . . The feminine character is a negative imprint of domination. But therefore equally bad.'

and state power. Since the proletariat has been integrated, and 'bourgeois society' possesses 'vast instruments of power, both actual physical instruments of power and also psychological instruments in the broadest sense', prospects for a revolution are 'highly problematic nowadays'.[50] So, even as he insists that a revolution is needed, Adorno concedes that a revolution is unlikely to occur in the foreseeable future, if it occurs at all: '[w]e do not live in a revolutionary situation, and actually things are worse than ever'. Things are much worse today because 'for the first time we live in a world in which we can no longer imagine a better one'.[51]

For his part, Foucault asks whether we are living in a period that marks the end of the age of revolution. However, immediately after asking this question, he responds that it is 'somewhat ridiculous [*un peu dérisoire*]' to condemn the revolution to death. At most, we may be 'living through the end of the historical period that, from 1789–1793, was dominated by the monopoly of the revolution, in the West at least'.[52] Indeed, Foucault is far from adopting a post-revolutionary stance, as some commentators have claimed.[53] He simply historicizes the discourse – including Marx's and, by extension, Adorno's – that advocates revolutionary change when he traces it back to the 'revolutionary discourse of seventeenth-century England, and … of nineteenth-century France and Europe'.[54] In fact, just as his genealogy of psychoanalysis by no means contests its validity, his genealogy of revolutionary discourse does not amount to a repudiation of it. Foucault only speculates that the monopoly of this discourse over other discourses about struggle – including his own – may have ended; he does not claim that the discourse is invalid.

Referring to Horkheimer, Foucault did ask whether a revolution is desirable.[55] Yet when the same question was put to him in an interview with Bernard-Henri Lévy, Foucault said that he could not answer it, adding that 'to engage in politics … is to try to know with the greatest possible honesty whether the revolution is desirable'.[56] To complicate matters, Foucault also rejected reformism. Against the reform of power relations, he argued that reform only serves to stabilize a system of power by making small changes to it. Rather than attempting to reform existing power relations, Foucault argues that struggles should

50   Adorno, *Lectures on 'Negative Dialectics'*, p. 45.
51   Adorno and Horkheimer, 'Towards a New Manifesto?', *New Left Review*, p. 61. Martin Shuster emphasizes this point about the failure of our imaginations in *Autonomy after Auschwitz*, p. 102ff.
52   Foucault, 'La Philosophie analytique de la Politique', *Dits et écrits* III, p. 547.
53   For example, in *Michel Foucault*, Rajchman claimed that Foucault adopted such a stance.
54   See Foucault, *Society Must be Defended*, p. 78. Cf. STP 356–7.
55   Foucault, 'Useless to Revolt?', *Essential Works: Power*, p. 450. Although Foucault says that it was Horkheimer who asked whether a revolution was desirable, I have found no textual support for this claim. In fact, in 'Towards a New Manifesto?' – the transcript of a conversation between Adorno and Horkheimer (cited above) – Horkheimer explicitly endorsed revolution.
56   Foucault, 'Power and Sex', *Politics, Philosophy, Culture*, p. 122.

aim at 'destabilizing power mechanisms, . . . endlessly destabilizing them'.[57] On Leslie Thiele's reading, this means that the 'ethicopolitical choice' that individuals must make 'every day consists in a judgment as to what form of power most threatens (the possibility of) . . . continued resistance'.[58]

Here, however, one should note two things. On the one hand, destabilizing the coercive mechanisms of disciplinary power and biopower could well result in radical – if not revolutionary (in the classical sense) – change to the extent that disciplinary power and biopower help to sustain capitalism. On the other hand, Foucault recognizes that resistive practices may simply reinforce individualizing and totalizing power. Indeed, despite his belief that an ethic of the self may foster the autonomy that will make resistance more effective, Foucault questions whether 'we have anything to be proud of in our current efforts to reconstitute an ethic of the self'. As 'urgent, fundamental and politically indispensable' as the task of reconstituting such an ethic may be, Foucault admits that it may be 'impossible today to constitute an ethic of the self, . . . if it is true after all that there is no first or final point of resistance to political power other than in the relation one has to oneself'.[59] Of course, this pessimism about the efficacy of resistance also permeates much of Adorno's work. Even as he underscores the importance of 'the factor of resistance, of refusing to be part of the prevailing evil', Adorno makes the melancholy observation that this refusal 'always implies resisting something stronger and hence always contains an element of despair'.[60]

FREEDOM

For Adorno, resistance to late capitalist society involves a measure of freedom. Insisting that 'the picture of freedom against society lies in the crushed, abused individual's features alone', Adorno also observes that '[f]reedom turns concrete in the changing forms of repression, as resistance to repression'. On his view, there has only been as much free will in the world as there have been people in the world with the will to be free (ND 265). And, if freedom in Adorno is virtually synonymous with resistance,[61] Foucault makes a similar claim. For Foucault, freedom manifests itself in practice; it exists only when it is exercised, and it is exercised in resistance to power.[62] To return to Thiele's Nietzschean reading of Foucault, freedom 'must be understood as resistance to the impositions of power, as the antimatter of power'.[63]

---

57 Foucault, 'La Philosophie analytique de la Politique', Dits et écrits III, p. 547.
58 Leslie Paul Thiele, 'The Agony of Politics', The American Political Science Review, p. 918.
59 Foucault, The Hermeneutics of the Subject, pp. 251–2 passim.
60 Adorno, Problems of Moral Philosophy, p. 7.
61 See also Adorno, History and Freedom, p. 174: 'freedom is nothing but the quintessence of resistance to the spell that I have been trying to explain to you'.
62 Foucault, 'Space, Knowledge, and Power', Essential Works: Power, pp. 354–5 passim.
63 Thiele, 'The Agony of Politics', The American Political Science Review, p. 907.

Colin Koopman indirectly undermines the central place that resistance occupies in Foucault's work when he argues that there is a stringent division of labour between critique and normative evaluation in Foucault's work.[64] I shall discuss this division of labour shortly, but Koopman does usefully note (following David Hoy and Nikolas Rose) that there are two types of freedom in Foucault. First, there is the prevailing idea of freedom. This idea is a by-product of disciplinary power and biopower; it is an idea to which these forms of power give rise even as they restrain individuals, or hem them in, with coercive techniques and security measures. It is the idea of freedom as emancipation from power *tout court* – an idea that Foucault emphatically rejects. Second, there is the freedom that Foucault champions, a freedom that manifests itself in resistance to power, or in counterconduct with respect to the conducts that power tries to inculcate in individuals.[65]

In contrast to Foucault, however, Adorno does not equate freedom exclusively with resistance. At the present time, freedom consists in resistance, but freedom will flourish only when exchange relations are radically transformed. For the exchange principle on which capitalism rests has always been a lie; its 'doctrine of like-for-like' is contradicted by the fact that 'the societally more powerful contracting party receives more than the other'. The 'repeatedly broken exchange contract' will be satisfied only on the condition that truly equal things are exchanged, that is, when exchange relations finally make good on the promise that is contained in the very idea of an exchange of *equivalents*.[66] If exchange were finally to become free and just, it 'would not just be abolished, but fulfilled' because 'no individual would be shortchanged of the yield of her labor' (ND 295–6).

Adorno thinks that it may be possible to transform existing conditions to such an extent that society becomes far more rational and individuals are no longer in thrall to exchange relations. Although he does not explicitly deny that there may be threats to freedom even after a revolution, Adorno does suggest that abolishing exchange relations will usher in a more substantive form of freedom. By contrast, even though Foucault believes that power may be transformed through resistance, he offers no hope of a complete escape from power. Although 'the recalcitrance of the will and the intransigence of freedom' lie at the 'very heart of the power relation', it is also the case that individuals will always be enmeshed in power relations (SP 341). Indeed, Foucault also denies that power and freedom are mutually exclusive. Power and freedom are engaged in a 'complicated interplay' because power is always exercised over free subjects, or over subjects 'who are faced with a field of possibilities in which several kinds of conduct . . . are available' (SP 342).

Freedom exists because power is not omnipotent. Far from it: Foucault argues that the deployment of 'so many power relations, so many systems of

64 Koopman, *Genealogy as Critique*, p. 17.
65 Ibid., pp. 152–3.
66 Adorno, 'Progress', *Critical Models*, p. 159.

control, so many forms of surveillance', only demonstrates how weak power actually is.[67] Moreover, power never shapes individuals 'all the way down'. After Ransom notes that the individual is 'formed into a productive and usable shape out of a multiplicity of drives, tensions, instincts, and capacities', he remarks that, for Foucault, 'some elements of the individual are left to the side, assigned a subordinate role, or otherwise left out of account'. As a result, Foucault believes that 'a great deal that has not been noticed by society is left over once society has finished shaping the individual to its needs'.[68] This selective shaping may allow individuals a margin of manoeuvre with respect to power. Equally important, since individuals impose norms on themselves (albeit often under coercion), the possibility for deviation remains. Not surprisingly, then, Foucault said that he was 'dumbfounded [*ahuri*]' that readers saw in his histories 'the affirmation of a determinism from which one cannot escape'.[69]

Yet Foucault was obviously concerned about the pernicious effects of power on individuals: he criticized our subjection to power, along with the forms of subjectivity that this subjection has engendered, and the submission and obedience that power has inculcated. When he argued that domination has taken three major forms in the West – social, economic and political – Foucault also claimed that it is political domination that prevails today, giving rise to struggles against power relations in disciplinary institutions and the biopolitical state (SP 331). Although we can never escape power, we may be able to escape existing forms of domination by struggling against the subjection in which domination now consists.

Foucault's extensive critique of domination belies Koopman's claim that Foucault follows Kant because he too sees critique as a 'prolegomenon' to judgement and avoids making value judgements himself.[70] Confusingly, however, Koopman also recognizes that Foucault wrote his genealogies of phenomena such as madness and sexuality precisely because these had become sites of resistance to domination. For his part, Adorno rejected the division of labour that Koopman wrongly attributes to Foucault when he said that 'it is foolish to demand that we should *first* understand a thing and only *then* criticize it'. On Adorno's view, '[i]nterpretation and critique come together at a profound level' because 'the process of understanding and interpreting' already 'entails negation'.[71] In Foucault as well, genealogy is constantly conjoined with criticism of domination. In fact, given Koopman's stress on the importance of Kant for Foucault, it is ironic that Koopman fails to see that Kant's influence is especially

---

67   Foucault, 'Précisions sur le Pouvoir. Réponses à certaines Critiques', *Dits et écrits* III, p. 629.

68   Ransom, *Foucault's Discipline*, p. 120. Many commentators (sympathetic or not) seem to miss this point: power may be ubiquitous, but it is by no means omnipotent.

69   Foucault, 'Interview with *Actes*', *Essential Works: Power*, p. 399; trans. mod.

70   Koopman, *Genealogy as Critique*, p. 17. Other commentators, including Jeffrey T. Nealon, also make this claim. I shall return to this issue at the end of this book.

71   Adorno, *History and Freedom*, p. 134 *passim*; italics in the text.

evident in Foucault's normative commitment to autonomy (a commitment that will be discussed at greater length in the next chapter).

Where Foucault sees freedom as a corollary to power, Adorno observes that there is a pre-existing disharmony between late capitalist society and the individual. Yet Adorno also makes the stronger claim that socialization finds 'its limits in the subject'. In fact, he thinks that individuals might resist the spell cast by exchange relations by mobilizing forces within the very stratum that allowed society to prevail in the first place – the stratum (*Schicht*) of individuality – and by asserting themselves 'against the process of civilization that is liquidating it'.[72] Although Adorno complains in *Minima Moralia* that most individuals will simply 'kick with the pricks' (MM 109) – or (in Freudian terms) identify with the aggressor – individuation itself may provide resources that can be turned back against society, resources that include the capacity for self-reflection. This is one reason why Adorno rejects determinism. But Adorno also objects that determinism is false because it 'acts as though dehumanization, the totally developed commodity character of labour power, were human nature pure and simple' (ND 264). Its 'thesis of unfreedom ... amounts to a metaphysically extended rule of the status quo' (ND 263).

Still, it is equally false to say that individuals are entirely free because this would ignore the fact that individuals have been commodified and reified. Arguing that the proponents of free will and determinism are both wrong, Adorno contends that individuals experience themselves as now free, now unfree (ND 261). They experience their unfreedom in their powerlessness against what society has made of them, and in their compulsive attempts to survive at any cost (ND 221). Freedom is illusory because our identities are tied inextricably to the socially conditioned process of individuation to the point where even those who channel their energy into resistance to society remain the 'involuntarily executors' of its law of value (ND 262). Yet we do experience ourselves as free when we oppose ourselves to society and attempt to do something against it. Here freedom involves pursuing ends that 'are not directly and totally exhausted by social ends'. To this, however, Adorno adds a characteristically sombre note: individuals can do 'incomparably less' against society than they believe (ND 261).

For Adorno, freedom largely manifests itself today in the practice of social criticism. To paraphrase a passage in *Negative Dialectics*, thought is free when it turns back on itself and discovers its own unfreedom (ND 220). Paradoxically, then, critique affords a freedom that largely consists in unmasking the extent to which critics themselves are unfree. By extension, of course, freedom is exercised when critics reflect on the conditions that have made other individuals dependent, weak and all too submissive to the forces that oppress them. Adorno makes this point in different ways throughout his work. So, for example, at the

---

72   Adorno, 'Postscriptum', *Soziologische Schriften* I, p. 92. Cited in Müller-Doohm, *Adorno*, p. 391.

end of his lectures on moral philosophy, he states that the highest point that moral philosophy can reach is 'that of the antinomy of causality and freedom which figures in Kant's philosophy in an unresolved and for that reason exemplary fashion'.[73]

Linking critique to self-reflection, Adorno also observes that 'the element of self-reflection has today become the true heir to what used to be called moral categories'.[74] On the one hand, it is imperative for those who criticize society to reflect critically on their own limitations. On the other hand, critics should provide others with contents, categories and forms of consciousness 'by means of which they can approach self-reflection'.[75] Foucault agrees: 'ethics is the conscious . . . practice of freedom'; it 'is the considered form that freedom takes when it is informed by reflection'.[76] As in Adorno, those who struggle, including social critics, exercise their freedom when they engage in practices that involve reflection on the forces that have produced them as individuals. Such reflection may also free individuals to think of themselves in new ways and, potentially at least, to transform themselves.

In later work, Foucault shows that self-reflection informed many of the practices in ancient Greece and Hellenistic Rome that enabled individuals to shape themselves autonomously. These practices of 'self-subjectivation' (involving memory, meditation and self-examination, for example[77]) consisted in a relation of the self to itself (*le rapport à soi*) in which individuals sought to master or to govern themselves.[78] Along with helping individuals to deal with a wide variety of situations and life experiences, care of the self had the aim of correcting bad habits and defective forms of training, while shaking off dependencies.[79] Indeed, caring for oneself involved a fundamentally critical relation to the self, and it is this critical function that Foucault stresses when he links freedom to self-government. Even today, freedom depends on establishing a critical relation to oneself because the *rapport à soi* may, by its very nature, counter the self-renunciation that power continues to foster. In Nietzschean terms, care of the self may promote a more healthy form of selfishness as it turns the self into 'the judge, the avenger, and the victim of its own law'.[80]

Since Adorno also championed critical self-awareness in conjunction with a sustained critique of existing conditions, he would probably have taken an

73   Adorno, *Problems of Moral Philosophy*, p. 176.

74   Ibid., p. 169. I made this point throughout *Adorno on Nature*. More recently, Freyenhagen stressed the importance of self-reflection for Adorno in *Adorno's Practical Philosophy*, pp. 169ff, and Martin Shuster made similar remarks in *Autonomy after Auschwitz*, pp. 132–7.

75   Adorno, 'Discussion of Professor Adorno's Lecture "The Meaning of Working through the Past"', *Critical Models*, p. 300.

76   Foucault, 'The Ethics of the Concern for Self as a Practice of Freedom', *Essential Works: Ethics*, p. 284.

77   Ibid., pp. 417ff.

78   Foucault, *The Hermeneutics of the Subject*, p. 214.

79   Ibid., p. 94.

80   Nietzsche, *Thus Spoke Zarathustra*, p. 226.

interest in the practices that Foucault studied, if not endorsed them. This is confirmed, albeit only indirectly, by Fabian Freyenhagen when he reveals that Adorno recommended (in an unpublished lecture on moral philosophy that he delivered in Frankfurt in the mid-1950s) that 'we should try, though we will almost inevitably fail, "to live as one believes one should live in a freed world"'. Freyenhagen explains that to live as one thinks one might live in a freed world would involve concerted attempts 'to anticipate those modes of existence, and to create models of them'. Yet he also notes that these models of living in a freed world 'are not meant to constitute (new) norms of behaviour'. Instead, Adorno simply thought that we might succeed in loosening the grip of damaged life 'by experimenting with ways of living'.[81]

Interestingly, Martin Shuster contends that Adorno may profitably be viewed as 'standing within a broader tradition of "spiritual exercises"'.[82] However, with respect to the kind of spiritual exercises that Foucault studied, Adorno might object that practices of self-mastery are repressive to the extent that they involve the domination of the ego over the id. Mark Kelly sees this problem clearly, but he nonetheless defends Foucault. On Kelly's reading, although 'government of the self is a matter of discipline and control' – one might even 'say in a Freudo-Nietzschean vein that the will is required to take up the role of master in respect of the drives' – it is also the case that government of the self 'is not a role of domination, necessarily, nor does it simply allow the drives free reign'. According to Kelly, 'Foucault does not . . . specifically forbid self-domination'. Nevertheless, his critique of domination 'might be taken to imply that he thinks self-domination might call for some kind of self-liberation'.[83]

But if Adorno would have taken an interest in Foucault's ideas about self-government, he was equally interested in making collective action more effective. By contrast, Foucault focussed almost exclusively on transforming individuals (albeit in social settings). Foucauldian practice involves a reflective and critical turn towards the self, a turn that affects collective action only indirectly. Still, Foucault sounds another Adornian note in a lamentably brief response to an objection from Richard Rorty to the effect that he never appeals 'to any "we" – to any of those "wes" whose consensus, whose values, whose traditions constitute the framework for thought and define the conditions in which it can be validated'. To this objection, Foucault responds that, before appealing to a 'we', one must first determine whether 'it is actually suitable to place oneself within a "we" in order to assert the principles one recognizes and the values one accepts'. And, if placing oneself in a 'we' is not suitable, it may be 'necessary to make the future formation of a "we" possible by elaborating the question'. Solidarity

---

81   Freyenhagen, *Adorno's Practical Philosophy*, p. 170. Freyenhagen is citing Adorno, 'Probleme der Moralphilosophie' (1956–7).
82   Martin Shuster, *Autonomy after Auschwitz*, p. 173.
83   Kelly, *The Political Philosophy of Michel Foucault*, p. 101.

cannot simply be presupposed; it can only be 'the result – and the necessarily temporal result – of the question as it is posed in the new terms in which one formulates it'.[84]

Even though he acknowledges in this late interview that social solidarity is a problem that critics must address, Foucault rarely thematized this problem. Indeed, to revisit a point made in the previous chapter, Adorno appears to differ from Foucault in another significant respect: although they both champion critical self-reflection, Adorno hopes that sustained criticism and self-criticism will enable individuals to come to terms with nature in themselves, or with the fact that they are always also instinctual beings. According to Adorno, we can progress beyond the absolute domination of nature, which is effectively also 'absolute submission to nature', only by means of reflection on nature in the self.[85] Specifically, the continued survival of our species (not to speak of the survival of other species) depends on our becoming cognizant of the degree to which self-preservation drives our behaviour. Such reflection is necessary if we are to extricate ourselves from the increasingly self-destructive pursuit of our survival *qua* individuals.

Nevertheless, I argued that there is an analogue in Foucault's work to Adorno's concerns. Where Adorno shows that late capitalist society has taken charge of the instincts and needs of individuals, Foucault demonstrates that Western states seek to manage and regulate the biological life of the population, especially its sexual and reproductive activities – activities which are obviously linked to its preservation. Much like Adorno, moreover, who tries to make us aware of how our instincts are manipulated, Foucault encourages reflection on the many ways in which disciplinary power and biopower have taken hold of our 'bodies, forces, energies, matters, desires, thoughts'.[86] Finally, where Adorno argues that the 'mechanism for reproducing life and for dominating and destroying it is exactly the same' (MM 53), Foucault warns about the threats that biopower poses to individuals; Western states now preserve their populations by procuring sophisticated military hardware that risks destroying the very lives it is supposed to protect.[87]

Foucault also conceives of freedom in much the same way that Adorno does. To be sure, he claims that our freedom to fashion our identities is

---

84   Foucault, 'Polemics, Politics, and Problematizations: An Interview with Michel Foucault', *Essential Works: Ethics*, pp. 114–15; trans. mod. Cf. Adorno, 'Introduction', *Critical Models*, p. 4, where Adorno gives the problem of collective action an aporetic form: 'Talk of a "we" one identifies with already implies complicity with what is wrong, as well as the illusion that goodwill and a readiness to communal action can achieve something where every will is powerless and where identification with *hommes de bonne volonté* is a disguised form of evil. A purist attitude, however, that refrains from intervening likewise reinforces that from which it timorously recoils. Such a contradiction cannot be settled by reflection.' See also ND 243: 'Whatever an individual or a group may undertake against the totality they are part of is infected by the evil of that totality; and no less infected is he who does nothing at all. This is how original sin has been secularized.'

85   Adorno, 'Progress', *Critical Models*, p. 152.

86   Foucault, *Society Must be Defended*, p. 28.

87   Ibid., p. 253.

compromised by the hold that power has on our bodies, a hold that extends to our ideas about ourselves. By contrast, Adorno argues that our freedom is undermined by exchange relations that target our instincts and needs, even as they shape us as individuals. Yet, in Foucault, those who struggle manifest their freedom when they attempt to wrest control of their bodies from disciplinary institutions and the biopolitical state by engaging in practices that are at once critical and self-critical. And in Adorno as well, those who resist exercise their freedom by becoming cognizant of the instincts that motivate their behaviour and by reflecting critically on how these instincts are controlled and manipulated. Foucauldian freedom consists in resisting the state's control over individual and collective life – a control that damages the lives of some even as it potentially threatens the lives of all. Freedom in Adorno involves escaping the prison of survival imperatives that isolate individuals from each other and undermine the solidarity that is needed for collective action. More generally, Adorno and Foucault both equate freedom with resistance (for the foreseeable future, at least), and they link resistance to activities that involve critical self-reflection.

One final point should be made before I examine the ends or goals of resistance: Adorno and Foucault agree that freedom is a thoroughly historical concept. Claiming that freedom is a modern concept, Adorno also contends that it would have been an 'anachronism to talk about freedom' before the modern individual was constituted 'as a unit by its own self-reflection' (ND 218). And, of course, Foucault too recognizes that freedom must be understood historically. Freedom for Foucault is relative to the prevailing form of power: since power today is largely characterized by its subjection of individuals, freedom consists in resistive activities that seek to free individuals from subjection, potentially freeing them to govern themselves and to constitute themselves more autonomously.

THE ENDS OF RESISTANCE

Adorno and Foucault both stress the contingency of history. Against Hegel and Marx, who dismissed 'all doubts about the inevitability of totality', Adorno argues in *Negative Dialectics* that doubts about whether the trajectory of history was a necessary one cannot but arise for those who are trying to change the world (ND 321). Despite his concerns about prospects for change, Adorno adopts the view that history is contingent, if only on heuristic grounds: 'Only if things might have gone differently; if the totality is recognized as socially necessary semblance . . .; if its claim to be absolute is broken – only then will a critical social consciousness retain its freedom to think that things might be different some day' (ND 323). Expressing a similar idea in his essay 'Progress', Adorno also states, more forthrightly, that 'rigidified institutions, and relations of production, are not Being as such' because 'even in their omnipotence they are man-made'. Since we made them, they are 'revocable'.[88]

Foucault sometimes appears to be more optimistic than Adorno about prospects for meaningful change. In his own gloss on the contingency of history, Foucault says that his genealogies reveal 'how that-which-is has not always been'; they demonstrate 'that the things which seem most evident to us are always formed in the confluence of encounters and chances, during the course of a precarious and fragile history'.[89] In fact, Foucault's optimism appears at times to be based on the contingency of history alone. His optimism consists 'in saying: "So many things can be changed, being as fragile as they are, tied more to contingencies than to necessities, more to what is arbitrary than to what is rationally established, more to complex but transitory historical contingencies than to inevitable anthropological constants."'[90]

Insisting that history is contingent and that it can be changed, Adorno and Foucault specifically suggest that resistance may succeed in transforming individuals, society and the relations between them. As Adorno puts it, the central task of a critical theory is 'to make transparent the dialectic of individual and species'.[91] Today, the species – which is represented 'in bourgeois thinking' by the state (ND 319) – and the individual are antagonistic because the state simply advances the aims of its capitalist paymasters. In the face of a situation in which individuals have been reduced to expendable pawns of the capitalist economy, Adorno asserts that there is only one model of freedom: 'that consciousness, as it intervenes in the total social constitution [*Gesamtverfassung*], will through that constitution, intervene in the complexion of the individual' (ND 265). In other words, our freedom will consist in exercising greater control over the many ways in which society shapes and controls us.

For his part, when Foucault criticizes power's individualizing and totalizing effects, he insists that 'liberation can come only from attacking not just one of these effects, but political rationality's very roots', namely the roots of modern arts of government in pastoral power.[92] Although we have not yet freed ourselves from pastoral power, Foucault does speculate about liberation from the rationality that underlies it. In fact, he suggests that liberation will involve transforming the asymmetrical relations between institutions (including the state) and individuals. He calls the transformation of these relations 'enlightenment': 'what *Aufklärung* has to do, and is in the process of doing, is precisely to redistribute the relationships between government of self and government of others'.[93] In his studies of resistance, Foucault detects a persistent question: 'How not to be

---

88   Adorno, 'Progress', *Critical Models*, p. 156.
89   Foucault, 'Critical Theory/Intellectual History', *Politics, Philosophy, Culture*, p. 37.
90   Foucault, 'So is it Important to Think?', *Essential Works: Power*, p. 458.
91   Adorno, *History and Freedom*, p. 264.
92   Foucault, ' "Omnes et Singulatim" ', *Essential Works: Power*, p. 325.
93   Foucault, *The Government of Self and Others*, p. 33.

governed like that, by that, in the name of these principles, in view of such objectives and by means of such methods, not like that, not for that, not by them?' Equally important, Foucault openly aligned himself with those who ask this question when he said that his own critical theory asks how we can avoid being governed so much.[94]

Unlike Foucault, however, Adorno has a more conventionally dialectical view of the relations between the species and the individual when he casts them as relations that obtain between the universal and the particular. Progress that is worthy of the name will require the universal species to accommodate itself to particular individuals and particular individuals to accommodate themselves to the species in such a way that both the individual and the species are preserved and enhanced. Indeed, despite Adorno's extensive criticisms of untrammelled self-preservation under late capitalism, David Kaufmann rightly remarks that it is not self-preservation *per se* that is the problem. Instead, it is 'the limited rationality of self-preservation ... that leads to the irrationality of a reason devoted exclusively to means, to *how* things should be done rather than to *what* should be done'.[95]

Far from viewing self-preservation as irrational, Adorno deems human behaviour to be rational precisely to the extent that 'it serves the principle that has been regarded ... as the truly fundamental principle of every existent being: [*suum*] *esse conservare*, self-preservation'.[96] Here Adorno implies that the pursuit of self-preservation is inherently rational because reason has always been the primary instrument for self-preservation. But self-preservation is rational for another reason: it is rational because the preservation of the self implicitly extends beyond the survival of individuals to embrace the survival of the species as a whole. Although humanity will become more fully rational only when 'it preserves its societalized subjects according to their unfettered potentialities', it is also the case that the individual, 'pursuing its self-preservation, is itself an actual universal, society – in its full logic, humanity'.[97]

To avoid misunderstanding, however, it is important to stress that the concepts 'species' and 'humanity' do not refer to universal essences.[98] Foucault

94   Foucault, 'What is Critique?', *What Is Enlightenment?*, p. 384. In 'Foucault and Hayek: Republican Law and Liberal Civil Society', *The Government of Life*, p. 182, Miguel Vatter politicizes the Nietzschean idea of becoming the judge, the avenger and the victim of one's own law when he argues that Foucault championed the revolutionary tradition in republican thought – a tradition in which law is rooted in the 'political self-organization of a people ... and turned into "judge-made law"'.

95   Kaufmann, 'Correlations, Constellations and the Truth', *Theodor W. Adorno*, p. 175.

96   Adorno, *Problems of Moral Philosophy*, p. 137, trans. mod.

97   Adorno, 'Marginalia to Theory and Praxis', *Critical Models*, pp. 272–3 passim.

98   Cf. Adorno, *Problems of Moral Philosophy*, p. 169: 'the term "humanity" ... is one of the expressions that reify and hence falsify crucial issues merely by speaking of them. When the founders of the Humanist Union asked me to become a member, I replied that "I might be willing to join if your club had been called an inhuman union, but I could not join one that calls itself "humanist"'.

himself wrongly implies that they do when he charges that the Frankfurt School wanted 'to recover our lost identity, . . . liberate our imprisoned nature, or discover our fundamental truth'.[99] Yet Adorno rejects prelapsarian views of progress, and he adopts Hegel's and Marx's view that the human species is 'a result, not an *eidos*'.[100] Like Foucault, moreover, Adorno wants to 'move toward something altogether different'. In fact, he would accept Foucault's gloss on Marx's phrase 'man produces man', namely that 'what ought to be produced is not man as nature supposedly designed him, or as his essence ordains him to be', but 'something that doesn't exist yet, without being able to know what it will be'.[101] To cite Adorno: since 'no progress is to be assumed that would imply that humanity in general already exists', progress would actually consist in the 'establishment of humanity in the first place'.[102]

Adorno's insistence that the individual should embrace the species, effectively bringing the species into being for the first time, is consonant with his view that only a global subject can pose an effective counter to late capitalism. Nevertheless, he also warns against hypostatizing the species. Of course, we should not hypostatize the species because we do not yet know what humanity is, but Adorno has a second reason for issuing this warning. Although it is 'part of the logic of the self-preservation of the individual that it should . . . embrace . . . the preservation of the species',[103] Adorno fears that the 'embrace' of the species risks pitting the 'general rationality' over and against 'particular individuals' (ND 318). As he remarks in one of his many criticisms of collective action, 'there is an intrinsic temptation for this universal to emancipate itself from the individuals it comprises' in both capitalist and socialist countries.[104]

Consequently, even as individuals free themselves from 'the particularity of obdurate particular interest', they must also free themselves from 'the no less obdurate particular interest of the totality'.[105] On the one hand, then, Adorno stresses the importance of developing new forms of collectivity and social solidarity that will address the interests and needs of individuals. On the other hand, in 'Progress', Adorno shares Peter Altenberg's view that the 'placeholder for humanity' is 'extreme individuation' on the grounds that we can conceive of humanity 'only through this extreme form of differentiation, individuation, not as a comprehensive generic concept'.[106] Here Adorno speculates that humanity will emerge only when individuals are more radically individuated – that is,

---

99 Foucault, 'Interview with Michel Foucault', *Essential Works: Power*, p. 275.
100 Adorno, 'On Subject and Object', *Critical Models*, p. 258; trans. mod.
101 Foucault, 'Interview with Michel Foucault', *Essential Works: Power*, p. 275.
102 Adorno, 'Progress', *Critical Models*, p. 145; trans. mod. See also Adorno, *History and Freedom*, p. 12, where Adorno argues that the human race does not exist because we have not yet created 'a society that is conscious of itself and [that] has its fate in its own hands'.
103 Adorno, *History and Freedom*, p. 44.
104 Ibid.
105 Ibid., p. 45.
106 Adorno, 'Progress', *Critical Models*, p. 151.

when each individual is able freely to develop in such a way that it can thrive as an autonomous and singular entity.[107]

Again, to thrive in this way, individuals must no longer 'frantically be guarding the old particularity' (ND 283). Currently, the individual is as shambolic as the species because its fixation on its own needs and desires – a fixation that is constantly reinforced by late capitalism when it confines individuals to the pursuit of ensuring their own survival – 'mars the idea of a happiness that will not arise until the category of the individual ceases to be self-seclusive' (ND 352). Indeed, in 'On Subject and Object', Adorno tried to envisage a resolution to the fraught dialectic between the individual and the species when he defined peace as a 'state of differentiation without domination, with the differentiated participating in each other'.[108]

Adorno seldom went beyond these broad and sweeping claims. This paucity of detail may explain why Jameson ventured to suggest that Adorno was promoting a utopia of 'misfits and oddballs, in which the constraints for uniformization and conformity have been removed, and human beings grow wild like plants in a state of nature: not the beings of Thomas More, . . . but rather those of the opening of Altman's *Popeye*, who, no longer fettered by the constraints of a now oppressive sociality, blossom into neurotics, compulsives, obsessives, paranoids, and schizophrenics whom our society considers sick but who, in a world of true freedom, may make up the flora and fauna of "human nature" itself'.[109] Here, however, Jameson travesties Adorno; he ignores his remark that 'the sickness of the normal does not necessarily imply as its opposite the health of the sick' (MM 60). Indeed, Adorno's view of neuroses as 'the pillars of society' also calls into question Jameson's interpretation (ND 298) .

For Adorno, it is not neuroses, but sustained and critical self-reflection that may make possible more 'extreme' forms of individuation. Foucault obviously agrees: he makes critical self-reflection one of the keys to shaping more fully differentiated, autonomous subjects because individuals can counter power more effectively only when they become aware of how power relations have shaped them. Criticizing his early work, Foucault said that it tended to focus on domination to the exclusion of exploring technologies of the self. These technologies, which foster self-government, may 'permit individuals to effect, by their own means, a certain number of operations on their own bodies, their own souls, their own thoughts, their own conduct, and this in a manner so as to transform themselves, modify themselves'.[110] Although many of these technologies will have been fashioned by the societies in which we live, some may help to free us from subjection precisely by enabling us to reflect critically on ourselves and the forces that have made us what we are.

---

107   Adorno, *History and Freedom*, p. 156; trans. mod.
108   Adorno, 'On Subject and Object', *Critical Models*, p. 247.
109   Fredric Jameson, *Late Marxism*, p. 102.
110   Foucault, 'Sexuality and Solitude', *Essential Works: Ethics*, p. 177.

If extreme individuation is the placeholder for humanity in Adorno, Paul Patton remarks that, for Foucault, more fully individuated individuals would also transform our ideas about what it is to be human – ostensibly because humanity is only instantiated in individuals.[111] Indeed, Foucault reformulated the widely cited proclamation that he made about the death of 'man' in *The Order of Things* when he told Duccio Trombadori that individuals 'have never ceased to construct themselves, that is, to continually displace their subjectivity, to constitute themselves in an infinite, multiple series of different subjectivities that will never have an end and never bring us in the presence of something that would be "man"'.[112] Nevertheless, it is also the case that, even if we succeed in revolutionizing the pastoral art of government, we will simply give another new face to humanity – albeit a face that may be far less docile and submissive than it is today.

When he criticizes the individualizing and totalizing effects of modern power, Foucault also notes that those who exercise their freedom by resisting disciplinary power's individualizing effects 'assert the right to be different and underline everything that makes individuals truly individual'. Opposing the totalizing tendencies of the biopolitical state, those who resist simultaneously attack 'everything that separates the individual, breaks his links with others, splits up community life, forcing the individual back on himself, and tying him to his own identity in a constraining way' (SP 330). In so doing, these individuals are responding to 'the political, ethical, social, philosophical problem of our days': the problem of liberating ourselves 'both from the state and from the type of individualization linked to the state'. Indeed, Foucault also claims that those who resist may eventually contribute to improving existing conditions as they 'imagine and build up what we could be' (SP 336).

Observing that many voters in France believed that the election of François Mitterrand in 1981 would finally make it possible to modify relations between individuals and the state, Foucault added, crucially, that this modification would have involved a change in the 'relation of obedience' between them. Rather than being subjected to government, voters thought that it might be possible to work together with the Mitterrand government.[113] In other words, they thought that Mitterrand might improve relations between governors and the governed by allowing citizens to become more active and egalitarian partners in government. This idea can be given a Marxist spin: we are the objects of our history – creatures of the societies that have made us what we are – but Foucauldian critique aims to transform the passive objects of history into more active historical agents.

Consequently, Adorno and Foucault both suggest that resistance might establish more radically democratic forms of government in which more

111 Paul Patton, 'Foucault's Subject of Power', *The Later Foucault*, pp. 70–1.
112 Foucault, 'Interview with Michel Foucault', *Essential Works: Power*, p. 276.
113 Foucault, 'So is it Important to Think?', *Essential Works: Power*, p. 455.

autonomous, self-reflective and self-critical individuals actively participate.[114] But resistance may have other goals as well. Among other things, it may aim to make the lives of individuals more pleasurable. So, for example, Adorno argues that the production process could be oriented to satisfying the needs of all so that individuals are no longer obliged to struggle against the pleasure principle by delaying the gratification of their needs and instincts, or by renouncing gratification altogether.[115] As things now stand, however, individuals cannot be reconciled with society because a real antagonism exists between their needs and the demands that are made on them under late capitalism. Indeed, Adorno believes that the resolution of this antagonism will remain 'mere ideology as long as the instinctual renunciation society expects of the individual can neither be objectively justified as true and necessary nor later provides him with the delayed gratification'.[116]

Adorno also questions the so-called 'sexual liberation' of the 1960s when he denies that late capitalist society liberated individuals by granting them greater sexual freedoms. Noting that society no longer requires 'abstinence, virginity, and chastity', Adorno argues that sexual activity has nonetheless been entirely 'absorbed, institutionalized, and administered by society'. Society now 'takes sexuality directly under its control without any intermediate authorities like the church, often even without any state legitimation'.[117] Furthermore, like his colleague Herbert Marcuse, who complained that sexual experience has been de-eroticized, Adorno claims that sex has been 'desexualized' because pleasure 'that is either kept cornered or accepted with smiling complaisance, is no longer pleasure at all'.[118] Adorno also echoes Marcuse when he notes that late capitalism ties pleasure almost exclusively to genital sex – and, by extension, to reproduction – even as the culture industry exploits and manipulates our sexual drives. Far from being liberated, drives that are not satisfied in genital sexual relations – following Freud, Adorno calls these partial drives (*Partialtriebe*) – continue to be 'repressed mentally and materially'.[119]

Foucault too denies that individuals have been liberated sexually. However, he also insists that progress should not be measured by sexual liberation as

---

114   Ransom's insightful reading of Foucault applies to Adorno as well: 'Where Weber worries that the spread of instrumentally rational forms of organization will inhibit the rise of leaders proficient at creating value structures, Foucault examines the tendency of the same structures to produce a quiescent population. In other words, Foucault takes the criticism of modern forms of subjectivity in Nietzsche and the concern over the inherently expansive drift of bureaucratic organizational forms in Weber and radicalizes them in a democratic direction. Neither Nietzsche nor Weber thinks "the crowd" is capable of value creation . . . For both, the masses are capable of little more than ill-informed support for this or that value which was created elsewhere . . . Foucault wishes . . . to democratize the insights and conclusions of his mentors.' See Ransom, *Foucault's Discipline*, pp. 182–3.

115   Adorno, 'Marginalia to Theory and Praxis', *Critical Models*, p. 262.

116   Adorno, 'Sociology and Psychology', *New Left Review* 47, p. 96.

117   Adorno, 'Sexual Taboos and Law Today', *Critical Models* p. 72 *passim*.

118   Ibid., p. 75. See also Herbert Marcuse, *One-Dimensional Man*, p. 73.

119   Ibid., p. 76.

defined by doctors and sexologists. Although we are told that our happiness depends on liberating our sexuality, Foucault warns that the equation of happiness with sexual liberation is a 'formidable trap'. Indeed, he argues that the claim that sexuality has been repressed and needs to be liberated has itself become a powerful 'tool of control and power'. Those who offer to liberate our repressed sexuality actually end by suppressing 'movements of revolt and liberation' because they constitute our sexuality in the very practices they deploy to liberate it.[120] Hence, liberation will not involve baring our souls to physicians, psychologists and psychoanalysts.

Adorno also denies that psychoanalysis will liberate us but he does so on the grounds that repression is not just a psychological problem. Rather, repression is rooted in economic conditions: considerable profit is made from a sexuality that is 'turned on and off, channeled and exploited in countless forms by the material and cultural industry'.[121] Of course, Foucault largely ignores the economic exploitation of sex, focussing instead on sex as a primary target of power. Still, in spite of these differences in perspective, it is interesting to note that Foucault and Adorno are equally critical of the construction of sex as something natural. For his part, Foucault criticizes the normalizing effects of the biopolitical conception of the natural. And when Adorno rails against our standardized, 'cellophane-wrapped' ideas about sex, he recommends that critical attention be paid to the idea of naturalness.[122] In this context, Adorno targets the construction of female sexuality, observing that our 'patriarchal' society has created an idea of femininity that exalts the passivity and docility of women; the ideal female character would be 'weaned from all personal affect, [and] if possible from all aspiration to her own pleasure'.[123] In fact, Adorno calls repressive the very sexualities that Foucault claims medicine constructed and targeted as anomalous: the sexualities of women, children and so-called sexual deviants.

Adorno and Foucault share the view that sexuality is a fundamentally normative construct. For both, the prevailing idea of sexuality presupposes that there are natural, normal or healthy sexual relations and roles. For both, moreover, this idea has had similar effects. To reiterate, on Adorno's view, the construction of so-called healthy sexuality under capitalism continues to demand the repression of partial drives. As for Foucault, he criticizes the distinction on the grounds that it helped to pathologize many sexual practices, but he essentially agrees with Adorno when he argues that what medicine distinguishes from 'normal' sexual practices and designates as pathological are 'incomplete' practices (*pratiques incomplètes*), or practices that circumvent genital sex.[124] In short, Adorno and Foucault contend that 'healthy' sexuality is modelled on the

120   Foucault, 'Power and Sex', *Politics, Philosophy, Culture*, p. 114.
121   Adorno, 'Sexual Taboos and Law Today', *Critical Models*, p. 72.
122   Ibid., p. 76.
123   Ibid., p. 75.
124   Foucault, *The History of Sexuality*, Vol. 1, p. 41.

ostensibly natural form of genital sex (between men and women), in comparison with which partial drives, which are channelled into 'incomplete' sexual practices, are considered perverse.

In response to a situation in which sex has become the privileged target of power, Foucault advocates resistance to the 'trend of "always more sex", and "always more truth in sex" which has enthralled us for centuries'. Those who resist may overcome 'the monarchy of sex' by 'inventing other forms of pleasures, of relationships, coexistences, attachments, loves, intensities'.[125] Foucault also discussed the possibility of inventing new forms of pleasure in the first volume of *The History of Sexuality* when he wrote that some individuals may succeed in breaking away from 'the agency of sex' by tactically inverting 'the various mechanisms of sexuality' and countering 'the grips of power with the claims of bodies, pleasures, and knowledges, in their multiplicity and their possibility of resistance'. In a passage that has perplexed, and sometimes perturbed, readers, Foucault asserts that it is not sex and desire, but bodies and pleasures, that can serve as the 'rallying point' for a counterattack against power.[126]

Of course, Adorno follows Freud when he links pleasure to polymorphous perverse sexualities – or to the very sexualities that Foucault claims were 'extracted from people's bodies and from their pleasures' and implanted by power.[127] Yet Adorno does appear to endorse the aim of 'desexualizing' pleasure – in Foucault's sense of the word 'desexualize' – when he objects that the 'focus on genitality has an element that is hostile to pleasure'.[128] For his part, Foucault seems to agree with Adorno that pleasure may be derived from the satisfaction of partial drives (or from sexual practices that psychologists have labelled 'incomplete') when he tells an interviewer that sado-masochism represents new possibilities for pleasure because it eroticizes different parts of the body and uses them as the source of numerous pleasures.[129] In other words, Foucault argues in this interview that the pleasures derived from so-called 'polymorphously perverse' sexual conducts (including sado-masochism) – conducts which he believes have been implanted by power – may effectively counter power.[130] Although I am only speculating, Foucault may believe that these pleasures can counter power because they lie outside the orbit of genital sex to which disciplinary power and biopower cling.

125   Foucault, 'Power and Sex', *Politics, Philosophy, Culture*, p. 116 *passim*.
126   Foucault, *The History of Sexuality*, Vol. 1, p. 157.
127   Ibid., p. 48.
128   Adorno and Horkheimer, 'Towards a New Manifesto?', *New Left Review*, p. 46.
129   Foucault, 'An Interview: Sex, Power and the Politics of Identity', *Advocate* 2, quoted in Macey, *The Lives of Michel Foucault*, p. 368.
130   In *Foucault's Critical Ethics*, p. 149, Lynch explains: 'even if . . . these "bodies and pleasures" are themselves contingent constructs, they can still function as the site and material for resistance, invention and transformation' by asserting themselves against power as countervailing forces. In this respect too, Foucault resembles Adorno who remarked (in a passage cited above) that the constructed stratum of individuality may serve as a resistive force against domination.

At this juncture, I shall return to an earlier point, namely that Adorno links the possibility of experiencing pleasure to the satisfaction of needs (whether these be, in Marx's phrase, needs of the stomach or needs of the imagination). Among other places, Adorno makes this point in *Negative Dialectics* when he gives the Christian notion of the resurrection of the flesh a secular interpretation and links it to liberation 'from the primacy of material needs in their state of fulfillment' (ND 207). Progress will occur only when everybody has enough to eat and when they can satisfy other needs as well. Recognizing that it is impossible to distinguish what is natural from what is social in needs, Adorno claims that society could be made more rational by gearing production to the satisfaction of all needs so that individuals are no longer obliged to struggle against the pleasure principle for the sake of self-preservation.[131]

For Adorno, a more rational society is not simply a pipe dream. A more rational society is not utopian in the pejorative sense of that term because it is, in principle at least, within reach owing to the advanced state of Western technology. The prospect of living lives that are no longer devoted primarily to self-preservation is viable even now because 'the technical forces of production are at a stage that makes it possible to foresee the global dispensation from material labor, its reduction to a limiting value'.[132] What was once thought utopian 'has now become a distinct possibility'. However, rather than eliminating poverty and misery, 'the triumphs of technological production' continue to 'bolster the illusion that a utopian world has already been realized within contemporary society'.[133] Here too, Adorno remarks that social integration under late capitalism has made it difficult even to imagine a world that differs from this one. As Slavoj Žižek puts it (in one of his many Adornian remarks), it is now easier to imagine the end of the world than it is to imagine the end of our unjust and destructive economic order.[134]

More problematically, Adorno also suggests that the radical changes he envisages may eventually bring humanity *tout court* into being, rather than simply giving humanity a new face. He sometimes implies that the dialectic between the individual and the species may be resolved definitively, bringing into being a 'truer' humanity, a more 'genuine' humanity. Although he does question whether this dialectic will ever be resolved, Adorno often gestures towards a world in which the individual and the species have been reconciled once and for all because society is no longer totalizing, and individuals are able

---

131 Adorno says that production should be oriented to the satisfaction of all needs – including the needs that capitalism creates – in 'Theses on Need', *Adorno Studies*, p. 103; trans mod. (italics in the text): '*If production were reorganized immediately, unconditionally and unrestrictedly for the satisfaction of needs – even and especially those needs produced by capitalism – then needs themselves would be transformed decisively.*'

132 Adorno, 'Marginalia to Theory and Praxis', *Critical Models*, p. 267.

133 Adorno, 'Late Capitalism or Industrial Society?' *Modern German Sociology*, p. 239.

134 'Slavoj Žižek Speaks at Occupy Wall Street: Transcript', cited in Bowie, *Adorno and the Ends of Philosophy*, p. 180.

to develop freely as individuals. At one and the same time, then, he denies that reconciliation and redemption are inevitable when he rejects teleological views of history, and he speculates about what utopia – or the 'transformation of the totality' – might look like.[135]

Foucault would certainly baulk at words like 'reconciliation' and 'redemption'; he would also object that resistance will not usher in humanity *tout court*, but simply a different, or new, instantiation of it. Nevertheless, he too suggests that resistance may bring about a substantively better society to the extent that individuals become more autonomous as power becomes less coercive. This 'better' society will not mark the end of history – as Adorno problematically implies at times – but it will mark a positive and radical change with respect to existing states of affairs. Since I shall respond in the next chapter to those who question the normative commitments on which Adorno's and Foucault's critiques are based, I shall simply reiterate here that, just as Adornian critique lends a voice to human suffering under late capitalism, Foucauldian critique targets those forms of power that individuals and groups of individuals find unbearable, while seeking to find ways to mitigate them.

Yet I have already remarked that Foucault also endorsed courses of action that would radically transform the 'totality' when he advocated the abolition of the state. In addition, he implied that resistive struggles could have other radical effects. As his genealogies reveal, it took a great deal of time and effort to produce individuals who would serve as efficient workers in capitalist countries. To harness individuals to the process of production, disciplinary mechanisms – or that 'set of techniques by which people's bodies and their time would become labor power and labor time so as to be effectively used and thereby transformed into hyperprofit [*sur-profit*]' – were indispensable.[136] And, since Foucault maintained that individuals feel compelled to work only because their bodies 'have been invested by political forces, [and] caught up in mechanisms of power',[137] I suggested earlier that, if resistance to these mechanisms should succeed in destabilizing them, it might radically transform society by undermining the work ethic on which capitalism depends.

To summarize, resistance in Adorno and Foucault aims to invent new pleasures, new modes of individuality and collectivity, and new relations between individuals and society. However, it should also be emphasized that these ideas about the ends or goals of resistance are not just broad and underdeveloped, they may always be challenged. As I shall discuss in more detail in 'Critique', Adorno and Foucault both insist on limiting the role that intellectuals – including themselves – play in struggles. Although their critiques do point towards possible dimensions of social change, they insist that it is not the task of

135   Adorno and Ernst Bloch, 'Something's Missing', *The Utopian Function of Art and Literature*, p. 3.
136   Foucault, 'Truth and Juridical Forms', *Essential Works: Power*, p. 86.
137   Foucault, 'Dialogue sur le Pouvoir', *Dits et écrits* III, p. 470.

intellectuals to dictate goals in an authoritarian manner. Instead, it is up to those who resist to determine the concrete goals that will direct their struggles.

Refusing to turn theory into a set of detailed instructions for political practice, Adorno declares that praxis is 'a source of power for theory but cannot be prescribed by it'. Praxis appears in theory only 'as a blind spot, as an obsession with what is being criticized'.[138] Also cautious about prescribing goals, Foucault insists that he is simply trying 'to pose problems, to make them active, to display them in such a complexity that they can silence the prophets and lawgivers, all those who speak for others or to others'.[139] In short, Adorno's and Foucault's critiques aim to give individuals who attempt to exercise their freedom by resisting the forces that have made them what they are a trenchant analysis of society's fault lines that may permit them to transform not just themselves, but the societies that hold them captive.

---

138   Adorno, 'Marginalia to Theory and Praxis', *Critical Models*, p. 278.
139   Foucault, 'Interview with Michel Foucault', *Essential Works: Power*, p. 288.

Chapter 5

Critique

'Immaturity', Kant declared in his famous essay on enlightenment, 'is the inability to use one's own understanding without the guidance of another'. Rather than thinking for themselves, individuals are immature to the extent that they allow authorities and experts to do their thinking for them, to act as their guardians.[1] Conversely, enlightenment presupposes maturity. In his gloss on Kant's essay, Adorno explains that maturity is achieved when individuals are able 'to resist established opinions and, one and the same, . . . to resist existing institutions, to resist everything that is merely posited, that justifies itself with its existence'. Critical theory itself presupposes maturity in the Kantian sense; it assumes that critics can speak for themselves because they have thought for themselves and are 'not merely repeating someone else'.[2]

By the late 1970s, Foucault placed himself squarely within this Kantian lineage. As I noted in the opening chapter, he explicitly situated himself in the tradition of critical philosophy that runs from Kant and Hegel 'to the Frankfurt School, passing through Nietzsche, Max Weber and so on'.[3] Claiming that his ideas about critique differ little from Kant's definition of enlightenment, Foucault also follows Kant and his successors when he opts for a 'critical thought which takes the form of an ontology of the present, of present reality, an ontology of modernity, an ontology of ourselves'. According to Foucault, the critical tradition that was inaugurated by Kant is animated by an 'attitude', or by a 'philosophical ethos that could be described as a permanent critique of our historical era'.[4] In addition, Foucault shares with the modern critical tradition the aim of finding an *Ausgang* that will release individuals from immaturity.[5]

Adorno's and Foucault's critical ontologies of the present will be studied in this chapter. The first section will explore the philosophical premises on which their ontologies are based; it will offer an account of Adorno's and Foucault's ideas about reality and our access to it. Kant was an important influence on their

---

1   Immanuel Kant, 'An Answer to the Question: What is Enlightenment?' *Kant's Political Writings*, p. 54.
2   Adorno, 'Critique', *Critical Models*, pp. 281–2 *passim*.
3   Foucault, *The Government of Self and Others*, p. 21. Apart from the texts cited here, see Foucault's remarks about the Kantian lineage he shares with the Frankfurt School in 'The Political Technology of Individuals', *Essential Works: Power*, p. 403. See also 'The Art of Telling the Truth', *Politics, Philosophy, Culture*, p. 95.
4   Foucault, 'What is Enlightenment?', *Essential Works: Ethics*, p. 312.
5   Ibid., p. 303.

conceptions of critique, but the next section of this chapter will show that Kantian ideas inform their ontologies as well. In the following section, I shall examine in more detail one of the primary motivations for Adorno's and Foucault's extensive critiques of existing conditions in the West: their concern that fascism might recur. Finally, the chapter will end with a discussion of the normative foundations of their critical theories, including their Kantian ideas about autonomy.

ONTOLOGIES OF THE PRESENT

Chapter Three asked about the 'stuff' from which individuals are made. However, it is also important to ask a more general question: how do Adorno and Foucault characterize the 'stuff' that makes up the world in which we live? To begin to answer this question, I shall make a very broad, and possibly contentious, claim: Adorno and Foucault conceptualize reality as simultaneously material and historical. Arguing that the material world is thoroughly historical, and that it is always grasped through an equally historical conceptual prism, Adorno and Foucault also deny that something can come from nothing. Reality is not constructed 'all the way down'. These ideas will be examined in what follows.

In a section of *Negative Dialectics* called 'Passage to Materialism', Adorno asserts: 'It is by passing to the object's preponderance [*Vorrang*] that dialectics is rendered materialistic' (ND 192). On Ståle Finke's reading, this thesis about the preponderance of the object means that objects are extraconceptual.[6] More specifically, Adorno thinks that objects are 'weighty' owing to their materiality: the preponderance of the object means that matter (*Stoff, Materie*) preponderates over mind. Although matter is always also mediated by concepts, Adorno warns against hypostatizing concepts, including the concept of matter itself. No concept can fully apprehend material things because concepts are abstract determinations, not concrete properties; universals, not particulars. Indeed, in contrast to Foucault, Adorno is less interested in examining the genesis of philosophical and scientific concepts than in criticizing the inadequacies of the prevailing form of conceptual mediation: identity thinking. Blindly identifying particulars with universal concepts, identity thinking commits what Adorno calls the fallacy of constitutive subjectivity because it implies that objects are constituted by concepts, or that matter can be reduced to mind.

In another prison metaphor, Adorno remarks that we invariably find ourselves captive 'in the prison of language', but we can at least 'recognize it as a prison'.[7] His thesis about the preponderance of the object elucidates this metaphor because it entails, in Kantian fashion, that material objects are distinct from, and not completely accessible to, the concepts we use to apprehend them.

6   Ståle Finke, 'Concepts and Intuitions', *Theodor W. Adorno*, p. 127 n. 17.
7   Adorno, *Metaphysics*, pp. 67–8 *passim*.

But this thesis also entails that concepts themselves are generated in our interaction with the material world in response to problems that arise at particular times. Specifically, concepts are 'moments of the reality that requires their formation, primarily for the control of nature' (ND 11). At one and the same time, then, the preponderance of the object means that objects are not reducible to concepts, and that concepts are firmly anchored in reality because what persists in their meanings is what their emergence in particular contexts under specific historical conditions has conveyed to them (ND 12).

Adorno praises Kant's postulate of the *Ding-an-sich*, or things-in-themselves, on the grounds that it rightly suggests that 'the object of nature that we define with our categories is not actually nature itself'.[8] Yet he also charges that Kant's conception of knowledge is 'tautological' because the Kantian subject effectively knows only its own categories.[9] Unlike Kant, who postulates the existence of an unknowable noumenal realm, Adorno argues that the caesura or block that separates concepts from things is not completely unbridgeable. Although Adorno emphasizes the nonidentity of concept and object, their nonidentity does not mean that concept and object are as radically distinct as Kant claims, precisely because concepts remain embedded in the material world to which their formation represents a response.

On Adorno's reading, the greatness of Kant's *Critique of Pure Reason* lies in the clash of two opposing ideas. On the one hand, Kant succumbed to identity thinking when he submitted 'synthetic *a priori* judgements and ultimately . . . all objectively valid experience, to an analysis of the consciousness of the subject'. Recognizing that our knowledge of objects is mediated, Kant wrongly concluded that we can apprehend only our own concepts and categories. On the other hand, Kant can be read as a nonidentity thinker. Rather than summarily reducing objects to our understanding of them, Kantian philosophy 'regards the idea that all knowledge is contained in humankind as a superstition and, in the spirit of the Enlightenment, it wishes to criticize it as it would any superstition'. According to Adorno, then, Kant's first critique contains both 'an identity philosophy – that is, a philosophy that attempts to ground being in the subject – and also a non-identity philosophy which attempts to restrict the claim to identity by insisting on the obstacles, the *block*, encountered by the subject in its search for knowledge'.[10]

If concepts are entwined with the nonconceptual, the preponderance of the object also means that the cognizing subject itself is material, something objective. It is not necessarily 'part of the meaning of objectivity' to be a subject, but it *is* necessarily part of the meaning of subjectivity to be an object. Concept formation involves both material particulars and material, corporeal subjects (ND 183). According to Adorno, '[n]o matter how the subject is defined,

8   Adorno, *Kant's 'Critique of Pure Reason'*, pp. 175–6.
9   Ibid., p. 129.
10   Ibid., p. 66.

existent being cannot be conjured away from it'.[11] Another reason why Adorno contests the 'supremacy of thinking over its otherness' is because mind is always 'otherness already, within itself' (ND 201). In fact, experience would not be possible if the subject did not belong 'a priori to the same sphere as the given thing' (ND 196).

In contrast to Kant, Adorno stresses our affinity with nature on the grounds that consciousness is 'part impulse itself, and also part of that in which it intervenes' (ND 265). Specifically, of course, Adorno insists that human history will never 'be divorced from self-preservation, from the satisfaction of human needs'.[12] At the same time, he is also concerned that our survival instincts are running wild under late capitalism. Where Foucault stressed the discontinuity in history in his early work, Adorno would counter that something does cement 'the discontinuous, chaotically splintered moments and phases of history'. No universal history 'leads from savagery to humanitarianism', but a universal history does lead from 'the slingshot to the megaton bomb'. Driven by survival instincts, we continue to dominate external nature, other human beings, and ourselves to the point where our survival is now threatened. In other words, it is our destructive and self-destructive domination of nature that cements the otherwise disparate phases of our history (ND 320).

Along with being part of the material, physical world owing to its drives and corporeality, the subject is obviously embedded in the social and historical world as well. The preponderance of the object also refers to the preponderance or weightiness of society over individuals. Again, Adorno adopts Marx's view that capitalist society preponderates over individuals by virtue of the 'law of value that comes into force without people being aware of it'. Informing social institutions, agencies, relations and practices, the law of value is the 'real objectivity' to which individuals are subjected (ND 300). Today, 'the standard structure of society is the exchange form'. It is the rationality underlying exchange that 'constitutes people'. What people 'are for themselves, what they think they are, is secondary'.[13]

I have already argued that Foucault shares these ideas about the preponderance of society over individuals. In Foucault, of course, society's preponderance manifests itself in the preponderance over individuals of disciplinary power, biopower and the social scientific knowledge that is linked to these. Yet, much like Adorno, who claims that our narcissistic view of ourselves as the very substance of society would suffer 'unbearable psychological harm' if we realized the extent to which we are the creatures of exchange relations (ND 312), Foucault also inflicts a narcissistic wound on our self-understanding. He inflicts this wound when he claims that power relations bypass consciousness, or 'the mediation of the subject's own representations', as they 'materially penetrate the body

---

11   Adorno, 'On Subject and Object', *Critical Models*, pp. 249–50; trans. mod.
12   Adorno, *Problems of Moral Philosophy*, p. 94.
13   Adorno, 'On Subject and Object', *Critical Models*, p. 248.

in depth'.[14] Just as 'social practices . . . engender domains of knowledge that . . . bring new objects, new concepts, and new techniques to light', practices that invest the body below the threshold of consciousness have given birth 'to totally new forms of subjects'.[15]

When the psychoanalyst Joel Whitebook took up the criticism that Foucauldian subjects are effectively fabricated *ex nihilo*, he objected that Foucault's constructivism is so thorough-going that 'the existence of a biological substratum is *virtually an illusion*'.[16] Along with many other critics of Foucault, however, Whitebook misinterprets Foucault because (as noted earlier) Foucault insists that power is directly or indirectly physical.[17] Furthermore, the targets of power are physical as well. In the somatocratic Western world, power shapes phenomena such as madness, delinquency and sexuality by materially investing the physical body. In fact, biopower specifically targets what Whitebook calls the 'biological substratum' when it attempts to regulate and control the 'biological processes that concern . . . the population', including the sexual activities of individuals.[18]

Responding to the objection that his analysis of sexuality elides the body, Foucault counters that his genealogy of sexuality attempts to show 'how deployments of power are connected directly to the body – to bodies, functions, physiological processes, sensations, and pleasures'. Far from eliding the body, he is trying to make visible how 'the biological and the historical . . . are bound together in an increasingly complex fashion in accordance with the development of the modern technologies of power that take life as their objective'. This is one reason why Foucault denied that he was writing a 'history of mentalities that would take account of bodies only through the manner in which they have been perceived and given meaning and value'. Rather, following Nietzsche, Foucault explores the history of bodies and tries to ascertain 'the manner in which what is most material and most vital in them has been invested'.[19]

Like Adorno, who remarks that matter can be apprehended only by means of universal concepts that invariably misrepresent it, Foucault maintains that material things can be grasped only through a prism of concepts. Employing Kantian terms in his discussion of this dimension of Foucault's work, Paul Veyne contends that, for Foucault, 'we can only reach a "thing in itself" by way of the idea that we have constructed of it in each different epoch'. In other words, 'we cannot separate the thing in itself from the "discourse" in which it is bound up for us or "buried in the sand", as Foucault put it'.[20] But if instinct is an example

---

14   Foucault, 'The History of Sexuality', *Power/Knowledge*, p. 186 *passim*.
15   Foucault, 'Truth and Juridical Forms', *Essential Works: Power*, p. 2.
16   Whitebook, 'Michel Foucault', *Thesis Eleven*, p. 60; italics in the text.
17   Foucault, *Discipline and Punish*, p. 26.
18   Foucault, *Society Must be Defended*, p. 251.
19   Foucault, *The History of Sexuality*, Vol. 1, pp. 151–2.
20   Paul Veyne, *Foucault: His Thought, His Character*, p. 11.

of a phenomenon that has been buried in the sand of discourse, it is also the case that, once the concept was invented, the nineteenth century witnessed 'the sudden emergence . . . of an object, or rather of a whole domain of new objects, of a whole series of elements that will be named, described, analysed, and . . . developed, within . . . psychiatric discourse'.[21]

However, it is important to reiterate that the discursive 'burial' of phenomena does not mean that there is nothing to which these concepts refer. Rather, and as Veyne says with respect to instincts, it means that when impulses, drives and tendencies, which had not previously been thematized in medicine and psychiatry, were postulated to explain monomania, instinct emerged as 'a strange little period piece, rare, irregular, never before seen'.[22] Furthermore, since it is a 'period piece', the concept of instinct may well vanish as an explanatory principle, as the postulate of the four humours (and other scientific postulates) have done. Referring specifically to madness, sexuality and civil society at the end of *The Birth of Biopolitics*, Foucault coins the phrase 'transactional reality' – a reality that is formed in the historical interaction between power and its targets – to refer to phenomena like these. These transactional and 'transitional figures' emerge in 'the interplay of relations of power and everything which constantly eludes them' (BB 297).

To complicate matters, however, Veyne says that, for Foucault, phenomena such as madness and sexuality 'are things that certainly exist'.[23] Yet Foucault seems to deny this when he states in *Security, Territory, Population* that 'it is certainly possible to say that madness "does not exist", but this does not mean that it is nothing' (STP 118; trans. mod.). To this statement, the editors of *Security, Territory, Population* appended a note that refers to a passage where Foucault appears to say the opposite: 'I have been seen as saying that madness does not exist, whereas the problem is exactly the converse: it was a question of knowing how madness, under the various definitions that have been given, was at a particular time integrated into an institutional field that constituted it as a mental illness, occupying a specific place alongside other illnesses' (STP 131, n. 9).[24] Yet in the following note, the editors cite a comment that Foucault reportedly made to Veyne: '"I personally have never written that *madness does not exist*; but it can be written; because . . . one has

---

21   Foucault, *Abnormal*, p. 131 *passim*.

22   Veyne, 'Foucault Revolutionizes History', p. 159.

23   Veyne, *Foucault*, p. 11.

24   The editors are citing Foucault, 'The Ethics of the Concern for Self as a Practice of Freedom', *Essential Works: Ethics*, p. 297. Cf. BB 19: 'it was not a question of showing how these objects [madness, disease, delinquency and sexuality] were hidden before finally being discovered . . . It was a matter of showing by what conjunctions a whole set of practices . . . was able to make what does not exist . . . become something . . . that continues not to exist. That is to say, what I would like to show is . . . how a particular regime of truth . . . makes something that does not exist able to become something. It is not an illusion since it is precisely a set of practices, real practices, which established it and thus imperiously marks it out in reality.'

to say ... that madness does not exist, but that it is not therefore nothing'" (STP 131 n. 10; italics in the text).

Arguably, however, the contradictions here are more apparent than real because it is possible to say, without contradiction, that madness (to give just one example) does not exist and that it is not nothing. Although power and knowledge do invest something real, material, they never completely capture the somatic singularities they invest. Again, Foucault claims that transactional figures – including madness and instinct – always elude their investment by power and knowledge. They elude complete capture by power and knowledge because the investment of power and knowledge in things is always selective and therefore partial. In this respect too, Foucault resembles Adorno: they both question the extent to which concepts can apprehend objects.

Foucault's 'systematic scepticism' regarding universals is also based on the fact that concepts are ephemeral historical constructs that are wielded by equally historical subjects.[25] This scepticism, which Foucault shares with Adorno, makes both thinkers powerful critics of science. Nevertheless, since Adorno believes that the caesura between concepts and objects is bridgeable, and that concepts can grasp things more satisfactorily than they currently do, he tries to find a way to mediate between them. Nonidentity thinking represents his attempt to supersede identity thinking by making a concerted effort to appre-hend what the blanket subsumption of particular things under universal concepts normally obscures. To return to another idea that was broached in Chapter One, Adorno proposes that concepts should be used to transcend concepts (ND 15).

Adorno's aspiration to conceptualize the nonconceptual certainly distin-guishes his work from Foucault's. Although they both deny that things are constructed *ex nihilo*, Foucault is more interested in the historical conjunctures that gave rise to the conceptual construction of things than in finding better ways to grasp the nonconceptual 'stuff' that power and knowledge target. This is not to say that the question of whether scientific discourse adequately captures things is irrelevant for Foucault. Although he believes that our ideas about truth are shaped by history, and he questions the Faustian pacts we have made in our pursuit of truth, Foucault readily admits that the question of the truth of a scien-tific discourse is 'an entirely legitimate problem'. Rather than investigating this problem, however, the problem that interests Foucault is of a different order: it is the problem of 'investigating the reasons for and the forms of the enterprise

---

25   Florence [pseudonym for Michel Foucault], 'Foucault', *Essential Works: Aesthetics*, p. 461. Those who call Foucault a nominalist should note that he also says (on the same page of this article) that he does not reject all universals 'from the start, outright, and once for all'. Instead, he is sceptical about them, and says that 'nothing of that order must be accepted that is not strictly indispensable'. In particular, anthropological universals must be 'tested and analyzed'. See also Foucault, *On the Government of the Living*, p. 80. Here Foucault explicitly refused to call himself a nominalist because 'nominalism is a very specific and technical conception, practice, and philosophical method'.

of truth-telling about things such as madness, illness, or crime'.[26] As Colin Gordon explains, one of Foucault's principal tasks was to discover the 'mobile systems of relationships and syntheses which provide the conditions of possibility for the formation of certain orders and levels of objects and of forms of knowledge of such objects'.[27]

When he charts the genealogy of social scientific concepts, Foucault does problematize science's grasp of the material to which its concepts refer, but he does so only implicitly. By contrast, of course, Adorno is a vociferous critic of identity thinking, and his criticisms extend to the natural sciences as well. Although he concedes that science 'works', that it often succeeds in predicting events and manipulating and controlling things, Adorno also complains that science has as its sole criterion 'the fact that it works'. In conjunction with this criticism, Adorno objects that science generally renounces 'any attempt to make any statement about the nature of things, and about what things really are'.[28] He believes that science might begin to work better if it prevented its abstractions from liquidating particulars by means of identification (ND 265). Science should acknowledge the preponderance of the object, or the asymmetrical relation between concepts and nonconceptual, material things because scientists fail adequately to apprehend things when they deploy concepts in subsumptive, identitarian ways.

To be sure, concepts will never make the nonconceptual 'their equal' owing to their abstract universality (ND 10). Yet they may succeed in grasping nonconceptual things in other ways. Nonidentity thinking tries to apprehend things by using constellations of concepts, but it also involves a proleptic or prospective apprehension of things, an apprehension that attempts to reveal the unrealized possibilities that inhere in them. Surprisingly, perhaps, Foucault adopts a similar view. Since I shall elaborate on his view in the final section of this chapter, I shall simply note here that Adorno and Foucault argue that thought invariably 'overshoots' the things that it attempts to think. This 'overshooting' has a positive dimension to the extent that it enables thought, at least in principle, to envisage things differently.

Foucault might also accept Adorno's criticisms of the fallacy of constitutive subjectivity because he too recognizes that concepts do not grasp things *wie sie eigentlich sind*. In his own Kantian reading of Foucault, Gary Gutting notes that Foucault endorses Kant's view 'that our thoughts and experiences occur only within fixed categorical boundaries'. As opposed to Kant, however, Gutting also points out that Foucault maintains – and Adorno certainly agrees – that these boundaries 'are themselves contingent products of our history and that, in

26 Foucault, *Wrong-doing, Truth-telling*, p. 21. As Gary Gutting convincingly argues, Foucault was by no means attempting to launch a 'universal assault on truth'. See Gutting, *Michel Foucault's Archaeology of Scientific Reason*, pp. 272-5.
27 Gordon, 'Afterword', in *Power/Knowledge*, p. 236.
28 Adorno, *Kant's 'Critique of Pure Reason'*, p. 134.

different epochs, there have been radically diverse systems ... governing thought and experience'.[29] Although Foucault does not fault science for failing to improve its cognitive grasp of objects, he does believe that science is thoroughly conditioned by history, and hence that it is an entirely fallible enterprise.

Another aspect of Adorno's and Foucault's critiques of science will be mentioned briefly here before I conclude this discussion. For they also question the motivations that lie behind scientific endeavours. On Adorno's view, of course, even scientific attempts to understand and explain the natural world are impelled by survival imperatives. As Espen Hammer observes, Adorno believes that science is entirely geared to 'identifying, controlling, and organizing a hostile and potentially dangerous environment'.[30] This point was made succinctly, if somewhat hyperbolically, in *Dialectic of Enlightenment* when Adorno and Horkheimer argued that self-preservation is the 'constitutive principle of science, the soul of the table of categories'.[31] With its instrumental orientation towards objects, science simply adjusts 'the world for the ends of self-preservation'; it 'recognizes no function other than the preparation of the object from mere sensory material in order to make it the material of subjugation'.[32]

According to Gutting, Foucault too sees 'all bodies of knowledge as originating from nondiscursive practices of social control'.[33] Yet, in contrast to Foucault, Adorno thought that practices like these might eventually be stemmed. Science now seeks compulsively to dominate external nature and our own internal nature in ways that have become life-threatening, but it could potentially enable us to reconcile ourselves with nature both within and without. Science could do so if it managed to escape 'the visual prison' by recognizing the primacy of the object – as Adorno thought post-Einsteinian physics was attempting to do (ND 188). To do justice to the preponderance of the object, science must become more self-aware. Specifically, science must acknowledge its own embeddedness in the nature that it attempts to control, along with its deep entanglement in the economic forces that drive late capitalism.

For his part, Foucault believes that power relations will always inform science. More generally, he adopts a Nietzschean view when he suggests that power inherently aims to seize, shape and transform its targets. According to Foucault, power relations are an ineradicable feature of all human societies, and control of some sort is an ineliminable feature of power. But, of course, it is also the case that Foucault criticizes the hypertrophy of power in both capitalist and socialist countries, along with the suffering that power now inflicts on individuals and groups

29   Gary Gutting, *Michel Foucault's Archaeology of Scientific Reason*, p. 275.
30   Hammer, *Adorno and the Political*, p. 45.
31   Horkheimer and Adorno, *Dialectic of Enlightenment*, p. 86; see also the later translation, p. 68.
32   Ibid., p. 83; see also the later translation, p. 65.
33   Gutting, *Michel Foucault's Archaeology of Scientific Reason*, p. 275.

of individuals, with a view to mitigating that suffering. Foucault's critical ontology of the present puts itself 'to the test of reality, of contemporary reality, . . . to grasp the points where change is possible and desirable'. Attempting to 'separate out, from the contingency that has made us what we are, the possibility of no longer being, doing, or thinking what we are, do, or think', Foucault seeks 'to give new impetus, as far and wide as possible, to the undefined work of freedom'.[34]

In this respect as well, Foucault's critique of the present finds a counterpart in negative dialectics. Indeed, in a phrase that could be applied to Foucault's own critical ontology of the present, Adorno calls negative dialectics an 'ontology of the wrong state of things' (ND 11). Like Foucault, who is concerned about the suffering that power inflicts on individuals in asylums, hospitals, schools and state institutions, Adorno gives to negative dialectics the tasks of lending a voice to the suffering that late capitalism has caused and of enabling those who suffer more effectively to resist, or to 'crash through' the barriers that have been erected by the 'power of the status quo' (ND 17). In the next section of this chapter, I shall examine more closely what Adorno's and Foucault's critical ontologies identify as the principal sources of suffering before turning to a discussion of the normative dimension of their critiques.

OUR INFERNAL PRESENT

The question that Adorno and Foucault raise throughout their work is one that animates Kant's essay on enlightenment, namely 'What is our present?' Adorno tries to answer this question by examining 'societal and political reality and its dynamic' in order to think the existing 'totality in its untruth'.[35] Yet Adorno goes much further than declaring that the social totality is untrue or false; he makes the moral judgement that the existing state of affairs is evil. One reason why Adorno believes that conditions today are evil is because they have made possible forms of social integration that are so far-reaching that they can be compared to genocide, 'the absolute integration' (ND 362). Individuals have been integrated into society to such an extent that they tend simply to adapt and conform to what exists, to perpetuate the status quo, obeying a 'principle of inertia'. And it is this principle that 'truly is . . . radically evil'.[36]

Individuals who adjust to late capitalism and conform to its norms effectively mutilate themselves by identifying with fungible commodities, inanimate objects, dead things. In a graphic passage where he takes up again Marx's

34 Foucault, 'What is Enlightenment?', *Essential Works: Ethics*, pp. 315–16 *passim*.
35 Adorno, 'Why Still Philosophy', *Critical Models*, p. 14.
36 Adorno, *Metaphysics*, p. 115. Adorno uses the word 'evil' frequently. See, for example, 'Why Still Philosophy', *Critical Models*, p. 10, where he calls unfreedom and oppression 'the evil whose malevolence requires as little philosophical proof as does its existence'. See also ND 219: evil 'is the world's own unfreedom. Whatever evil is done comes from the world.' For an extended discussion of Adorno's use of this word, see Freyenhagen, *Adorno's Practical Philosophy*, pp. 158–61.

thematic distinction between the living and the dead, Adorno quips that even individuals 'who burst with proofs of exuberant vitality could easily be taken for prepared corpses', albeit corpses 'from whom the news of their not-quite-successful demise has been withheld for reasons of population policy' (MM 59; trans. mod.). However, those who refuse, or who are unable, to adjust to society and its norms fare no better. They not only suffer from their maladjustment, they may be marginalized and excluded, or exposed 'to the vengeance of society, even if they are not yet reduced to going hungry and sleeping under bridges'.[37]

In extremis, these individuals may simply be killed. Adorno claimed in *Minima Moralia* that there is a 'straight line' that leads from our thraldom to reifying exchange relations to 'Gestapo torturers and the bureaucrats of the gas-chambers' (MM 183). The literal extermination of individuals in concentration camps was just a more extreme example of the extermination of all vestiges of individuality by homogenizing exchange relations. In his gloss on this passage, Freyenhagen remarks that 'what happened to the victims of the concentration camps is what late capitalism is moving towards: the liquidation of anything individual, the degradation of people to things, and the triumph of bureaucratic rationality at the expense of deeper reflection about means and ends'.[38] To be sure, countertendencies exist that may prevent this: late capitalism will not necessarily become totalitarian, and Adorno does distinguish between Nazi Germany and other Western states. Nevertheless, if he is right about our fearful submission to authority figures and our inability to think for ourselves, the possibility of totalitarianism persists.

Adapting to existing conditions simply in order to survive, individuals currently lack the psychological strength they need to resist demagogues such as Adolf Hitler and his ilk. With their weak, narcissistic egos and authoritarian personality traits, individuals make easy prey for charismatic leaders. Following Freud, Adorno notes that members of a group led by a charismatic leader behave in similar ways because their behaviour is motivated by instincts – which are shared by everyone – rather than by more egocentric interests. Groups like these also act as a 'negatively integrating force' because they distinguish themselves (violently, in the case of Nazism) from other groups. Exhibiting negative attitudes and emotions towards other groups, followers of the in-group believe that 'simply through belonging to the in-group', they are 'better, higher and purer than those who are excluded'.[39] Today, individuals tend to adopt as their own the credo that Adorno claims lies at the heart of anti-Semitism: 'Whoever is not with me is against me.' In so doing, they are all too ready to consign 'for mere difference to the enemy camp' those who fail, for whatever reason, to identify

---

37   Adorno, 'Sociology and Psychology', *New Left Review* 46, p. 71; trans. mod.
38   Freyenhagen, 'Moral Philosophy', *Adorno*, p. 100.
39   Adorno, 'Freudian Theory and the Pattern of Fascist Propaganda', *The Essential Frankfurt School Reader*, p. 130.

with and adapt to prevailing norms (MM 131).

In previous chapters, I noted that identity thinking also helps to account for racism. Adorno's critique of identity thinking reveals the cognitive mechanisms involved in racism, even as it links these mechanisms to broader socio-economic tendencies and trends. Underlying prejudice is the pervasive and coercive subsumption of the different under the same which characterizes both identity thinking and its 'social model', exchange (ND 146). Where exchange relations equate heterogeneous things, identity thinking equalizes the unequal by treating things as if they were merely instances of a more general kind. Thought will tolerate nothing that falls outside the parameters of its abstract concepts and categories. What it cannot assimilate, or what fails to match up to its concepts, will often be rejected or excluded. According to Adorno, thought has become totalitarian: it is 'blinded to the point of madness by whatever would elude its rule' (ND 172).

Adorno says that Western societies are evil, and Foucault calls them demonic.[40] Western societies are demonic because the Christian pastorate introduced a 'strange game' into Western history – a game 'whose elements are life, death, truth, obedience, individuals, self-identity'.[41] Again, Western states not only adopted pastoral techniques that make self-abnegation and obedience to norms corollaries of the modern process of individuation, they simultaneously reduced their citizens to members of a population that is biologically defined. In short, Foucault thinks that Western states are demonic because they are informed by a political rationality that seeks to correlate 'an increasing individualization and the reinforcement of . . . totality'.[42] Foucault also believes that this political rationality impedes maturity in the Kantian sense. Among other things, and to cite Ransom, the state prevents us from becoming mature when it gives to professionals and experts 'the task of self-constitution', the task of shaping even the 'subjective experiences that we . . . believe are uniquely our own'.[43] Indeed, Foucault even questions at one point whether individuals will ever become mature.[44]

As disciplinary power began to impinge on bodies, constituting the modern 'soul', the soul, in a kind of rebound effect, imprisoned the body inasmuch as the

40 See Foucault, ' "Omnes et Singulatim" ', *Essential Works: Power*, p. 325, and SP 332.

41 Foucault, ' "Omnes et Singulatim" ', *Essential Works: Power*, p. 311.

42 Foucault, 'The Political Technology of Individuals', *Essential Works: Ethics*, p. 416.

43 Ransom, *Foucault's Discipline*, p. 75.

44 Foucault, 'What is Enlightenment?', *Essential Works: Ethics*, p. 318: 'I do not know whether we will ever reach mature adulthood. Many things in our experience convince us that the historical event of the Enlightenment did not make us mature adults, and we have not reached that stage yet.' Cf. Foucault, 'Interview with Michel Foucault', *Essential Works: Power*, p. 294: 'As an intellectual, I don't wish to prophesy or play the moralist, to announce that the Western countries are better than the Eastern ones, and so on. People have reached political and moral adulthood [*l'âge de la majorité politique et moral*]. It's up to them to choose, individually and collectively. It is important to say how a certain regime functions, what it consists in, and to prevent a whole series of manipulations and mystifications. But the choice has to be made by people themselves.'

body served as the repository and vehicle for disciplinary norms.[45] Trying to avoid standing out from the crowd, normalized individuals perpetually and anxiously search for signs of deviance in themselves, not least because conformity is rewarded and failure to conform may be punished severely. Those who deviate from disciplinary norms may be incarcerated in prisons, asylums and reform schools (among other institutions) where they will be turned into 'cases' to be normalized by ever more finely tuned mechanisms of control.

Resistance to discipline calls for more discipline, for more concerted attempts to subjugate and assimilate deviants, to make them 'normal'. In the final analysis, however, deviants may be eliminated. Again, since the biopolitical state now assumes the task of ensuring the survival of the population, it has allowed those it judged deviant to die, or it has killed them.[46] Although biological racism can be traced back to the historical and political discourse that portrayed history as a struggle between races in a non-biological sense, Foucault remarks that, from the nineteenth century on, struggles were recast in openly biological terms as struggles between a superior race and a sub-race. At this point, racism became 'the discourse of power itself', and state racism was turned into 'one of the basic dimensions of social normalization'. Portrayed 'as the one true race, the race that holds power', the superior race is entitled 'to define the norm . . . against those who deviate from that norm, against those who pose a threat to the biological heritage'. Subsequently, theories of degeneracy developed, as did institutions that 'made the discourse of race struggle function as a principle of exclusion and segregation and, ultimately, as a way of normalizing society'.[47]

A mechanism that allows biopower to work in the West, racism helps to account for the genocides that blighted the twentieth century. Foucault argues that, if 'genocide is . . . the dream of modern powers, it is because power is situated and exercised at the level of life, the species, the race, and the large-scale phenomena of population'.[48] To be sure, in *The Birth of Biopolitics*, Foucault calls the neoliberal view of the state 'inflationary' on the grounds that it postulates 'a kinship . . . between different forms of the state, with the administrative state, the welfare state, the bureaucratic state, the fascist state, and the totalitarian state all being . . . successive branches of one and the same great tree of state control in its continuous and unified expansion' (BB 187).[49] Nevertheless, he

45 Foucault, *Discipline and Punish*, p. 30.
46 Foucault, *Society Must be Defended*, pp. 255–6.
47 Ibid., pp. 61–2 *passim*.
48 Foucault, *The History of Sexuality*, Vol. 1, p. 137.
49 Given Foucault's criticisms of neoliberalism in *The Birth of Biopolitics*, Koopman warns against 'inflated' conceptions of the biopolitical state, specifically targeting Giorgio Agamben's and Robert Exposito's appropriations of Foucault's notion of biopower. See Koopman, 'Michel Foucault's Critical Empiricism Today', *Foucault Now*, pp. 96–101. Yet, as problematic as these appropriations may be, Koopman ignores Foucault's claims about the similarities between Nazi Germany and other Western states – claims based on Foucault's studies of the mechanisms and technologies that the former inherited from the latter.

argues in 'The Subject and Power' that Nazi Germany 'used and extended mechanisms already present in most other societies'; it 'used, to a large extent, the ideas and the devices of our political rationality' (SP 328). Remarks like these also appear in the first volume of *The History and Sexuality* and in *Society Must be Defended*: Nazism represented 'the paroxysmal development of the new power mechanisms that had been established since the eighteenth century'. Not only was no state more disciplinary than the Nazi regime, but Nazism 'generalized biopower in an absolute sense'; it generalized 'the sovereign right to kill'.[50]

Studying some of the techniques and mechanisms in the West that were adopted by Nazi Germany and the USSR, Foucault also contends in 'La Philosophie analytique de la Politique' that there are 'permanent potentialities – structural in some sense, intrinsic to our systems – that may emerge at any time, making perpetually possible those great excrescences of power, the excrescences of power that were the Mussolinian, Hitlerian, Stalinist systems'.[51] On a more personal note, Foucault also told Trombadori that the experience of the Second World War had demonstrated to his generation the 'urgent need for a society radically different from the one in which we were living, this society that had permitted Nazism, that had lain down in front of it, and that had gone over en masse to de Gaulle'.[52] Although Marxism provided tools for analyzing poverty and exploitation in the nineteenth century, Foucault told another interviewer that the twentieth century had shown that many economic problems could be solved without solving the pernicious problem of power.[53]

For Adorno too, racism is built in to Western culture; it is an odious effect of the pathic form of reason in the West. Furthermore, Adorno claims that the world in which we live often obliges us to act, wittingly or unwittingly, in such a way that we perpetuate the radical evil that culminated in Auschwitz (ND 218–19). On the one hand, since individuals now tend to submit to authority figures and demagogic leaders, they may also be persuaded to direct their remaining energy to combating enemies who are more apparent than real. On the other hand, to defend themselves against the possibility – however remote – of a violent backlash to recurrent economic crises, Western states may resort to calling on their military and police forces, allowing the power motive to supplant the profit motive, if only temporarily.

In short, Adorno and Foucault reveal that Western societies have perfected sophisticated techniques for ensuring our conformity and adaptation to social norms even as they marginalize and exclude – to the point of murder – those who deviate from them. And, since they view Western societies as evil, or demonic, Adorno and Foucault are trying to find a way out of our infernal

---

50   Foucault, *Society Must be Defended*, pp. 259–60 *passim*. See also Foucault's comments on disciplinary power, biopower and fascism in *The History of Sexuality*, Vol. 1, pp. 149–50.

51   Foucault, 'La Philosophie analytique de la Politique', *Dits et écrits* III, p. 536.

52   Foucault, 'Interview with Michel Foucault', *Essential Works: Power*, p. 247.

53   Foucault, 'Pouvoir et Savoir', *Dits et écrits* III, p. 401.

present. Although Adorno wants to overcome the totalitarian tendencies in identitarian reason and exchange relations, and Foucault wants to supersede the coercive arts of government, rooted in the Christian pastorate, that sustain disciplinary power and biopower, they both hope that their critiques will enable individuals to become more mature in the sense that they are able to think for themselves without relying on guardians.

MATURITY AND CRITIQUE

In a conversation with Hellmut Becker (who was, among other things, a lawyer at the Nuremberg trials), Adorno said that Kant's idea of maturity remains 'extraordinarily relevant today'.[54] But while he adopts many of Kant's ideas about maturity, Adorno does not think that immaturity is entirely self-incurred. It is not just laziness and cowardice that make individuals unable to think for themselves.[55] Rather, Adorno attributes immaturity to factors that Kant never considered. Not only have we fallen under the spell cast by levelling and homogenizing exchange relations, but cultural and educational institutions also cripple independent thought.[56] In schools, for example, individuals are encouraged not just to behave but to think in socially approved ways – in terms of stereotypes and other categorical schema – to the point where they simply reproduce the status quo rather than thinking for themselves. Although he believes that prospects for autonomy confront 'indescribable difficulties' today, Adorno thinks that autonomy might be achieved if education were to become 'an education for contradiction and resistance'.[57]

The previous chapter showed that critical self-reflection is also needed if resistance to our exchange-based society is to become more effective. Unmasking the forces that prevent us from thinking for ourselves, Adornian critique gives individuals 'insight into society's laws of motion' with the ultimate aim of promoting maturity. In fact, Adorno defines resistance in Kantian terms as 'the ability to distinguish between what is known and what is accepted merely by the constraint of authority'. To this he adds that resistance is 'one with critique'.[58] In a much less Kantian vein, however, Adorno argues that '[s]omething would already be achieved if philosophy . . . sought to bring people's consciousness of

---

54   Adorno and Hellmut Becker, 'Education for Autonomy', *Telos* 56, p. 103. Cited in Jarvis, *Adorno*, p. 77. For a later translation of this conversation between Adorno and Becker, see 'Education for Maturity and Responsibility', *History of the Human Sciences* 12.

55   Yet Adorno does suggest that intellectuals and academics are cowardly in *History and Freedom*, p. 165.

56   See, for example, ND 41; trans. mod.: 'Under social conditions – educational ones, in particular – which prune and often cripple the forces of mental productivity, . . . it would be fictitious to assume that all people might understand, or even perceive, all things. To expect this would be to make cognition accord with the pathic features of a humankind stripped of its capacity for experience by a law of perpetual sameness – if it ever had this capacity.'

57   Adorno and Becker, 'Education for Autonomy', pp. 108–9 *passim.*

58   Adorno, 'Critique', *Critical Models*, p. 282.

themselves to the same state of knowledge that they have of nature'.[59] Indeed, if individuals were aware of 'what the world has done to them', they would be 'different from what they are and could not be turned into whatever it is that the course of the world has made of them'.[60]

Tracing the critical tradition in philosophy all the way back to Xenophanes, Adorno also endorsed 'Kant's famous dictum that the critical path is the only one still open to us'.[61] According to Adorno, moreover, it is no accident that Kant – 'who taught autonomy, that is, judgment according to one's own insight in contrast to heteronomy, obedience to what is urged by others' – named his three major works 'critiques'. Yet Adorno went much further than Kant when he linked critique and maturity to democratic forms of government, arguing that the 'separation of powers, upon which every democracy is based, from Locke and Montesquieu and the American constitution up to today, has its lifeblood in critique'. Since this separation enables each power to criticize the others, critique 'and the prerequisite of democracy, political maturity, belong together'.[62]

As for Foucault, he says that he belongs to the critical tradition inaugurated by Kant because he is trying to discover the modes of subjectivation that make it possible for subjects to be constituted as individuals. But Foucault obviously situates himself within the Kantian tradition for other reasons as well. Endorsing the Kantian project of a critical ontology of the present, Foucault follows Kant when he tries to unearth the practices and mechanisms that impede maturity. He accepts Kant's equation of critique with enlightenment because, in both, there is a refusal to submit blindly to the will of authorities.[63] Like Adorno, however, Foucault differs from Kant when he links critique to democracy (if only indirectly) and advocates 'the art of not being governed, . . . the art of not being governed like that and at this price', or 'the art of not being governed so much'.[64] Again, Foucault claims that enlightenment requires a redistribution of relations between government of self and the government of others.[65]

In a related definition of critique, Foucault states that critique is 'the movement through which the subject gives itself the right to question truth concerning its power effects and to question power about its discourses of truth'. To this, Foucault adds that his view of critique resembles Kant's idea of enlightenment because both critique and enlightenment involve 'the art of voluntary inservitude, of reflective indocility'.[66] According to Foucault, moreover, philosophy exemplifies this art: the entire history of philosophy is the history of *parrēsia*, a history of the courageous practice of speaking truth to power. This practice has

59   Adorno, 'Why Still Philosophy', *Critical Models*, p. 15.
60   Adorno, *History and Freedom*, p. 73.
61   Adorno, 'Why Still Philosophy', *Critical Models*, p. 7.
62   Adorno, 'Critique', *Critical Models*, pp. 281–2 *passim*.
63   Foucault, 'What is Critique?', *What Is Enlightenment?*, p. 386.
64   Ibid., p. 384.
65   Foucault, *The Government of Self and Others*, p. 33.
66   Foucault, 'What is Critique?', *What is Enlightenment?*, p. 386.

been a permanent feature of philosophy for 'at least two and a half millennia'.[67] More germane to the present discussion, Foucault contends that the Greek notion of *parrēsia* foreshadows Kant's idea of critique: 'Kant's text on the *Aufklärung* is a certain way for philosophy, through the critique of the *Aufklärung*, to become aware of problems which were traditionally problems of *parrēsia* in antiquity.'[68]

Gordon observes that Foucault distinguished between two senses of enlightenment. The first is 'an Enlightenment of sure identity, conviction and destiny', and the second is an 'Enlightenment which is question and questioning, which is committed to uncertainty'.[69] Adopting the latter idea of enlightenment, Foucault criticized the former. Here Gordon implicitly makes a point some of whose ramifications will be discussed at the end of this book, namely that Foucault challenged enlightenment in the name of enlightenment. In so doing, Foucault acknowledged that he was raising a question that had already been asked by the Frankfurt School: whether 'the Enlightenment's promise of attaining freedom through the exercise of reason has been turned upside down, resulting in a domination by reason itself, which increasingly usurps the place of freedom'.[70]

In Adorno as well, critique challenges enlightenment in the name of enlightenment when it reveals that we have become entangled in mechanisms of domination that the 'enlightened' scientific age developed when it disenchanted nature and began to subject human beings themselves to increasingly coercive mechanisms of manipulation and control.[71] In other words, to become more enlightened, we must reflect critically on the legacy of enlightenment. Indeed, in his essay on enlightenment, Foucault offers another definition of enlightened critique that Adorno would undoubtedly accept: critique involves imagining the present as other than what it is now, and transforming it, but only 'by grasping it in what it is'. To this, Foucault adds that critique involves transforming our relation to ourselves by turning ourselves into 'the object of a complex and difficult elaboration'.[72]

---

67   Foucault, *The Government of Self and Others*, p. 230. See also Foucault, 'The Ethics of the Concern for Self as a Practice of Freedom', *Essential Works: Ethics*, pp. 300–1. When asked whether it is philosophy's role to 'warn of the dangers of power', Foucault responded: 'This has always been an important function of philosophy. In its critical aspect – and I mean critical in a broad sense – philosophy . . . calls into question domination at every level and in every form in which it exists, whether political, economic, sexual, institutional, or what have you.'

68   Ibid., p. 350.

69   Gordon, 'Question, Ethos, Event', *Economy and Society*, pp. 74–5.

70   Foucault, 'Interview with Michel Foucault', *Essential Works: Power*, p. 273.

71   Foucault refers indirectly to what Weber called the disenchantment of the world in STP 234–7. There, he calls it the 'degovernmentalization of the cosmos' (STP 236). Once the idea of God's pastoral government of the world had been called into question, Western states began to assume many pastoral functions.

72   Foucault, 'What is Enlightenment?', *Essential Works: Ethics*, p. 311. Since I am arguing here that Adorno himself adopts this Marxist perspective on critique, and that he is looking for alternatives, I also take issue with Robert Lanning in *In the Hotel Abyss*. See for example, page 5, where Lanning claims that Adorno comes up short with regard to change and alternatives.

Questioning 'over and over again what is postulated as self-evident', Foucauldian critique aims to disturb 'people's mental habits, the way they do and think things, to dissipate what is familiar and accepted, to reexamine rules and institutions'.[73] Echoing Adorno, Foucault also believes that, once 'people begin to have trouble thinking things the way they have been thought, transformation becomes at the same time very urgent, very difficult, and entirely possible'.[74] Consequently, one goal of Foucauldian critique is to achieve a Brechtian *Verfremdungseffekt*: critique consists in estranging individuals from 'the assumptions, . . . familiar notions, [and] unexamined ways of thinking' on which 'accepted practices are based'.[75] What lies at the heart of critique is '[t]he experience through which we grasp the intelligibility of certain mechanisms . . . and the way in which we are enabled to detach ourselves from them by perceiving them differently'.[76] As for Adorno, he too recommends that social critics should fashion perspectives on the world that seek to 'displace and estrange' it by making what is familiar, or taken for granted, appear strange (MM 247).

Since critique is 'an attitude at once individual and collective, to emerge, as Kant said, from one's immaturity', Foucault implies that critics themselves must become enlightened.[77] Adorno obviously shares his view: critics must examine their own entanglement in mechanisms of domination – they must be critical of themselves. By extension, Adorno and Foucault suggest that critique may serve as a model for maturity.[78] Their critiques of the West are performative because they attempt to model the critical self-reflection that they aim to foster in others. Consequently, on one reading of the claim that humanity can be conceived only through an 'extreme form of differentiation', namely 'individuation', Adorno implies that critics may act, at least temporarily – and with a profound sense of their own fallibility – as stand-ins for the species.[79] Critics may stand in for the species because their concerted attempts to think for themselves, to criticize the conditions that adversely affect their own thought and behaviour, make them more autonomous than those who simply adapt and conform to these conditions. For Adorno, once again, '[t]he freedom of philosophy is nothing other than the capacity to lend a voice to its own unfreedom' (ND 19).

Making visible the social, political and economic forces that have shaped all individuals, including themselves, Adorno and Foucault do more than provide a model for maturity. For by encouraging individuals to look more critically at themselves and the forces that have shaped them as they question the meaning,

---

73   Foucault, 'The Concern for Truth', *Politics, Philosophy, Culture*, p. 265.
74   Foucault, 'So is it Important to Think?', *Essential Works: Power*, p. 457.
75   Ibid., p. 456.
76   Foucault, 'Interview with Michel Foucault', *Essential Works: Power*, p. 244.
77   Foucault, 'What is Critique?', *What is Enlightenment?*, p. 398; trans. mod.
78   Viewing critique as a form of practice in its own right, Adorno called two collections of his critical essays 'models'. See Adorno, *Critical Models*.
79   Adorno, 'Progress', *Critical Models*, p. 151.

conditions and goals of their actions,[80] Adorno and Foucault also hope to make it possible for individuals to find effective ways to refuse the identities that have been foisted on them and to constitute their identities autonomously. Even as they unearth the processes of individuation and social integration that make a mockery of our individuality, they aim to promote in individuals a more conscious and critical sense of their nonidentity with respect to the social forces that have shaped them.

When he shows that our identities have been constituted by socio-economic forces that operate over our heads and through them, Adorno only underscores his interest in 'the utopian particular that has been buried beneath the universal – with that nonidentity which would not come into being until realized reason has left the particular reason of the universal behind' (ND 318). Freed from coercive identity-formation, from the compulsive internalization of, and adaptation to, social norms, individuals would shape themselves more independently than they currently do precisely by exercising their capacity for critical reflection and self-reflection. However, to reiterate a point that was made in the previous chapter, Adorno denies that critique alone can put an end to modes of individuation which effectively make all individuals the same by restricting their life activity to ensuring their own survival. To release individuals from 'the idol in the mirror', society must be completely transformed (ND 349). Critique is a necessary, but not a sufficient, condition for this transformation. Critique may reveal what is wrong about society by showing how and why human life has been damaged, but it cannot make the wrong life right.

Of course, Foucault insists that critique should be accompanied by political action in local sites, but he too recognizes that, as a form of resistance in its own right, 'criticism (and radical criticism) is utterly indispensable for any transformation.'[81] Involving 'an attitude, an ethos, a philosophical life', his critical ontology of the present combines an 'historical analysis of the limits imposed on us and an experiment with the possibility of going beyond them' (SP 319). Since it reveals how our identities have been shaped by our guardians – or by what physicians, teachers, psychologists and other experts consider normal or natural – Foucauldian critique simultaneously promotes desubjection and desubjectification.[82] It aims to liberate 'our subjectivity, our relation to ourselves'.[83]

Although critics may serve as models for more autonomous individuals, it is not possible to say precisely what autonomous individuals will ultimately look

---

80   I am paraphrasing Foucault in 'Polemics, Politics, and Problematizations', *Essential Works: Ethics*, p. 116.

81   Foucault, 'So is it Important to Think?', *Essential Works: Power*, pp. 456–7 *passim*.

82   Foucault, 'What is Critique?', *What is Enlightenment?*, p. 386. In *The Politics of Our Selves*, p. 60, Allen notes that Foucault uses the word '*désassujettisement*' here. She translates this word as 'desubjection', but it also means desubjectification. I am using both words because Foucault often emphasized the double meaning of '*assujettissement*'.

83   Foucault, 'Foucault étudie la Raison d'Etat', *Dits et écrits* III, p. 802.

like (not to speak of envisaging a society that accommodates them). To reiterate, with his study of ancient practices of the self in later work, Foucault was by no means proposing that we model ourselves after Seneca or Marcus Aurelius, or even after the Cynics whose aim of 'changing the value of the currency' – of 'changing the custom, breaking with it, breaking up the rules, habits, conventions, and laws' – he so clearly admired.[84] Individuals must invent new ways to constitute themselves, and they may use ancient practices as resources but only to the extent that these exemplify the critical reflexivity that is needed to make resistance more effective. Here too, Adorno mirrors Foucault's intransigence: 'in the right condition . . . things would differ only a little from the way they are; but not even the least can be conceived now as it would be then' (ND 300).

But if this is the case, and Adorno and Foucault can only gesture towards alternative conceptions of the individual and society, one might be tempted to question the normative bases for their critiques of our historical present. On what normative grounds do Adorno and Foucault claim that Western society is evil or demonic? One of the more prominent figures who has raised this issue is Jürgen Habermas. On his reading of Adorno in *The Philosophical Discourse of Modernity*, for example, Habermas objects that Adorno's confidence in modernity was shaken so badly by Nazism and Stalinism that his scepticism extended to reason itself.[85] Yet since Adorno realized that he needed 'at least one rational criterion' to account for 'the corruption of *all* rational criteria',[86] he opted for 'the paradoxical concept of the nonidentical' and 'the mimetic content hidden in avant-garde works of art'.[87] Posing a similar challenge to Foucault, Habermas asks why he prefers struggle to submission: 'Why ought domination . . . be resisted?' According to Habermas, Foucault could answer this question only if he had normative criteria against which to judge the 'modern power-knowledge regime'.[88] Here, Habermas implies that Foucault lacks even 'paradoxical' concepts to ground his critique.

Since these criticisms have been so influential, I shall respond here to Habermas' charge that Adorno's and Foucault's critiques not only lack, but require, more adequate normative grounding. To begin with Adorno, the basis for his critique lies in determinate negation, or in the negation of the negative social conditions in which we live. In an inversion of Baruch Spinoza's dictum, Adorno states in his essay 'Critique' that it is the false, 'determinately known and precisely expressed', that provides 'an index of what is right and better'.[89] He repeats this remark in his lectures on *Negative Dialectics* where he goes so far as

---

84   See Foucault, *The Courage of Truth*, p. 242.
85   Jürgen Habermas, *The Philosophical Discourse of Modernity*, p. 116.
86   Ibid., p. 127.
87   Ibid., p. 129.
88   Ibid., p. 284.
89   Adorno, 'Critique', *Critical Models*, p. 288. In this discussion of determinate negation, I am developing ideas that I advanced in much of my work, most recently in 'Through a Glass Darkly', *Adorno Studies*.

to call determinate negation a 'methodological principle'. Challenging Spinoza's claim 'that *verum index sui et falsi*, or that the true and the false can both be read directly . . . from the truth', Adorno again counters 'that the false, that which should not be the case, is *in fact* the standard of itself: . . . the false, namely that which is not itself in the first instance – i.e. not itself in the sense that it is not what it claims to be – that this falseness proclaims itself in what we might call a certain immediacy, and this immediacy of the false, this *falsum*, is the *index sui atque veri*'. To this, Adorno adds that determinate negation offers 'a certain pointer' to '"right thinking"'.[90]

The false is an index of the true because it points dialectically to its own reversal.[91] With respect to our ideas about freedom, for example, Adorno argues that they are derived from the negation of unfree conditions: freedom 'can only be grasped in determinate negation in accordance with the concrete form of a specific unfreedom' (ND 231). Consequently, and as Elizabeth Pritchard also observes, far from banning ideas about a better world, Adorno attempts to arrive at ideas about improved conditions by inverting our ideas about existing ones.[92] Determinate negation can serve as a basis for critique because it enables critics to envisage – albeit only indirectly – an improved state of affairs against which damaged life can be judged. In fact, Adorno suggests that there are fragments of good in the world, but these can be glimpsed only obliquely by those who resist, in their critiques of damaged life, the injustice, unfreedom and oppression that lie at the root of so much human suffering.

Hence, I disagree with Freyenhagen when he denies that Adorno points, even obliquely, towards positive ideas of 'the good'.[93] For Adornian critique relies on weak, and entirely fallible, ideas about the good (including ideas about maturity and autonomy) derived from a critical assessment of life under late capitalism. Although determinate negation does not provide a clear and distinct idea of the good (let alone an idea of the good in itself), the practical orientation that its intimations of a better future offer is important in its own right. Indeed, Adorno remarked in a conversation with Ernst Bloch that, if we cannot speak at all about a better state of affairs, then we cannot even say why critique is necessary.[94] Here too, Adorno claimed that the false is an index of the true.[95] This claim is repeated in 'Individuum und Organisation' where Adorno wrote: 'we may not know what people are and what the correct arrangement of human affairs should be but we do know what they should not be and what

90   Adorno, *Lectures on 'Negative Dialectics'*, pp. 28–9; trans. mod.
91   Adorno, 'Progress', *Critical Models*, p. 149.
92   Elizabeth Pritchard, '*Bilderverbot* Meets Body in Adorno's Inverse Theology', p. 193.
93   Freyenhagen, *Adorno's Practical Philosophy*, p. 215.
94   Adorno and Bloch, 'Something's Missing', *The Utopian Function of Art and* Literature, p. 13. Unfortunately, the translation of this conversation between Bloch and Adorno is faulty and I am paraphrasing Adorno's ideas here.
95   Ibid., p. 12.

arrangement of human affairs is false'. Only in this knowledge of the false is 'the other, positive, knowledge open to us'.[96]

Ideas of a better life can be gleaned from 'resistance to the forms of the bad life that have been seen through and critically dissected'.[97] In a more poetic vein, Adorno also said that '[g]rayness could not fill us with despair if our minds did not harbor the concept of different colors, scattered traces of which are not absent from the negative whole' (ND 377). Still, it is important to stress that, since these scattered traces of different colours are derived from a critique of damaged life, they are also tainted by the negativity of that life. Even if we could 'imagine all things radically altered', our images of things would remain chained to ourselves and 'to our present time as static points of reference, and everything would be askew' (ND 352). For these reasons, then, critique encounters insuperable limits. Employing another vivid metaphor that only underscores these limits, Adorno avers that critics must do 'what the miner's adage forbids: work their way through the darkness without a lamp, without possessing the positive through the higher [viz. Hegelian] concept of the negation of the negation, and immerse themselves in the darkness as deeply as they possibly can'.[98] Of course, by problematizing critique in this way, Adorno demands humility from critics. Individuals who 'will not be stopped from differing and criticizing' are not authorized to put themselves in the right because their criticisms are sullied by the very reality they hope to change (ND 352).

Acknowledging both the limits of critique and its fallibility, Adorno nonetheless argues that determinate negation offers the only viable leverage on existing conditions because it enables critics to envisage something that lies beyond these conditions and to indicate directions for change. Adorno's colleagues in the Frankfurt School adopted similar views. For example, Marcuse argued in *One-Dimensional Man* that the emphatic concepts derived from determinate negation 'conceptualize the stuff of which the experienced world consists, and they conceptualize it with a view of its possibilities, in light of their actual limitation, suppression and denial'.[99] For his part, Horkheimer emphasized the historicity of these concepts when he wrote: 'At all times, the good has shown the traces of the oppression in which it originated.' For Horkheimer, it is the very 'shackling' of our thoughts and actions that creates 'the prerequisites of the emancipation of reason'.[100] To give an example that is relevant to the present discussion, the concept of autonomy, which is indelibly marked by traces of the heteronomy that prompted its formation, points to a potential that remains unrealized. It expresses 'the possibility of which their reality has cheated' individuals, but 'which is nonetheless visible in each one' (ND 52).

---

96   Adorno, 'Individuum und Organisation', *Soziologische Schriften* I, p. 456.
97   Adorno, *Problems of Moral Philosophy*, pp. 167–8.
98   Adorno, *Metaphysics*, p. 144.
99   Marcuse, *One-Dimensional Man*, p. 215.
100 Horkheimer, *Eclipse of Reason*, p. 177 *passim*.

Although he realizes that Adorno made use of determinate negation, Habermas alleges that Adorno later appealed to nonidentity and mimesis as normative grounds for his critical theory. On this point, however, Habermas is simply mistaken. With respect to Adorno's much-touted but largely misunderstood concept of mimesis, Bernstein rightly notes that Adorno wanted to expand both reason and the 'scope and character of cognitive life' by rethinking conceptuality; he by no means wanted to replace reason 'with aesthetic praxis and judgement'.[101] Furthermore, Habermas fails to see that nonidentity is bound up with determinate negation since it is, in part, through the determinate negation of existing conditions that the nonidentity of concept and object, society and the individual, comes to the fore. In other words, determinate negation may bring to light the better potential that Western societies are 'containing' (to borrow Marcuse's phrase) – not to say crushing.

On Habermas' reading of *Dialectic of Enlightenment*, however, determinate negation was practised by Adorno and Horkheimer 'on an ad hoc basis' as a way of standing 'firm against that fusion of reason and power that plugs all crevices'. Arguing that Adorno and Horkheimer were trying to occupy 'the very spot once occupied by philosophy with its ultimate groundings', Habermas argues that they could legitimately occupy that position only if they made it 'at least minimally plausible' that there was no other way out. Since it is beyond the scope of this study to respond to Habermas' counterclaim that communicative rationality provides a viable *Ausgang* (and I have done so elsewhere), I shall confine myself here to addressing his objection that determinate negation, or the 'practiced spirit of contradiction', is 'all that remains' of Adorno's theory.[102]

On this point, it must be conceded that Habermas is essentially right. In fact, Fotini Vaki adds more critical weight to Habermas' highly polemical interpretation of Adorno when she asks just how far Adorno can go 'by relying only on the recognition of contradictions'.[103] Vaki also objects that Adorno's normative standpoint 'is only glimpsed indirectly in a completely unspecified way', and that he never clarifies the conditions under which ideas derived from determinate negation would become 'a concrete possibility'.[104] Yet Vaki fails to see that Adorno readily concedes these points. His 'negative prescription' to critique damaged life in order to arrive at entirely fallible ideas about a less damaged one is the sole form of guidance he is willing to give.[105] Adorno admits

---

101   Bernstein, *Adorno*, p. 4.
102   Habermas, *The Philosophical Discourse of Modernity*, p. 128. See my criticisms of Habermas' notion of communicative rationality in *Adorno, Habermas, and the Search for a Rational Society*.
103   Fotini Vaki, 'Adorno *contra* Habermas and the Claims of Critical Theory as Immanent Critique', *Historical Materialism*, p. 114.
104   Ibid., p. 116.
105   Adorno, *Problems of Moral Philosophy*, pp. 167–8.

that he cannot clarify the conditions under which a better life would be realized because determinate negation can do no more than offer a glimpse of something better. Finally, to the related charge that determinate negation is a weak methodological principle, Adorno would reply that no more secure standpoint for critique exists.

Those who seek the kind of grounding for critique that Habermas claims to have found will probably remain dissatisfied with determinate negation.[106] For Adorno argues that we have no choice but to start from where we are: our ideas about improved conditions are always forged in the crucible of our experiences of damaged life and in our resistance to it. Pain and negativity are 'the moving forces of dialectical thinking' because they have prompted individuals to seek reality's better potential (ND 202). Equally important, Adorno objects that it is an 'outrage' to demand the kind of philosophical justification that Habermas believes is needed to legitimate acts that aim to alleviate suffering (ND 365). Since the conditions that cause suffering today are also those that made Auschwitz possible, it would be outrageous to insist that, before attempting to change these conditions, we find ultimate moral groundings for our actions.[107] Indeed, Adorno also argues that the very presumption of moral certainty 'would be immoral'; it 'would falsely relieve the individual of anything that might be called morality'. Today, no moral decision can be 'warranted as the right one' (ND 242–3).

Like Adorno, Foucault also admits that he lacks ultimate grounding for his critique of the present. This fact has exercised many commentators, including Nancy Fraser, who first posed the question that Habermas takes up in *The Philosophical Discourse of Modernity*, namely, why struggle?, why resist?[108] Noting that Foucault seems to appeal to norms when he criticizes our subjection to power, Fraser asks about the 'normative framework' that grounds his critique. According to Fraser, Foucault rules out liberal and Marxian normative frameworks[109] because he, like the early Frankfurt School theorists (including Adorno), was 'openly suspicious of attempts to formulate a positive, theoretical basis for critique'. However, Fraser revises her argument when she goes on to claim that Foucault surreptitiously made use of a liberal humanist framework.[110] Since this framework appeals to autonomy, dignity and human rights, Fraser

---

106   Referring indirectly to *The Theory of Communicative Action*, Habermas argues that, if Adorno and Horkheimer had not 'surrendered to an uninhibited scepticism regarding reason', they might have understood 'the grounds that cast doubt on this scepticism itself'. They might also have been able to set (as Habermas thinks he has done) 'the normative foundations of critical social theory so deep that they would not have been disturbed by the decomposition of bourgeois culture that was then being enacted in Germany for all to see'. See Habermas, *The Philosophical Discourse of Modernity*, p. 129.

107   In Chapter Seven of *Adorno's Practical Philosophy*, Freyenhagen offers a more extended discussion of Adorno's views on this issue than I can provide here.

108   Nancy Fraser, *Unruly Practices*, p. 29.

109   Ibid., pp. 29–30.

110   Ibid., p. 56.

praises Foucault for trying to keep humanism honest by criticizing it from within.[111]

Against Fraser, however, one could question whether autonomy is a specifically liberal or humanist norm, especially since Foucault convincingly traces the concern for autonomy all the way back to ancient Greece, noting that Hellenistic and Roman culture adopted ancient Greek techniques oriented towards care of the self, even as it reactivated and reorganized them.[112] But one could also try to clarify the grounds on which Foucault's appeal to autonomy rests. Here one could invoke, in Adornian fashion, autonomy's counterconcept – heteronomy – and point to the constraints that are placed on individuals by disciplinary power and biopower. In fact, Gutting has advanced an argument like this, thereby bringing Foucault into closer proximity with Adorno.[113] Still, it is also important to note that, rather than offering a philosophical justification for resistance, Foucault often shows that some individuals and groups simply do struggle against the constraints of power. On the basis of his studies of resistance, Foucault observed that 'a system of constraint becomes truly intolerable when the individuals who are affected by it don't have the means of modifying it', when they are denied 'the liberty to transform the system', or to alter the constraints that are placed on them.[114]

Nevertheless, Foucault's interest in autonomy is not simply a function of his insights into what motivates struggles in the West because autonomy is one of the principal normative commitments of his own critique. In fact, Foucault explicitly opposes his work to the 'humanist thematic' on the grounds that he endorses 'the principle of a critique and a permanent creation of ourselves in our autonomy'.[115] Leslie Thiele offers a Nietzschean reading of this goal. Targeting Fraser, Thiele contends that, rather than defending autonomy on humanist

---

111   Ibid., pp. 64–5. Lynch also defends Foucault against Fraser in *Foucault's Critical Ethics*. However, our arguments differ in important respects, and I emphasize Foucault's normative commitment to autonomy.

112   See Foucault, *The Hermeneutics of the Subject*, p. 50. In fact, on page 254, Foucault says that care of the self became 'an autonomous, self-finalized art imparting value to the whole of life' in Hellenistic and Roman culture. See also Foucault, *Subjectivité et Vérité*, p. 110; my translation: 'at one and the same time, autonomy is the goal and the form of philosophical existence. Autonomy entails self-mastery.' Moreover, it makes no sense to speak, as Koopman does in *Genealogy as Critique*, of a transformative freedom that works through power to recreate itself while denying that freedom requires autonomy. Allen also stresses the importance of autonomy for Foucault throughout *The Politics of Our Selves*. Koopman does not successfully refute her.

113   See Gutting, *Michel Foucault's Archaeology of Scientific Reason*, p. 284. Here Gutting argues that Foucault grounds normative judgements, not in philosophical principles, but in 'our direct, practical encounters with alleged sources of domination . . . There are, of course, many errors to which judgments formed from direct experience are susceptible. But these errors are much more limited and more readily corrected by further experiences than are judgments rooted in general philosophical theories. Indeed, such theories have themselves proved to be among the greatest dangers to human freedom.'

114   Foucault, 'Sexual Choice, Sexual Act', *Essential Works: Ethics*, pp. 147–8 *passim*.

115   Foucault, 'What is Enlightenment?', *Essential Works: Ethics*, p. 314.

grounds, Foucault adopts a perspective in which we always find ourselves 'involved in the struggle of becoming', of creating and recreating ourselves. Since self-creation occurs within specific historical conditions – conditions that may be more or less favourable to the aspirations of those who are situated within them – what must be preserved or created 'are the political, social, and cultural conditions under which individuals are allowed the possibility of struggling to change these same conditions'. By extension, individuals must also be able to change 'the conditions that influence their means of understanding and identifying themselves'.[116]

Like Adorno, Foucault also refuses to dictate what is to be done. One of the primary functions of Foucauldian critique is simply 'to analyse, to elucidate, to make visible and thus to intensify struggles against power'.[117] As is well known, Foucault called himself a specific intellectual. Intellectuals are specific when they work within local sectors, including the sectors where 'their own conditions of life and work situate them'.[118] Collaborating with others who are also struggling against power in these sectors, the role of specific intellectuals is confined to raising 'questions in an effective, genuine way', to raising them 'with the greatest possible rigor, with the maximum complexity and difficulty so that a solution doesn't spring from the head of some reformist intellectual or suddenly appear in the head of a party's political bureau'.[119]

Nevertheless, it is important to reiterate that Foucault often complained about the poverty of our political imaginations, and he tried to stimulate them by asking penetrating questions about our present.[120] Moreover, I have already shown that Foucault's refusal to provide positive blueprints for what is to be done did not prevent him from speculating about the future. In *The Order of Things*, for example, Foucault spoke about a decisive rupture, caesura or paradigm shift that could result in the death of 'man'. He speculated about the emergence of a new form of reason in *History of Madness*, about instituting an antidisciplinarian form of right in *Discipline and Punish*, and about a new ethic of bodies and pleasures in *The History of Sexuality*. Such speculation can be defended on the Adornian grounds that every critical assessment of society outlines, if only indirectly, alternatives. Again – and like Marx, who said that he did not want 'dogmatically to prefigure the future, but . . . to find the new world only through criticism of our own'[121] – Foucault remarks that he is trying to imagine the present as other than what it is but only by understanding what it is.

116   Thiele, 'The Agony of Politics', *The American Political Science Review*, p. 919.
117   Foucault, 'La Philosophie analytique de la Politique', *Dits et Écrits* III, p. 540.
118   Foucault, 'Truth and Power', *Essential Works: Power*, p. 126.
119   Foucault, 'Interview with Michel Foucault', *Essential Works: Power*, p. 288.
120   I am paraphrasing Foucault in 'Méthodologie pour la Connaissance du Monde', *Dits et écrits* III, p. 599.
121   Marx and Engels, *The Marx-Engels Reader*, p. 13. Cited in Lynch, *Foucault's Critical Ethics*, p. 4. It is Lynch who points out, quoting Fraser, that Foucault agrees with Marx, though neither he nor Fraser refers to Foucault's remark in 'What is Enlightenment?' to illustrate this point.

Still, given his concerns about the poverty of our imaginations, Foucault's spec-
ulations may also be interpreted as an attempt to provoke those who resist to
think 'outside of the box', rather than to provide an ironclad blueprint for the
future.

Foucault was also well aware that there are important limits to what critics
can imagine because critics 'are themselves agents of this system of power'.[122] He
gave due consideration to the objection that his attempt to restrict critique to an
'always partial and local inquiry or test' ran the serious risk that critics might be
'determined by more general structures' of which they are not conscious.
Acknowledging the legitimacy of this objection, Foucault concedes that 'we
have to give up hope of ever acceding to a point of view that could give us access
to any complete and definitive knowledge of what may constitute our historical
limits'. For Foucault, 'the theoretical and practical experience we have of our
limits, and of the possibility of moving beyond them, is [itself] always limited
and determined'. This is why critics 'are always in the position of beginning
again'.[123] Like Adorno, then, Foucault recognized that critics are entirely fallible,
human, all too human; their ability to imagine alternatives is occulted by the
very conditions they seek to change.

In this context, it is also interesting to note that Adorno and Foucault had
strikingly similar ideas about the nature of thought. According to Adorno,
thought inherently resists 'mere things in being' (ND 19). In thought, human
beings distance themselves from the world, if only unwittingly, refusing passively
to accept what is given. Examples of resistive thought range 'from the primitive,
who contemplates how he can protect his small fire from the rain or where he
can find shelter from the storm, to the Enlightenment philosopher who
construes how humanity can move beyond its self-incurred tutelage by means
of its interest in self-preservation'.[124] But the resistance of thought to mere things
in being is all the more powerful when it takes the form of a critique that is
based on ideas derived from the determinate negation of damaged life. Resolutely
critical, negative dialectics indicts damaged life by virtue of the orientation that
some concepts (such as freedom and autonomy) may provide towards the unrealized possibilities that are embedded in it. These concepts give critics the freedom 'to step out of the object, a freedom which the identity claim cuts short'
(ND 28).

It is just this critical and speculative approach that distinguishes negative
dialectics from positivism. Criticizing positivism, Adorno remarks that, by failing to detach itself from the objects on which it is reflecting, and doggedly stick-
ing to facts, positivism 'loses not only its autonomy in the face of reality but,
with it, the power to penetrate reality'. Critics can engage with damaged life only
if they remain at a remove from it. Indeed, criticism requires 'an element of

122   Foucault, 'Intellectuals and Power', *Language, Counter-Memory, Practice*, p. 207.
123   Foucault, 'What is Enlightenment?', *Essential Works: Ethics*, pp. 316–17.
124   Adorno, 'Marginalia to Theory and Praxis', *Critical Models*, pp. 264–5; trans. mod.

exaggeration'. By 'exaggeration', Adorno means an element 'of over-shooting the object, of self-detachment from the weight of the factual, so that instead of merely reproducing being, thought can, at once rigorous and free, determine it' (MM 126–7). Although he freely admits that exaggeration 'harbors the potential for delusion as well as for truth', Adorno also claims that all thinking 'is exaggeration in so far as every thought that is a thought at all goes beyond its confirmation by the existing facts'.[125]

Adorno associated speculative thought, not just with resistance, but with freedom: the 'speculative surplus that goes beyond whatever is the case, beyond mere existence, is the element of freedom in thought'.[126] And Foucault values the speculative dimension of thought for the same reason. He claims that thought 'is what allows one to step back' from a particular 'way of acting or reacting, to present it to oneself as an object . . . and to question it as to its meaning, its conditions, and its goals'. For Foucault too, thought is inherently resistive; it involves 'freedom in relation to what one does, the motion by which one detaches oneself from it, establishes it as an object, and reflects on it as a problem'.[127] Foucauldian critique exemplifies the resistive dimension of thought when it shows 'that things are not as obvious as people believe, making it so that what is taken for granted is no longer taken for granted'.[128]

Foucault famously called his genealogies historical fictions, adding that what he had written was partial and exaggerated from an historical perspective.[129] He made this provocative remark in several interviews, but he suggested how it might be interpreted in a 1977 conversation with Lucette Finas that was originally published in *La Quinzaine Littéraire*. Telling Finas that he had never written anything but fictions, Foucault nonetheless insisted that truth is not completely absent from his work because 'fiction can function within truth'. Fictitious in the sense that it '"manufactures" something that does not exist', his work also rests on 'a political reality that makes it true'. Or, in another formulation, his work '"fictions" a politics not yet in existence on the basis of a historical truth'.[130] Here too Foucault highlights the speculative dimension of his genealogies: struggles waged against existing modes of subjection in the West outline a fictitious world – a world that does not yet exist and that may never exist – in which these modes of subjection have ended.

125   Adorno, 'Opinion Delusion Society', *Critical Models*, p. 108 *passim*; trans. mod.
126   Adorno, *Lectures on 'Negative Dialectics'*, p. 108.
127   Foucault, 'Polemics, Politics, and Problematizations', *Essential Works: Ethics*, p. 117.
128   Foucault, 'So is it Important to Think?', *Essential Works: Ethics*, p. 456.
129   Foucault, 'Foucault étudie la Raison d'Etat', *Dits et écrits* III, p. 40.
130   Foucault, 'The History of Sexuality', *Power/Knowledge*, p. 193. I originally made this point in 'History as Fiction', *The Journal of the British Society for Phenomenology*. Indeed, I agree with Martin Saar about the importance of the shock value of exaggeration and hyperbole, not just in Foucault but in Adorno as well. See Saar, 'Genealogy and Subjectivity', *European Journal of Philosophy*. Moreover, Allen is right to say that this is what Nietzsche meant by 'philosophizing with a hammer'. See Allen, *The End of Progress*, p. 195.

Attempting to stimulate our impoverished political imaginations, Adorno's and Foucault's speculative critiques of our present also seek to foster maturity in the Kantian sense, not just with a view to aiding those who resist, but to serve as a bulwark against fascism. Indeed, James Bernauer notes that Foucault has been called the patron saint of the study of fascism, but this epithet certainly applies to Adorno as well.[131] Adorno's critique of the historical conditions that made fascism possible also included important empirical studies of prejudice and authoritarianism.[132] Auschwitz became a cipher in his work for the fascist tendencies that continue to plague the West. According to Adorno, Hitler imposed a new categorical imperative 'on unfree humankind: to arrange their thoughts and actions so that Auschwitz will not repeat itself, so that nothing similar will happen' again (ND 365). Echoing Adorno, Foucault declares that fascism remains the 'strategic adversary'. How, Foucault asks, can we cultivate an art of living that will counter all forms of fascism?[133] Of course, Adorno's and Foucault's concerns about a resurgence of fascism also help to explain their strong normative commitments to autonomy – an autonomy that, in Kant, remained a mere postulate of reason, and that continues to elude individuals in the Western world.

---

131   Bernauer, 'Michel Foucault's Philosophy of Religion', *Michel Foucault and Theology*, p. 81. Bernauer is quoting Geoff Eley, 'Scholarship Serving the Nazi State I', *Ethnic and Racial Studies*.

132   See Adorno et al., *The Authoritarian Personality*. See also Adorno, *Guilt and Defense*.

133   Foucault, 'Preface' to Deleuze and Guattari, *Anti-Oedipus*, p. xii.

Chapter 6

Remarks on Western Reason

To end this book, I shall discuss a more general issue that Adorno and Foucault address throughout their work, namely the problem of the rationality that undergirds Western societies. Towards the end of the 1970s, and until his death in 1984, Foucault noted on several occasions that his interest in this problem marks another point of convergence between his work and the work of the Frankfurt School. Before broaching this discussion of Western rationality, however, I shall review some of the points made in previous chapters, while emphasizing once again that none of the differences between Adorno and Foucault that are discussed in this book fatally compromises a rapprochement between them. Although Adorno's and Foucault's critical ontologies of our present highlight distinct dimensions of society, this book has demonstrated that the aims of their critiques and their analyses of the problems that afflict the West are remarkably similar.

I began by showing that Adorno and Foucault were influenced by some of the same thinkers. These shared influences only facilitate the rapprochement that I have attempted here. The influence of Kant and Nietzsche on their work is relatively uncontroversial, but I also argued that Marx was an important interlocutor for both theorists, as were Hegel and Freud. After examining these influences briefly, I observed that Adorno's and Foucault's critical theories generally revolve around two sets of questions: questions concerning concepts and concept formation and questions that concern Western societies and their effects on individuals. In other words, their critical theories converge in their common focus on relations between concepts and objects and between society and individuals. Importantly, they also reveal that things always elude concepts, and that individuals evade complete capture by exchange relations and power relations. In fact, Foucault has his own version of what Adorno calls the nonidentical.

'Is Power Always Secondary to the Economy?' plumbed Adorno's and Foucault's relations to Marx in more detail. Among other things, it showed that Adorno and Foucault retain Marx's view that Western society is stratified into classes even as they rethink and revise it. Nevertheless, given the emergence of Nazism and Stalinism in the twentieth century, Foucault chose to focus his genealogies on the hypertrophy of power in the West. Moreover, where Adorno maintained that Western states remain subordinate to the economy, Foucault often described relations between the economy and the state as reciprocal and complex. Even when he seemed to acknowledge the primacy of the economy in *The Birth of Biopolitics*, Foucault also challenged Adorno indirectly when he denied that Western societies are regulated by exchange relations. However, since Foucault failed to provide support for the neoliberal view that competition has superseded exchange, and he recognized that economic forces now predominate, I concluded that exchange relations should remain the principal target of a critical social theory. At the same time, I argued that Foucault's contention that power is not always subordinate to the economy is defensible, and on Adorno's own terms.

'Notes on Individuation' began by assessing the impact of Freud on Adorno and Foucault. Of course, this assessment challenges the widespread belief that Foucault simply rejected psychoanalytic theory, including Freud's repressive hypothesis and his instinct theory. Against this, I argued that Foucault not only acknowledged the reality of repression, he was interested in the vicissitudes of our impulses or drives. Like Freud, moreover, Adorno and Foucault believed that individuation involves the internalization of norms and the emergence of a moral 'conscience'. Yet they most obviously disagreed about the role that Christianity played in the process of individuation: Adorno largely ignored Christianity's influence on individuation and Foucault highlighted it when he traced disciplinary power and biopower back to pastoral power. Although they both linked individuation to self-reflection, Adorno also thought that self-reflection came into its own with the rise of capitalism whereas Foucault claimed that practices involving self-reflection were already highly developed in the Hellenistic age. In spite of these differences, however, Adorno and Foucault share the view that instincts are the 'stuff' that is fashioned into individuals. They also characterize individuals in similar ways, namely as conformist, submissive, unquestioningly obedient and often prejudiced or racist.

Chapter Four examined Adorno's and Foucault's ideas about resistance. Not only did they both advocate resistance, resistance in their work is broadly directed against the forces that compromise our autonomy. Adorno and Foucault also agreed that resistance has an instinctual component and that it is often motivated by suffering. After comparing Foucault's critique of individualization and totalization to Adorno's critique of individualism and collectivism, Chapter Four demonstrated that they make similar claims about the freedom of individuals. I also defended these claims against the objection that resistance would not be possible given the coercive process of individuation that they describe. Noting that Adorno and Foucault emphasize the importance of self-reflection for resistance, this chapter concluded with a consideration of the goals of resistive struggles. Very generally, Adorno and Foucault contend that resistance seeks to transform individuals, society and the relations between them with the aim of promoting greater autonomy.

Chapter Five compared Adorno's and Foucault's ideas about critique. Since they both referred to their critiques as ontologies, this chapter began with a discussion of their Kantian conceptions of reality and our relation to it. Subsequently, I elaborated on a central theme in this book, namely that Adorno and Foucault devoted their critiques to combating 'the fascism in us all, in our heads and in our everyday behavior, the fascism that causes us to love power, to desire the very thing that dominates and exploits us'.[1] With this aim in mind, their critiques attempted to make the familiar appear strange in order to estrange individuals from the conditions that made fascism possible, thereby potentially enabling individuals to fashion their identities with a greater degree of autonomy. Nevertheless, since the normative basis for their critiques has been contested, I also defended Adorno and Foucault against the criticisms of Jürgen Habermas and others. Conceding that critique is an entirely fallible enterprise, that it does not have an unassailable normative basis, Adorno and Foucault acknowledge the limits of critique, even as they view it as a resistive force in its own right.

Despite his reservations about some aspects of critical theory, Foucault recognized that his work complements Adorno's. However, since he mentioned Adorno by name only once, and that in the context of a private conversation, this book has provided support for his claim that there are indeed striking parallels between his analysis of our carceral society and Adorno's critique of our administered world. As Foucault noted in 'What is Critique?', he considered himself to be a 'brother' of the Frankfurt School because both he and the Frankfurt School make the problem of enlightenment a central concern.[2] Enlightenment is a problem for both because fascism and Stalinism reactivated 'the series of problems that distinguished Max Weber's analyses', namely problems that revolve around reason in the Western world.[3]

When he commented on his affinity with the Frankfurt School in his interview with Trombadori, Foucault praised its theorists for posing problems 'that we are still laboring over today: in particular, the problem of the effects of power and their relation to a rationality that is defined historically and geographically, in the West, from the sixteenth century onward'. He followed up this commendation with a question cited in the previous chapter. Like the Frankfurt School, Foucault also asked whether enlightenment's promise of emancipation through reason has been transformed into domination by reason.[4] I shall parse this question in these concluding remarks by examining Adorno's and Foucault's claims about Western reason in more detail. To begin, I shall describe briefly Adorno's account of reason's historical trajectory.

In *Dialectic of Enlightenment*, Adorno and Horkheimer locate the origins of reason in ancient Greece. They cite *The Odyssey* to show how reason developed as an organ of adaptation to the environing world, comparing reason to the teeth

---

1 Foucault, 'Preface' to Deleuze and Guattari, *Anti-Oedipus*, p. xii.
2 Foucault, 'What is Critique?', *What Is Enlightenment?*, p. 391; trans. mod.
3 Ibid., p. 390.
4 Foucault, 'Interview with Michel Foucault', *Essential Works: Power*, p. 273.

of a bear on the grounds that they both serve the same purpose.[5] Reason enabled human beings, not simply to adapt to their surroundings, but to survive in an environment that was often exceedingly hostile. Odysseus' encounters with the Cyclops and the Sirens illustrate this point. Developing a cunning streak as a means to the end of preserving himself, Odysseus was able to outwit forces that were far more powerful than himself. By shrewdly adapting to nature in order to escape its full force, Odysseus was able to bring nature under his control.

Adorno believes that reason originated as a means to the end of self-preservation and that it remains an adaptive response to a world that we fear because we continue to perceive it as hostile. Here, of course, Adorno underscores the continuity in reason's history: attempting to control the natural world and to diminish the threats that it posed, reason eventually extended its control to human beings themselves to the point where it now seeks to control our inner nature as well (ND 320). Western societies have become increasingly totalitarian because they have forced themselves all the way into our psychological makeup using psychotechnologies that demagogues like Hitler and Stalin turned to their own advantage – and that Western leaders and the media continue to use. Hence, *Dialectic of Enlightenment* opens with a strident warning: if enlightened reason was supposed to emancipate humanity, the 'fully enlightened earth radiates disaster triumphant'.[6]

Drawing on Weber's idea of the disenchantment of the world through progressive rationalization, as well as on the dialectic of faith and enlightenment in Hegel's *Phenomenology of Spirit*, *Dialectic of Enlightenment* maintains that, far from superseding the mythic worldview, enlightenment grew out of myth, and it ends by reverting to myth. Our supposedly enlightened reason – which, to borrow Nietzsche's phrase, conceptually mummifies living things[7] – confuses 'the animate with the inanimate, just as myth compounds the inanimate with the animate'. In fact, the fear of nature, which enlightenment and myth share, reaches such a fever pitch in the modern age that nothing is allowed to remain outside of our conceptual grasp.[8] Again, when it subsumes all things under explanatory schema in order to dominate and control them, reason continues to be driven by nature. Enlightened reason merely makes nature 'audible in its estrangement' because its compulsive attempts to dominate nature simply enslave it all the more to nature.[9]

'In fear', Adorno argues, our 'bondage to nature is perpetuated by a thinking that identifies, that equalizes everything unequal' (ND 172). Although his

5   Horkheimer and Adorno, *Dialectic of Enlightenment*, p. 222; see also the later translation, p. 184.
6   Ibid., p. 3; see also the later translation, p. 1.
7   Nietzsche, *Twilight of the Idols*, in *The Portable Nietzsche*, p. 479.
8   Horkheimer and Adorno, *Dialectic of Enlightenment*, p. 16; see also the later translation, p. 11.
9   Ibid., p. 39; see also the later translation, p. 31.

criticisms of the contemporary form of reason – identity thinking – have already been discussed, I shall reiterate a point I made in Chapter One, namely that Adorno follows Sohn-Rethel when he contends that our summary identification of things with concepts is a function of a society that is built on exchange relations. With the emergence and spread of increasingly abstract exchange relations, which turn disparate things into equivalents, thought itself became abstract and totalitarian. Tolerating nothing outside of itself, the 'imprisonment' of thought in what Adorno calls the 'circle of identification' is thought's 'own handiwork' (ND 172).

Since our domination of nature may well end by destroying us, Adorno promotes a more salutary form of enlightenment that would entail recognizing our affinity with nature – an affinity that is all too apparent in our compulsive attempts to dominate nature. Yet he also cautions that our affinity with nature should not be regarded as a 'positive, ontological determination' because this would allow the dialectic of enlightenment to 'grind it to bits as a relic, a warmed-up myth that agrees with domination' (ND 270). Communicating with nature by virtue of our affinity with it as embodied and instinctual beings, individuals must also learn to distinguish themselves from nature, to respect nature's heterogeneity. Indeed, we may be able more fully to differentiate ourselves from nature by reflecting critically on nature in ourselves precisely because self-reflection is one of the few capacities that does distinguish us from other animals. This is why Adorno declares that mindfulness of nature is the harbinger of freedom: freedom depends on nature becoming conscious of itself.[10]

Of course, Foucault does not advocate mindfulness of nature in the self. Nor does he emphasize the role that self-preservation has played in humanity's underground history. Yet he does observe that the overriding concern for security in the West led modern states to focus on the preservation of the population and its welfare. And while he does not explicitly connect the development of modern rationality to the historical vicissitudes of our survival instincts, he does attempt to make us aware of how disciplinary power and biopower target our bodies – and in particular, our sexual and reproductive behaviours. Here Foucault echoes Adorno to the extent that they both claim that Western states and institutions shape our drives by manipulating and controlling them, by forcing them into certain channels and diverting them from others. Again, Foucault also points to the threats that biopower now poses to our survival. Like Adorno, moreover, who highlights the pathic features of Western reason that endanger our species, Foucault attributes these dangers to the 'antinomies of our political reason'. Reason today is antinomic because it engages in a 'life and death game' in which 'large destructive mechanisms' coexist uneasily with 'institutions oriented toward the care of individual life'.[11] In the West, Foucault

10   Adorno, *Problems of Moral Philosophy*, p. 104. I first made these points in *Adorno on Nature*.
11   Foucault, 'The Political Technology of Individuals', *Essential Works: Power*, p. 405 *passim*.

argues, the politics of life – biopolitics – is vying with the politics of death, thanatopolitics.[12]

Noting that his work converges with the work of the Frankfurt School by virtue of their shared interest in Western reason, Foucault nonetheless criticizes some aspects of the School's account of reason. Before exploring the points of convergence in their ideas, I shall review these criticisms in order to assess the differences in their accounts of modern reason. First, Foucault suggested on at least two occasions that Critical Theory traced modern rationality only as far back as enlightenment. To this, he objected that Western rationality originated in 'more remote historical processes than enlightenment'.[13] Specifically, Foucault argued, modern reason is rooted historically in Christianity and pastoral power. However, as *Dialectic of Enlightenment* shows, Adorno stressed the historical continuity between the emergence of reason as an organ of self-preservation in human prehistory and the prevailing form of rationality in the West. He therefore took a much longer view of the history of reason than Foucault believes. Indeed, Foucault himself takes a longer view of the history of Western reason when he explores the historical links between pastoral practices and practices in the Hellenistic Age.

Foucault also implies that the Frankfurt School failed to differentiate between the types of reason that inform distinct spheres of human activity. In this context, he observes that our 'political rationality is linked with other forms of rationality', including those that underlie 'economical, social, cultural, and technical processes'.[14] Yet Foucault neither studies these other forms of rationality himself, nor shows how they interact. In fact, just as Adorno confines himself to examining the rationalities underlying exchange and thought (including science), Foucault is interested almost exclusively in political rationality and scientific rationality. And where Adorno argues that scientific rationality is grounded in exchange relations, Foucault often subordinates knowledge to power. Furthermore, Foucault tries to distinguish his account of reason from the Frankfurt School's when he says that he is interested in the relations between modern rationality and power in different 'fields', including madness, sexuality and crime.[15] *Pace* Foucault, however, Adorno shows how exchange relations and identity thinking insinuate themselves in a variety of 'fields', including mass culture, law and female sexuality.

In *The Birth of Biopolitics*, Foucault also alleges that his work differs from the Frankfurt School's because he does not seek to denounce reason. Here he implies that his critique aspires to a degree of neutrality because it is limited to exploring the historical conditions that gave rise to modern rationality (BB

12   Ibid., p. 416.
13   Foucault, '"Omnes et Singulatim"', *Essential Works: Power*, p. 299. See also SP 328.
14   Foucault, 'The Political Technology of Individuals', *Essential Works: Power*, p. 416.
15   Foucault, '"Omnes et Singulatim"', *Essential Works: Power*, p. 299. See SP 329.

35-6).[16] On this point, however, Foucault was not consistent: his claim that we are subjected to coercive power mechanisms that took extremely pathological forms in the twentieth century is hardly value-neutral. Nor is his view that Western societies are demonic. More to the point, when he comments again on our antinomic political rationality – on the fact that 'the moment when the state concerns itself with health is the moment when it begins to massacre people' – Foucault deems Western reason to be dangerous because violence is 'profoundly anchored' in it.[17] For Foucault, 'the central issue of philosophy and critical thought since the 18th century . . . is, and will, I hope, remain . . . what is this reason we use?', what are its limits and its dangers? To this Foucault adds that, if it is dangerous to say that 'reason is the enemy that should be eliminated', it is equally dangerous 'to say that any critical questioning of this rationality risks sending us into irrationality'. For we 'should not forget [that] it was on the basis of the flamboyant rationality of social Darwinism that racism was formulated, becoming one of the most enduring and powerful ingredients in Nazism'.[18]

To revisit a point raised in the previous chapter, some commentators – among them, Koopman and Nealon – claim that Foucault refrained from making value judgements.[19] To support this claim, they point to the fact that he once said in an interview that 'not everything is bad, but . . . everything is dangerous'. However, it might be useful to note that Foucault did not say that nothing is bad. Far from it: his strong condemnation of Nazism and Stalinism, along with his criticisms of the fascism that is inside our heads, shows that he thinks that the hypertrophy of power can become a very bad thing indeed. Foucault also implies that some things can be both bad and dangerous, even though being dangerous is 'not exactly the same thing as being bad'. Finally, when he insists that identifying the main danger is the ethical and political choice that we need to make every day of our lives,[20] Foucault equates ethical behaviour with looking persistently, and critically, at society.

Foucault's critique does diverge from Adorno's in one important respect. For he argued that it is 'not enough to do a history of rationality: one needs to do the history of truth itself'.[21] In contrast to Adorno, who criticized the culture of expertise but never examined in any detail or depth the truths against which individuals are judged, Foucault was interested in how subjects are constituted (and how they constitute themselves) in relation to truths that define who and what they are and that profoundly affect how they think about themselves. Again, Christianity defines individuals in relation to a truth about their souls – a

---

16   Cf. Foucault, '"Omnes et Singulatim"', *Essential Works: Power*, p. 299, and SP 329 where Foucault seems to distinguish those who 'put reason on trial' from the Frankfurt School.

17   Foucault, 'Foucault étudie la Raison d'Etat', *Dits et écrits* IV, pp. 38–9.

18   Foucault, 'Space, Knowledge, Power', *Essential Works: Power*, p. 358.

19   See Jeffrey T. Nealon, *Foucault Beyond Foucault*, p. 22, and Koopman, *Genealogy as Critique*, pp. 62 and 92.

20   Foucault, 'On the Genealogy of Ethics', *Essential Works: Ethics*, p. 256 *passim*.

21   Foucault, 'Interview with Michel Foucault', *Essential Works: Power*, p. 253.

truth that it unearths in practices such as confession. But in the modern age, the truths to which individuals submit in constant examinations are largely defined by medicine and the social sciences. Still, even this difference between Adorno and Foucault does not undermine the complementarity of their work. If anything, Foucault could be said to supplement Adorno's critical social theory with his Nietzschean genealogy of truth.

Adorno's and Foucault's ontologies of our present are also complementary because they offer similar critiques of Western reason. As I have argued here, they are both concerned about what 'enlightened' reason has wrought in its pursuit of ever more finely tuned, insidious and coercive mechanisms of social control. At the same time, they also share a more positive concern for what enlightenment – in the form of maturity and autonomy – might offer by way of remedying this situation. It is in this respect that Foucault can be said to challenge enlightenment in the name of enlightenment. As Foucault explains, he follows critical theory in 'examining a reason, the autonomy of whose structures carries with it a history of dogmatism and despotism – a reason . . . which can have an effect of emancipation on condition that it manages to liberate itself from itself'.[22] Although reason has engendered despotic forms of subjection, Foucault seems to agree with Adorno that a trenchant critique of the West may 'prepare the way for a positive notion of enlightenment which will release it from entanglement in blind domination'.[23]

Encouraging critical reflection on ourselves and how we have become what we are, Adorno and Foucault simultaneously attempt to release us from the tutelage of the guardians who are currently doing our thinking for us. Anti-authoritarianism is a constant feature of their work. Rather than submitting blindly to the dictates of our political leaders, scientific experts, physicians, psychologists and others, individuals must learn to think for themselves. Since Adorno believes that critique is imperative for a healthy democracy, he argues that one prerequisite for democracy is an education that fosters 'the capacity and courage of each individual to make full use of her reasoning powers'.[24] Much like Adorno, Foucault too links our release from tutelage to the promotion of a resolutely critical attitude. In Foucault, this attitude manifests itself in

---

22   Foucault, 'Introduction', in Canguilhem, *The Normal and the Pathological*, p. 12. Cited in Gordon, 'Question, Ethos, Event', *Economy and Society*, p. 72; I am citing Gordon's translation.

23   Horkheimer and Adorno, *Dialectic of Enlightenment*, p. xvi; *Dialectic of Enlightenment: Philosophical Fragments*, p. xviii. However, in 'What is Enlightenment?', *Essential Works: Ethics*, p. 313, Foucault warns against 'introducing "dialectical" nuances while seeking to determine what good and bad elements there may have been in enlightenment'. However, on one reading of it, his warning is problematic because Foucault himself recognizes that enlightenment has a Janus face: even as it engendered the critical attitude that Foucault associates with Kant and adopts in his own work, it gave rise to disciplinary and biopolitical subjection. In the passage I cited above from his introduction to Canguilhem's *The Normal and the Pathological*, Foucault called the latter form of enlightenment 'despotic'.

24   Adorno and Becker, 'Education for Maturity and Responsibility', *History of the Human Sciences* 12, p. 21; trans. mod.

the capacity and courage of individuals to speak truth to power by contesting the many ways in which they are being governed too much or in unbearable ways.

Adorno and Foucault see critique as one of the hallmarks of modernity. According to Foucault, when the government of individuals became a central objective in the Christian West, critique emerged to counter 'the ecclesiastical magisterium', to question the legitimacy and adequacy of existing laws, and to challenge appeals to authority.[25] Of course, Adorno does not explore the connection between the Christian art of governing individuals and the emergence of critique. Nevertheless, when he endorses Arthur Rimbaud's dictum – 'Il faut être absolument moderne'[26] – Adorno notes that modernity's conception of itself includes critique. Following Kant, he also claims that the modern concept of reason is virtually synonymous with critique.[27]

Prospects for the emergence of a more positive form of enlightenment depend on promoting this critical attitude, which is rooted in enlightenment, towards the obedience and submission that enlightenment has inculcated. But where Foucault contends that this critical disposition animated resistive movements centuries ago – the Reformation is 'the first critical movement that takes the form of an art of not being governed'[28] – Adorno stresses the extent to which the equation between the modern concept of reason and critique has frequently been belied. He complains that the critical disposition has rarely been fully exercised, and that it is often actively discouraged, if not vilified. Critique has been held in check, not just in philosophy (where even Kant wanted to punish reason for exceeding its bounds, and to bridle its use), but in post-war Germany and other parts of the Western world.[29]

Nevertheless, when he links the critical attitude to modernity, Adorno suggests that reason has a better potential on which it can continue to draw. Adorno's and Foucault's critiques draw on this potential when, to cite Foucault, they ask: 'What is it about this rationalization that . . . characterizes not only Western thought and science since the sixteenth century but also social relations, state organizations, economic practices, and . . . the behavior of individuals?' In fact, Foucault claims that his approach to this question resembles the approach of the Frankfurt School because they both engage in 'an historico-philosophical practice' that studies the links between 'structures of rationality and the mechanisms of subjugation that are tied to it'.[30] In addition, they 'desubjectify' modern reason by historicizing it. Finally, they both define

25 Foucault, 'What is Critique?', What is Enlightenment?, p. 385.
26 Adorno and Peter von Haselberg, 'On the Historical Adequacy of Consciousness', Telos, p. 98.
27 Adorno, 'Critique', Critical Models, p. 282.
28 Foucault, 'What is Critique?', What is Enlightenment?, p. 389; trans. mod.
29 Adorno, 'Critique', Critical Models, p. 282.
30 Foucault, 'What is Critique?', What is Enlightenment?, pp. 390–1.

enlightenment – a moniker for the period in which the modern form of reason emerged – broadly so that it encompasses a variety of phenomena, including 'the formation of capitalism, the constitution of the bourgeois world, the establishment of the state system, the foundation of modern science with all its correlative techniques', as well as the 'opposition between the art of being governed and that of not being governed in such a manner'.[31]

Examining the conditions that made Western reason possible, Foucault and Adorno obviously view modern reason as a contingent phenomenon. For his part, when Adorno calls Western reason a 'particular rationality', he indicates that the identity thinking that characterizes reason today is peculiar to the modern age (ND 172). And, as a product of history, identity thinking can be changed. In order to change, however, reason must first subject itself to a thoroughgoing critique. Like Foucault, who speaks (in a passage cited above) about reason liberating itself from itself, Adorno avers that only reason – 'the principle of societal domination inverted into the subject – would be capable of abolishing this domination'. Reason must become self-critical; it must apply reason 'to itself and in its self-restriction emancipate itself from the demon of identity'.[32]

For his part, Foucault explores the rationality that underlies the mechanisms of coercion that modern power relations have engendered; he also studies the connections between these mechanisms and modern forms of social scientific knowledge. However, he refuses to equate reason with 'the totality of rational forms which have come to dominate – at any given moment, in our own era and even very recently – in types of knowledge, forms of technique and modalities of government or domination'.[33] Foucault refuses to do so because these forms 'can perfectly well be shown to have a history'. Indeed, since they have been made, they can also be unmade, 'as long as we know how it was that they were made'.[34] Here too, Foucault defers to the Frankfurt School: 'since Max Weber, in the Frankfurt School, and . . . for many historians of science since Canguilhem, it was a question of isolating the form of rationality presented as dominant and endowed with the status of the one-and-only reason in order to show that it is only *one* possible form among others'.[35]

Foucault's genealogical critique tries to 'separate out, from the contingency that has made us what we are, the possibility of no longer being, doing, or thinking what we are, do, or think'.[36] Gesturing towards the possibility of other forms of reason, Foucault also refuses to succumb to the 'blackmail' that says: you either accept reason as it is, or you 'fall prey to the irrational'. For those who say this wrongly imply that 'a rational critique of reason' is impossible; they act 'as

31 Ibid., p. 392.
32 Adorno, 'Progress', *Critical Models*, p. 152; trans. mod.
33 Foucault, 'Critical Theory/Intellectual History', *Politics, Philosophy, Culture*, p. 35.
34 Ibid., p. 37.
35 Ibid., p. 27.
36 Foucault, 'What is Enlightenment?', *Essential Works: Ethics*, pp. 315–16.

though a rational history of all the ramifications, and all the bifurcations, a contingent history of reason, were impossible'.[37] That Adorno also rejects this 'blackmail' is evidenced by his attempts to trace the history of reason in *Dialectic of Enlightenment* and elsewhere. In fact, what Adorno says about Kant holds for both him and Foucault: what makes a critique of reason possible is just 'the self-reflective nature of reason'. Reason can criticize itself because, 'as a rational being, I am capable of reflecting on my own reason, and through this reflection I am able to give myself an account of what it can and cannot achieve'.[38]

Foucault and Adorno deny that there was once a pristine form of reason that fell from grace and that we need to restore. There is no nostalgia for the past in their work. Before I bring this study to a close, however, I shall comment briefly on their ideas about inaugurating a new form, or forms, of rationality. Arguing that other forms of rationality are possible, Adorno and Foucault agree that these may also transform relations between individuals and society in more positive ways. Yet where Adorno often gestures towards a more salutary form of reason that would finally make possible a definitive reconciliation between the individual and society, Foucault would deny that overcoming the mechanisms of subjection that are rooted in pastoral power will lead to reconciliation in Adorno's sense. Indeed, even as Adorno casts serious doubt on the prospects for a revolution, he problematically suggests at times that a revolution will solve everything.

Foucault's intimations of a better future in which the 'ideas and devices of our political reality' have been overcome in a 'new economy of power relations' (SP 328) by no means preclude the possibility that new struggles will be needed to combat new, and entirely unforeseeable, dangers. In this respect, Foucault could be said to be more realistic than Adorno. Nevertheless, since they both encourage readers to exercise their political imaginations with the aim of envisaging something better, I believe that Adorno can be defended, particularly since he conceded that images of the future – even and especially his own images of the future – invariably fall short. Agreeing with Adorno on this point as well, Foucault only echoed his pessimistic views about the efficacy of critique when he remarked that philosophy is an enterprise that is fraught with 'effort and uncertainty, dreams and illusions'. Yet Adorno and Foucault continued to hope that their critiques would contribute to displacing and transforming familiar 'ways of thinking' by detaching them 'from what is accepted as true'.[39] In fact, it is especially here, mired in an often disheartening uncertainty about the efficacy of critique, while clinging stubbornly to the hope that Western reason will change as they draw on the legacy of enlightenment, that the critical theories of Adorno and Foucault join forces.

---

37 Foucault, 'Critical Theory/Intellectual History', *Politics, Philosophy, Culture*, p. 27.
38 Adorno, *Kant's 'Critique of Pure Reason'*, p. 7; trans. mod.
39 Foucault, 'The Masked Philosopher', *Philosophy, Politics, Culture*, p. 330.

Bibliography

CITED WORKS BY THEODOR W. ADORNO

With Else Frenkel-Brunswik, Daniel J. Levinson and R. Nevitt Sanford. *The Authoritarian Personality*, abridged edition. New York: Harper & Brothers, 1950.

'Probleme der Moralphilosophie' (1956–7). Frankfurt: Adorno Archiv, Vo 1289–1520.

'Sociology and Psychology'. Translated by Irving N. Wohlfarth. *New Left Review* 46 (1967), pp. 63–80.

'Sociology and Psychology'. Translated by Irving N. Wohlfarth. *New Left Review* 47 (1968), pp. 79–97.

'Society'. Translated by Fredric Jameson. *Salmagundi*, Vol. 3 (1969–70), pp. 144–53.

With Max Horkheimer. *Dialectic of Enlightenment*. Translated by John Cumming. New York: Continuum, 1972.

Soziologische Schriften I. Edited by Rolf Tiedemann. Frankfurt: Suhrkamp Verlag, 1972.

The Jargon of Authenticity. Translated by Knut Tarnowski and Frederic Will. Evanston IL: Northwestern University Press, 1973.

Negative Dialectics. Translated by E. B. Ashton. New York: Continuum, 1973.

Minima Moralia: Reflections from Damaged Life. Translated by E. F. N. Jephcott. London: New Left Books, 1974.

'Freudian Theory and the Pattern of Fascist Propaganda'. *The Essential Frankfurt School Reader*. Translated by Andrew Arato and Eike Gebhardt. New York: Urizen Books, 1978, pp. 118–37.

Against Epistemology: A Metacritique. Studies in Husserl and the Phenomenological Antinomies. Translated by W. Domingo. Cambridge MA: The MIT Press, 1982.

With Hellmut Becker. 'Education for Autonomy'. Translated by David J. Parent. *Telos* 56 (Summer 1983), pp. 103–10.

With Peter von Haselberg. 'On the Historical Adequacy of Consciousness'. Translated by Wes Blomster. *Telos* 56 (Summer 1983), pp. 97–103.

'The Essay as Form'. Translated by Robert Hullot-Kentor and Frederic Will. *New German Critique*, no. 32 (Spring-Summer 1984), pp. 151–71.

'Late Capitalism or Industrial Society?' Translated by Fred van Gelder. *Modern German Sociology*. Edited by V. Meja, D. Misgeld and N. Stehr. New York: Columbia University Press, 1987, pp. 232–47.

With Ernst Bloch. 'Something's Missing: A Discussion with Ernst Bloch and Theodor W. Adorno on the Contradictions in Utopian Longing'. *The Utopian Function of Art and Literature: Selected Essays*. Translated by Jack Zipes and Frank Mecklenburg. Cambridge MA: The MIT Press, 1988, pp. 1–17.

Notes to Literature, Vol. 2. Translated by Shierry Weber Nicholsen. New York: Columbia University Press, 1992.

Hegel: Three Studies. Translated by Shierry Weber Nicholsen. Cambridge MA: The MIT Press, 1993.

'Theory of Pseudo-Culture'. Translated by Deborah Cook. *Telos* 95 (Spring 1993), pp. 15–38.

Aesthetic Theory. Edited by Gretel Adorno and Rolf Tiedemann. Translated by Robert Hullot-Kentor. Minneapolis: University of Minnesota Press, 1997.
Critical Models: Interventions and Catchwords. Translated by Henry W. Pickford. New York: Columbia University Press, 1998.
With Hellmut Becker. 'Education for Maturity and Responsibility'. Translated by Robert French, Jem Thomas and Dorothee Weymann. *History of the Human Sciences* 12, no. 3 (1999), pp. 21–34.
Introduction to Sociology. Edited by Christoph Gödde. Translated by Edmund Jephcott. Stanford: Stanford University Press, 2000.
Problems of Moral Philosophy. Edited by Thomas Schröder. Translated by Rodney Livingstone. Stanford: Stanford University Press, 2000.
Kant's 'Critique of Pure Reason'. Edited by Rolf Tiedemann. Translated by Rodney Livingstone. Stanford: Stanford University Press, 2001.
Metaphysics: Concept and Problems. Edited by Rolf Tiedemann. Translated by E. F. N. Jephcott. Stanford: Stanford University Press, 2001.
With Max Horkheimer. *Dialectic of Enlightenment: Philosophical Fragments.* Translated by Edmund Jephcott. Stanford: Stanford University Press, 2002.
'Reflections on Class Theory'. Translated by Rodney Livingstone. *Can One Live After Auschwitz?: A Philosophical Reader.* Edited by Rolf Tiedemann. Stanford: Stanford University Press, 2003, pp. 93–110.
History and Freedom: Lectures 1964–1965. Edited by Rolf Tiedemann. Translated by Rodney Livingstone. Cambridge: Polity Press, 2006.
Lectures on 'Negative Dialectics': Fragments of a Lecture Course 1965/1966. Edited by Rolf Tiedemann. Translated by Rodney Livingstone. Cambridge: Polity Press, 2008.
Guilt and Defense: On the Legacies of National Socialism in Postwar Germany. Edited and translated by Jeffrey K. Olick and Andrew J. Perrin. Cambridge MA: Harvard University Press, 2010.
With Max Horkheimer. 'Towards a New Manifesto?' Translated by Rodney Livingstone. *New Left Review* 65 (September–October 2010), pp. 33–61.
'Theses on Need'. Translated by Martin Shuster and Iain Macdonald. *Adorno Studies* I, no. 1 (January 2017), pp. 102–4.

CITED WORKS BY MICHEL FOUCAULT

'Introduction'. In Ludwig Binswanger, *Rêve et existence.* Translated by J. Verdeaux. Paris: Desclée de Brouwer, 1954.
Folie et déraison: histoire de la folie à l'âge classique. Paris: Plon, 1961.
The Archaeology of Knowledge & The Discourse on Language. Translated by A. M. Sheridan-Smith and Rupert Swyer. New York: Pantheon Books, 1972.
The Birth of the Clinic: An Archaeology of Medical Perception. Translated by A. M. Sheridan. London: Tavistock Publications Limited, 1973.
The Order of Things. Translated by Alan Sheridan. New York: Vintage, 1973.
'Intellectuals and Power'. *Language, Counter-Memory, Practice: Selected Essays and Interviews.* Edited by Donald F. Bouchard. Translated by Donald F. Bouchard and Sherry Simon. Ithaca, NY: Cornell University Press, 1977, pp. 205–17.
Sexualität und Wahrheit, Band 1: *Der Wille zum Wissen.* Translated by Ulrich Raulff and Walter Seitter. Frankfurt: Suhrkamp Verlag, 1977.
The History of Sexuality, Vol. 1: *An Introduction.* Translated by Robert Hurley. New York: Random House, 1978.

Discipline and Punish: The Birth of the Prison. Translated by Alan Sheridan. New York: Vintage Books, 1979.

Power/Knowledge: Selected Interviews and Other Writings, 1972-1977. Edited by Colin Gordon. Translated by Colin Gordon, Leo Marshall, John Mepham and Kate Soper. New York: Pantheon Books, 1980.

'Questions of Method'. Translated by Colin Gordon. *The Foucault Effect: Studies in Governmentality.* Edited by Graham Burchell, Colin Gordon and Peter Miller. Chicago: University of Chicago Press, 1981, pp. 73–86.

'Preface'. In Félix Guattari and Gilles Deleuze, *Anti-Oedipus: Capitalism and Schizophrenia.* Translated by Robert Hurley, Mark Seem and Helen R. Lane. Minneapolis: University of Minnesota Press, 1983, pp. xiii–xvi.

'An Interview: Sex, Power and the Politics of Identity'. *Advocate* 2 (August 1984), pp. 163-73.

The History of Sexuality, Vol. 2: *The Use of Pleasure.* Translated by Robert Hurley. London: Penguin, 1986.

Politics, Philosophy, Culture: Interviews and Other Writings 1977-1984. Edited by Lawrence D. Kritzman. Translated by Alan Sheridan et al. New York and London: Routledge, Chapman & Hall, Inc. 1988.

'Rituals of Exclusion'. *Foucault Live (Interviews 1966-84).* Edited by Sylvère Lotringer. Translated by John Johnston. New York: Semiotext(e), 1989, pp. 63–72.

'Introduction'. In Georges Canguilhem, *The Normal and the Pathological.* Translated by Carolyn R. Fawcett with Robert S. Cohen. New York: Zone Books, 1991, pp. 7–24.

Dits et écrits 1954–1988, Vol. II: *1970–1975.* Edited by Daniel Defert and François Ewald. Paris: Gallimard, 1994.

Dits et écrits 1954–1988, Vol. III: *1976–1979.* Edited by Daniel Defert and François Ewald. Paris: Gallimard, 1994.

Dits et écrits 1954–1988, Vol. IV: *1980–1988.* Edited by Daniel Defert and François Ewald. Paris: Gallimard, 1994.

'What is Critique?' Translated by Kevin Paul Geiman. *What Is Enlightenment? Eighteenth-century Answer and Twentieth-century Questions.* Edited by James Schmidt. Berkeley and Los Angeles: University of California Press, 1996, pp. 382–98.

Essential Works of Foucault (1954–1984), Vol. 1: *Ethics: Subjectivity and Truth.* Edited by Paul Rabinow. Translated by Robert Hurley et al. New York: The New Press, 1997.

Essential Works of Foucault (1954–1984), Vol. 2: *Aesthetics, Method, and Epistemology.* Edited by James D. Faubion. Translated by Robert Hurley et al. New York: The New Press, 1998.

Essential Works of Foucault (1954–1984), Vol. 3: *Power.* Edited by James D. Faubion. Translated by Robert Hurley et al. New York: The New Press, 2000.

Abnormal: Lectures at the Collège de France 1974–1975. Edited by Valerio Marchetti and Antonella Salomoni. Translated by Graham Burchell. New York: Picador, 2003.

Society Must be Defended: Lectures at the Collège de France 1975–1976. Edited by Mauro Bertani and Alessandro Fontana. Translated by David Macey. New York: Picador, 2003.

The Hermeneutics of the Subject: Lectures at the Collège de France 1981–1982. Edited by Frédéric Gros. Translated by Graham Burchell. New York: Palgrave Macmillan, 2005.

History of Madness. Edited by Jean Khalfa. Translated by Jonathan Murphy and Jean Khalfa. London and New York: Routledge, 2006.

Psychiatric Power: Lectures at the Collège de France 1973–1974. Edited by Jacques Lagrange. Translated by Graham Burchell. New York: Picador, 2006.

'The Meshes of Power'. Translated by Gerald Moore. *Space, Knowledge and Power: Foucault and Geography*. Edited by Jeremy W. Crampton and Stuart Elden. Aldershot: Ashgate Publishing Limited, 2007, pp. 153–62.

Security, Territory, Population: Lectures at the Collège de France 1977–1978. Edited by Michel Senellart. Translated by Graham Burchell. New York: Picador, 2007.

The Birth of Biopolitics: Lectures at the Collège de France 1978–1979. Edited by Michel Senellart. Translated by Graham Burchell. New York: Palgrave Macmillan, 2008.

Introduction to Kant's Anthropology. Edited by Roberto Nigro. Translated by Roberto Nigro and Kate Briggs. Los Angeles: Semiotext(e), 2008.

The Government of Self and Others: Lectures at the Collège de France 1982–1983. Edited by Frédéric Gros. Translated by Graham Burchell. New York: Palgrave Macmillan, 2010.

The Courage of Truth (The Government of Self and Others II): Lectures at the Collège de France 1983–1984. Edited by Frédéric Gros, François Ewald and Alessandro Fontana. Translated by Graham Burchell. New York: Palgrave Macmillan, 2011.

Lectures on the Will to Know: Lectures at the Collège de France 1970–1971. Edited by Daniel Defert. Translated by Graham Burchell. New York: Palgrave Macmillan, 2013.

On the Government of the Living: Lectures at the Collège de France 1979–1980. Edited by Michel Senellart. Translated by Graham Burchell. New York: Palgrave Macmillan, 2014.

Subjectivité et vérité: cours au Collège de France 1980–81. Edited by Frédéric Gros. Paris: Seuil/Gallimard, 2014.

Wrong-doing, Truth-telling: The Function of Avowal in Justice. Edited by Fabienne Brion and Bernard E. Harcourt. Translated by Stephen W. Sawyer. Chicago: University of Chicago Press, 2014.

The Punitive Society: Lectures at the Collège de France 1972–1973. Edited by Bernard E. Harcourt. Translated by Graham Burchell. New York: Palgrave Macmillan, 2015.

OTHER WORKS CITED

Allen, Amy. *The Politics of Our Selves: Power, Autonomy, and Gender in Contemporary Critical Theory*. New York: Columbia University Press, 2008.

———. *The End of Progress: Decolonizing the Normative Foundations of Critical Theory*. New York: Columbia University Press, 2016.

Audier, Serge. *Néolibéralisme(s): une archéologie intellectuelle*. Paris: Grasset, 2012.

Balibar, Étienne. 'Foucault and Marx: The Question of Nominalism'. *Michel Foucault Philosopher*. Edited and translated by Timothy J. Armstrong. New York: Routledge, 1992, pp. 38–58.

Becker, Gary, Ewald, François and Harcourt, Bernard E. 'Becker on Ewald on Foucault on Becker'. University of Chicago Institute for Law & Economics Olin Research Paper, no. 614; University of Chicago, Public Law, Working paper, no. 401 (September 5, 2012).

Behrent, Michael. 'La Querelle du Néolibéralisme'. *Sciences Humaines. Hors série*, no. 19: *Michel Foucault: numéro anniversaire* (May-June 2014), pp. 50–1.

Benjamin, Walter. *Charles Baudelaire: A Lyric Poet in the Era of High Capitalism*. Translated by Harry Zohn. London: Verso, 1973.

Bernauer, James W. 'Michel Foucault's Ecstatic Thinking'. *The Final Foucault*. Edited by James W. Bernauer and David Rasmussen. Cambridge MA: The MIT Press, 1987, pp. 45–82.

———. 'Michel Foucault's Philosophy of Religion: An Introduction to the Non-Fascist Life'. *Michel Foucault and Theology: The Politics of Religious Experience*. Edited by James Bernauer and Jeremy Carrette. Aldershot: Ashgate, 2004, pp. 77–97.

———. 'Secular Self-Sacrifice: On Michel Foucault's Courses at the Collège de France'. *Foucault's Legacy*. Edited by C. G. Prado. London and New York: Continuum, 2009, pp. 146–60.

Bernstein, J. M. *Adorno: Disenchantment and Ethics*. Cambridge: Cambridge University Press, 2001.

———. 'Negative Dialectic as Fate: Adorno and Hegel'. *The Cambridge Companion to Adorno*. Edited by Tom Huhn. Cambridge: Cambridge University Press, 2004, pp. 19–50.

Bowie, Andrew. *Adorno and the Ends of Philosophy*. Cambridge: Polity Press, 2013.

Burckhardt, Jacob. *The Civilization of the Renaissance in Italy*. Translated by S. Middlemore. London: Penguin Books, 1990.

———. *The Greeks and Greek Civilization*. Edited by Oswyn Murray. Translated by Sheila Stern. New York: St. Martin's Press, 1999.

Canguilhem, Georges. *The Normal and the Pathological*. Translated by Carolyn R. Fawcett and Robert S. Cohen. New York: Zone Books, 1991.

Cook, Deborah. 'History as Fiction: Foucault's Politics of Truth'. *The Journal of the British Society for Phenomenology* 22, no. 3 (October 1991), pp. 139–47.

———. *Adorno, Habermas, and the Search for a Rational Society*. London and New York: Routledge, 2004.

———. *Adorno on Nature*. Stocksfield: Acumen, 2011.

———. 'Foucault, Freud, and the Repressive Hypothesis'. *The Journal of the British Society for Phenomenology* 45, no. 2 (2014), pp. 148–61.

———. 'Through a Glass Darkly: Adorno's Inverse Theology'. *Adorno Studies* 1, no. 1 (January 2017), pp. 66–78.

Cooper, Melinda. 'The Law of the Household: Foucault, Neoliberalism, and the Iranian Revolution'. *The Government of Life: Foucault, Biopolitics, and Neoliberalism*. Edited by Vanessa Lemm and Miguel Vatter. New York: Fordham University Press, 2014, pp. 29–58.

Deleuze, Gilles. *Foucault*. Translated by Seán Hand. Minneapolis: University of Minnesota Press, 1988.

Dews, Peter. *Logics of Disintegration: Post-structuralist Thought and the Claims of Critical Theory*. London and New York: Verso, 1987.

Dreyfus, Hubert L. and Rabinow, Paul. *Michel Foucault: Beyond Structuralism and Hermeneutics*, 2nd edition. Chicago: University of Chicago Press, 1982.

Dubiel, Helmut. *Theory and Politics: Studies in the Development of Critical Theory*. Translated by Benjamin Gregg. Cambridge MA: The MIT Press, 1985.

Elden, Stuart. *Foucault's Last Decade*. Cambridge: Polity Press, 2016.

Eley, Geoff. 'Scholarship Serving the Nazi State I: Studying the East'. *Ethnic and Racial Studies* 12, no. 4 (1989), pp. 574–81.

Eribon, Didier. *Michel Foucault*. Translated by Betsy Wing. Cambridge, MA: Harvard University Press, 1991.

———. 'Toward an Ethic of Subjectivation: French Resistances to Psychoanalysis in the 1970s'. *Foucault Now: Current Perspectives in Foucault Studies*. Edited by James D. Faubion. Cambridge: Polity Press, 2014, pp. 71–87.

Faubion, James D. 'Introduction'. In Michel Foucault, *Essential Works of Foucault (1954–1984)*, Vol. 2: *Aesthetics, Method, and Epistemology*. Edited by James D. Faubion. Translated by Robert Hurley et al. New York: The New Press, 1998, pp. xiii–xliii.

Finke, Ståle. 'Concepts and Intuitions: Adorno after the Linguistic Turn'. *Theodor W. Adorno*, Vol. 1: *Philosophy, Ethics and Critical Theory*. Edited by G. Delanty. London: Sage, 2004, pp. 103–33.

Fraser, Nancy. *Unruly Practices: Power, Discourse and Gender in Contemporary Social Theory*. Minneapolis: University of Minnesota Press, 1989.

Freud, Sigmund. 'A Difficulty in the Path of Psycho-analysis'. *The Standard Edition of the Complete Psychological Works of Sigmund Freud*, Vol. 17. Translated by James Strachey. London: The Hogarth Press, 1955, pp. 135–44.

———. 'An Outline of Psycho-analysis'. *The Standard Edition of the Complete Psychological Works of Sigmund Freud*, Vol. 23. Translated by James Strachey. London: The Hogarth Press, 1964, pp. 139–208.

———. *Civilization and its Discontents. The Standard Edition of the Complete Psychological Works of Sigmund Freud*, Vol. 21. Translated by James Strachey. London: The Hogarth Press, 1968, pp. 64–125.

———. *The Future of an Illusion. The Standard Edition of the Complete Psychological Works of Sigmund Freud*, Vol. 21. Translated by James Strachey. London: The Hogarth Press, 1968, pp. 5–56.

———. 'Instincts and their Vicissitudes'. *The Standard Edition of the Complete Psychological Works of Sigmund Freud*, Vol. 14. Translated by James Strachey. London: The Hogarth Press, 1975, pp. 109–40.

———. 'On the History of the Psycho-analytic Movement'. *The Standard Edition of the Complete Psychological Works of Sigmund Freud*, Vol. 14. Translated by James Strachey. London: The Hogarth Press, 1975, pp. 7–66.

Freyenhagen, Fabian. 'Moral Philosophy'. *Theodor Adorno: Key Concepts*. Edited by Deborah Cook. Stocksfield: Acumen, 2008, pp. 99–114.

———. *Adorno's Practical Philosophy: Living Less Wrongly*. Cambridge: Cambridge University Press, 2013.

Gandesha, Samir. 'Leaving Home: On Adorno and Heidegger'. *The Cambridge Companion to Adorno*. Edited by Tom Huhn. Cambridge: Cambridge University Press, 2004, pp. 101–28.

Geuss, Raymond. 'Suffering and Knowledge in Adorno'. *Constellations* 12, no. 1 (2005), pp. 3–20.

Gordon, Colin. 'Afterword'. In Michel Foucault, *Power/Knowledge: Selected Interviews and Other Writings, 1972-1977*. Edited by Colin Gordon. Translated by Colin Gordon, Leo Marshall, John Mepham and Kate Soper. New York: Pantheon Books, 1980, pp. 229–59.

———. 'Question, Ethos, Event: Foucault on Kant and Enlightenment'. *Economy and Society* 15, no. 1 (February 1986), pp. 71–87.

———. 'The Soul of the Citizen: Max Weber and Michel Foucault on Rationality and Government'. *Max Weber: Rationality and Modernity*. Edited by Scott Lash and Sam Whimster. London: Allen & Unwin, 1987, pp. 293–316.

———. 'Introduction'. In Michel Foucault, *Essential Works of Foucault (1954-1984)*, Vol. 3: *Power*. Edited by James D. Faubion. Translated by Robert Hurley et al. New York: The New Press, 2000, pp. xi-xli.

Gordon, Peter E. *Adorno and Existence*. Cambridge MA: Harvard University Press, 2016.

Gros, Frédéric. 'Course Context'. In Michel Foucault, *The Hermeneutics of the Subject: Lectures at the Collège de France 1981-1982*. Translated by Graham Burchell. New York: Palgrave Macmillan, 2005, pp. 507–50.

———. 'Is There a Biopolitical Subject? Foucault and the Birth of Biopolitics'. Translated by Samantha Bankston. *Biopower: Foucault and Beyond*. Edited by Vernon W.

Cisney and Nicholae Morar. Chicago and London: University of Chicago Press, 2016, pp. 259–73.

Gutting, Gary. *Michel Foucault's Archaeology of Scientific Reason*. Cambridge and New York: Cambridge University Press, 1989.

Habermas, Jürgen. *The Philosophical Discourse of Modernity: Twelve Lectures*. Translated by Frederick Lawrence. Cambridge MA: The MIT Press, 1987.

Hacking, Ian. *The Social Construction of What?* Cambridge MA: Harvard University Press, 1999.

Hammer, Espen. *Adorno and the Political*. London and New York: Routledge, 2005.

Held, David. *Introduction to Critical Theory: Horkheimer to Habermas*. Berkeley and Los Angeles: University of California Press, 1980.

Honneth, Axel. *The Critique of Power: Reflective Stages in a Critical Social Theory*. Translated by Kenneth Barnes. Cambridge MA: The MIT Press, 1991.

———. 'Foucault's Theory of Society: A Systems-Theoretic Dissolution of the *Dialectic of Enlightenment*'. Translated by Kenneth Baynes. *Critique and Power: Recasting the Foucault/Habermas Debate*. Edited by Michael Kelly. Cambridge MA: The MIT Press, 1994, pp.157–83.

Horkheimer, Max. *Eclipse of Reason*. New York: The Seabury Press, 1974.

Hoy, David Couzens and McCarthy, Thomas. *Critical Theory*. Oxford: Blackwell, 1994.

Jameson, Fredric. *Late Marxism: Adorno, or, the Persistence of the Dialectic*. New York: Verso, 1990.

Jarvis, Simon. *Adorno: A Critical Introduction*. New York: Routledge, 1998.

Jay, Martin. *The Dialectical Imagination: A History of the Frankfurt School and the Institute for Social Research, 1923–1950*. Boston and Toronto: Little, Brown and Company, 1973.

———. *Adorno*. London: Fontana, 1984.

Kant, Immanuel. 'An Answer to the Question: What is Enlightenment?' *Kant's Political Writings*. Translated by H. B. Nisbet. Cambridge: Cambridge University Press, 1971, pp. 54–60.

Kaufmann, David. 'Correlations, Constellations and the Truth: Adorno's Ontology of Redemption'. *Theodor W. Adorno*, Vol. 1: *Philosophy, Ethics and Critical Theory*. Edited by Gerard Delanty. London: Sage, 2004, pp. 163–81.

Kellner, Douglas. *Critical Theory, Marxism and Modernity*. Baltimore: The Johns Hopkins University Press, 1989.

Kelly, Mark G. E. *The Political Philosophy of Michel Foucault*. New York and London: Routledge, 2009.

Koopman, Colin. *Genealogy as Critique: Foucault and the Problems of Modernity*. Bloomington: Indiana University Press, 2013.

———. 'Michel Foucault's Critical Empiricism Today: Concepts and Analytics in the Critique of Biopower and Infopower'. *Foucault Now: Current Perspectives in Foucault Studies*. Edited by James D. Faubion. Cambridge: Polity Press, 2014, pp. 88–111.

Lanning, Robert. *In the Hotel Abyss: A Hegelian-Marxist Critique of Adorno*. Chicago: Haymarket Books, 2014.

Lasch, Christopher. *Haven in a Heartless World: The Family Besieged*. New York: Basic Books, 1979.

Legrand, Stéphane. 'Le Marxisme oublié de Foucault'. *Actuel Marx: Marx et Foucault*, no. 36 (2004), pp. 27–43.

Lynch, Richard A. 'Is Power All There Is? Michel Foucault and the "Omnipresence" of Power Relations'. *Philosophy Today* 42, no. 1 (Spring 1998), pp. 65–70.

———. *Foucault's Critical Ethics*. New York: Fordham University Press, 2016.

Macey, David. *The Lives of Michel Foucault: A Biography*. London: Hutchinson, 1993.

McGushin, Edward F. *Foucault's Askesis: An Introduction to the Philosophical Life*. Evanston IL: Northwestern University Press, 2007.

Marcuse, Herbert. *One-Dimensional Man: Studies in the Ideology of Advanced Industrial Society*. Boston: Beacon Press, 1964.

Marx, Karl. *Grundrisse*. Translated by Martin Nicolaus. New York: Vintage Books, 1973.

———. *Le Capital*, Livre Premier, Tome 1. Translated by Joseph Roy. Paris: Editions Sociales, 1975.

———. *Capital: A Critique of Political Economy*, Vol. 1. Translated by Ben Fowkes. New York: Vintage Books, 1976.

Marx, Karl and Engels, Friedrich. *The Marx-Engels Reader*, 2nd edition. Edited by Robert C. Tucker. New York: Norton, 1978.

May, Todd and McWhorter, Ladelle. 'Who's Being Disciplined Now? Operations of Power in a Neoliberal World'. *Biopower: Foucault and Beyond*. Edited by Vernon W. Cisney and Nicholae Morar. Chicago and London: University of Chicago Press, 2016, pp. 245–58.

Miller, James. *The Passion of Michel Foucault*. New York: Simon & Shuster, 1993.

Mitcheson, Katrina. 'Foucault's Technologies of the Self: Between Control and Creativity'. *The Journal of the British Society for Phenomenology* 43, no. 1 (2012), pp. 59–75.

Müller-Doohm, Stefan. *Adorno: A Biography*. Translated by Rodney Livingstone. Cambridge: Polity Press, 2005.

Nealon, Jeffrey T. *Foucault Beyond Foucault: Power and its Intensification since 1984*. Stanford: Stanford University Press, 2008.

Nietzsche, Friedrich. *On The Genealogy of Morals*. Translated by Walter Kaufmann and R. J. Hollingdale. New York: Vintage Books, 1969.

———. *Thus Spoke Zarathustra* in *The Portable Nietzsche*. Edited and Translated by Walter Kaufmann. New York: Penguin Books, 1982.

———. *Twilight of the Idols* in *The Portable Nietzsche*. Edited and Translated by Walter Kaufmann. New York: Penguin Books, 1982.

O'Connor, Brian. *Adorno's Negative Dialectic: Philosophy and the Possibility of Critical Rationality*. Cambridge MA: The MIT Press, 2004.

O'Farrell, Clare. *Foucault: Historian or Philosopher?* Houndsmills: Macmillan, 1989.

O'Neill, John. 'The Disciplinary Society: From Weber to Foucault'. *The British Journal of Sociology* 37, no. 1 (1986), pp. 42–60.

Owen, David. *Maturity and Modernity: Nietzsche, Weber, Foucault and the Ambivalence of Reason*. London and New York: Routledge, 1994.

Patton, Paul. 'Foucault's Subject of Power'. *The Later Foucault: Politics and Philosophy*. Edited by Jeremy Moss. London: Sage, 1998, pp. 67–77.

Pollock, Friedrich. 'State Capitalism: Its Possibilities and Limitations'. *Studies in Philosophy and Social Research* 9, no. 2 (1941), pp. 200–25.

Pritchard, Elizabeth A. '*Bilderverbot* Meets Body in Adorno's Inverse Theology'. *Theodor W. Adorno*, Vol. I: *Philosophy, Ethics and Critical Theory*. Edited by Gerard Delanty. London, Thousand Oaks, New Delhi: Sage Publications, 2004, pp. 184–211.

Rajchman, John. *Michel Foucault: The Freedom of Philosophy*. New York: Columbia University Press, 1985.

Ransom, John S. *Foucault's Discipline: The Politics of Subjectivity*. Durham NC: Duke University Press, 1997.

Riccio, Franco and Vaccaro, Salvo, eds. *Adorno e Foucault: Congiunzione disgiuntiva*. Palermo: Renzo e Rean Mazzione, 1990.

Riesman, David with Denny, Reuel and Glazer, Nathan. *The Lonely Crowd: A Study of the Changing American Character*. New Haven: Yale University Press, 1950.

Rusche Georg and Kirchheimer, Otto. *Punishment and Social Structure*. New York: Columbia University Press, 1939.

Saar, Martin. 'Genealogy and Subjectivity'. *European Journal of Philosophy* 10, no. 2 (2002), pp. 231–45.

Scheuerman, William. *Between the Norm and the Exception: The Frankfurt School and the Rule of Law*. Cambridge MA: The MIT Press, 1994.

Shuster, Martin. *Autonomy after Auschwitz: Adorno, German Idealism, and Modernity*. Chicago: University of Chicago Press, 2014.

Siedentop, Larry. *Inventing the Individual: The Origins of Western Liberalism*. London: Penguin, 2014.

Smart, Barry. *Foucault, Marxism and Critique*. London: Routledge & Kegan Paul, 1983.

Stone, Alison. 'Adorno and the Disenchantment of Nature'. *Philosophy and Social Criticism* 32, no. 2 (2006), pp. 231–53.

Thiele, Leslie Paul. 'The Agony of Politics: The Nietzschean Roots of Foucault's Thought'. *The American Political Science Review* 84, no. 3 (September 1990), pp. 907–25.

Vaki, Fotini. 'Adorno *contra* Habermas and the Claims of Critical Theory as Immanent Critique'. *Historical Materialism* 13, no. 4 (2005), pp. 79–120.

Van der Wee, Herman. *Prosperity and Upheaval: The World Economy (1945–1980)*. Translated by Robin Hogg and Max R. Hall. Berkeley and Los Angeles: University of California Press, 1986.

Vatter, Miguel. 'Foucault and Hayek: Republican Law and Liberal Civil Society'. *The Government of Life: Foucault, Biopolitics and Neoliberalism*. Edited by Vanessa Lemm and Miguel Vatter. New York: Fordham University Press, 2014, pp. 162–184.

Veyne, Paul. 'Foucault Revolutionizes History'. Translated by Catherine Porter. *Foucault and his Interlocutors*. Edited by Arnold I. Davidson. Chicago: University of Chicago Press, 1997, pp. 146–82.

———. *Foucault: His Thought, His Character*. Translated by Janet Lloyd. Cambridge: Polity Press, 2010.

Weber, Max. *The Protestant Ethic and the Spirit of Capitalism*. Translated by Talcott Parsons. London: Unwin Hyman, 1950.

Weber Nicholsen, Shierry and Shapiro, Jeremy J. 'Introduction'. In Theodor W. Adorno, *Hegel: Three Studies*. Translated by Shierry Weber Nicholsen. Cambridge MA: The MIT Press, 1993, pp. ix–xxxiii.

Weberman, David. 'Foucault's Reconception of Power'. *The Philosophical Forum* XXVI, no. 3 (Spring 1995), pp. 189–217.

Whitebook, Joel. *Perversion and Utopia: A Study in Psychoanalysis and Critical Theory*. Cambridge MA: The MIT Press, 1995.

———. 'Michel Foucault: A Marcusean in Structuralist Clothing'. *Thesis Eleven* 71 (November 2002), pp. 52–70.

———. 'Weighty Objects: On Adorno's Kant-Freud Interpretation'. *The Cambridge Companion to Adorno*. Edited by Tom Huhn. Cambridge: Cambridge University Press, 2004, pp. 51–78.

Žižek, Slavoj. 'Slavoj Žižek Speaks at Occupy Wall Street: Transcript'. *Impose*, 10 October 2011.

Zuidervaart, Lambert. *Social Philosophy After Adorno*. Cambridge: Cambridge University Press, 2007.

Index

perversion 26, 63–4, 118–19; *see also*
    deviance, sexuality
phenomenology 11–13, 12n55
philosophy
    Adorno on 18, 19n83, 19–20, 65, 70,
        137–8, 140, 145, 160
    Foucault on 6, 13n62, 20, 91n125, 123,
        138–9, 139n65, 158, 162
physics 63, 131
Plato 18
pleasure
    Adorno on 62, 117, 118, 119–20, 121
    Foucault on 68, 73, 83, 119, 121, 127,
        148
Pollock, F. 33
Popeye 115
population 17–18, 25, 42–3, 46, 51, 57, 75,
    76, 84–5, 89, 95, 101, 117n114, 127,
    134, 135, 156; *see also* species
power (relations) ix, 9, 31, 36–9, 47, 48–51,
    55, 58–9, 61, 68, 70, 72, 83, 105–6; *see
    also* government
    biopower 20, 23, 26, 31, 39n40, 43, 49,
        50–1, 52, 57, 59, 61, 72–4, 76n54, 84–5,
        86, 89, 94, 98, 105, 110, 127, 135–6,
        153, 156
    disciplinary 8, 14–15, 26, 30, 31, 39n40,
        42–3, 49–50, 52, 54, 57n100, 59, 61,
        68–9, 72–3, 73n51, 74, 75–6, 76n64,
        80, 82–4, 88–90, 93, 94–5, 98, 104,
        105–6, 126, 134–6, 148, 156
    pastoral 74, 75, 78–80, 84, 87, 94–5, 96,
        99–100, 112–13, 116, 134, 137, 139n71,
        157, 162
praxis 100–1, 122, 145
prejudice 51–2, 134, 151; *see also* racism
preponderance of object *see* object
    (preponderance of)
Pritchard, E. 143
profit motive 33–4, 58, 92, 136
proletariat 7, 35, 101, 101n45, 103; *see also*
    bourgeoisie, class, revolution
Protestantism 79, 79n77; *see also*
    Reformation
psychiatry 65–6, 101, 128
psychoanalysis *see* Freud

Rabinow, P. 13, 15, 24
race 36, 36n23, 50–1
racism ix, 18, 89–90, 96, 134–7; *see also*

fascism, Nazism, prejudice
    Adorno on 51–2, 134, 135
    Foucault on 50–1, 52, 63–4, 89, 134–5,
        158
Rajchman, J. 4, 103n53
Ransom, J. 9, 83, 99, 106, 117n114, 134
rapport à soi 78, 108–9
rationality 15, 152; *see also* reason
    Adorno on 14–15, 113–14, 126, 157, 161
    Foucault on 14–15, 46, 49, 112, 134,
        135–6, 152, 157–8, 160, 161
Raulet, G. 25, 38
reason 15; *see also* rationality
    Adorno on 30, 39, 62, 65, 70, 82, 97,
        113–14, 136–7, 141, 142, 144–5,
        146n106, 154–6, 157, 159, 160–2
    Foucault on 38, 139, 148, 154, 156–8, 159,
        160–2
reconciliation 91,120–1, 131,162
redemption 120–1
Reformation 50, 160; *see also* Protestantism
reification 16n73, 41–2, 48, 71, 71n45,
    90n123, 107
repression 61
    Adorno on 10, 61–2, 66–7, 69–70, 73, 81,
        91, 104, 109, 117, 118
    Foucault on 50, 63, 67–9, 83, 109, 118,
        153
revisionism 62
revolution; *see also* collective action, global
    subject
    Adorno on 33, 58, 60, 102–3, 105, 162
    Foucault on 50, 60, 101n45, 103–4
Riccio, F. 2n8
Riesman, D. 14, 87
Rimbaud, A. 160
Rorty, R. 109
Rose, N. 105
Rusche, G. 1
Ryle, G. 11

Saar, M. 150n130
sado-masochism 119; *see also* sex
Sartre, J.-P. 12, 13
Scheuerman, W. 33n7
Schlabrendorff, F. von 97
Schönberg, A. 16
Schumpeter, J. 53
self-preservation 10, 17, 24, 64–5, 77, 82,
    84–5, 110, 113, 114, 120, 126, 131, 149,

Printed by Printforce, United Kingdom